Storm Cycle 2014
The Best of Kind of a Hurricane Press

Edited by: A.J. Huffman
and April Salzano

Cover Art: "Breaking the Blue" by A.J. Huffman

Copyright © 2015 A.J. Huffman

All rights reserved. Except for brief quotations in critical articles or reviews, no part of this book may be reproduced in any manner without prior written permission from the publisher:

Kind of a Hurricane Press
www.kindofahurricanepress.com
kindofahurricanepress@yahoo.com

CONTENTS

	Thank You from the Editors	23

From the 2014 Editor's Choice Contest Winners

Donna Barkman	Scavenger Hunt	27
Denise Weuve	Visitation Tuesday	29
Christopher Hivner	Mathematics	31
Mary Newell	The Traffic in Old Ladies	34
Alexis Rhone Fancher	this small rain	36
Terri Simon	Signs of the Apocalypse	38

From the 2014 Pushcart Prize Nominees

Michael H. Brownstein	Before the Winter Storm Drifted East	41
Theresa Darling	Another Departure	42
Amanda Kabak	Common Grounds	43
Marla Kessler	Twenty Eight Seconds	45
Emily Pittman Newberry	Signs	47
Leland Seese	Until Next Time	48

From the 2014 Best of the Net Nominees

Ben Rasnic	Urban Still Life	51
Richard Schnap	Domestic Dispute	52
Marianne Szlyk	Walking Past Mt. Calvary Cemetery in Winter	53
Jon Wesick	A Postindustrial Romance	54
Joanna M. Weston	I Meant to Tell You	55
Deborah L. Wymbs	Spooning	77

From The Anthologies

Sheikha A	Alzheimer's	61
Amanda Anastasi	Half-Past	62
Steve Ausherman	Closing Time	63
Mary Jo Balistreri	The Steaming Cup Café	64
	Coffee at the Double Perk	65
Pattie Palmer-Baker	The Truth About Dahlias	66
David J. Bauman	Recurrents	67
Sarah Bence	DSM-V	69
Aaron Besson	Sestina Omerta	70
Ali Carey Billedeaux	Vintage Vinyl	72

Andrew M. Bowen	Morning Goes Down to Night	75
Shirley J. Brewer	Iced Latté	77
Andrew Campbell-Kearsey	The Alliterative Assassin	78
Alan Catlin	Jean Cocteau's Shadow Play of Life	80
	Mapplethorpe's Hand and Flower	82
Cathleen Chambless	Going Steady in 2013	83
Aidan Clarke	Revenge of the Flowers	85
Daniel Clausen	Again	86
Cathleen Cohen	Writing Poems in Beersaba'h	87
SuzAnne C. Cole	Beehives	88
Larry Crist	I Broke into the House of Writing	91
Dah	In Streetlight, His Wet Hair	93
Susan Dale	Spaces Among Spaces	95
Tim Dardis	Driving to Physical Therapy After Reading Delmore Schwarty	97
Bruce Louis Dodson	The Time of My Life	98

Liz Dolan	We Hope You Come Again to Funland*	99
Chiyuma Elliott	Why I Called So Late	100
Alexis Rhone Fancher	Tonight We Bloom for One Night Only	101
Cyd Ferree	Unadulterated	102
Claire T. Field	A Bouquet of Glads	103
Pattie Flint	Beggar Lattés	104
	Talk to Me in Marzipan	106
Sarah Flint	Moon-Fat Moths	107
Nancy Flynn	Weather Hysteria	108
Linda Gamble	Dragonfire	111
Sue Mayfield Geiger	Noir Couture	112
Phil Ginsburg	Assorted Centers	115
Jessica Gleason	Misshapen Adulthood	116
Nancy J. Hayden	Coffee Break on the Western Front, 1918	118
Damien Healy	Learning a New Language	121
Harmony Hodges	The Dancer	123
Trish Hopkinson	Trash Bag Burial	125
Liz Hufford	Fall Follies	126

Diane Jackman	BBC Radio Interview	127
Miguel Jacq	Nine Year Microwave Sky	128
David James	A Poem in Praise of the Morning	130
Sonja Johanson	In the Church of the Holy Coffee Bean	131
Michael Lee Johnson	Mindful, Mindless October Date	132
	She	133
Babo Kamel	I Tunneled Out of Bone	134
Clyde Kessler	Spring Sequence	135
Marla Kessler	The Job Interview	138
Irene Koronas	Chance Show	140
Laura Lovic-Lindsay	Summer Sacrament	141
Jacqueline Markowski	Of Pigs and Pizza	143
Bradley McIlwain	Winter Eulogy	145
Jane Miller	Making What We Can	146
James Mirarchi	The Shelleys Visit a 20th Century Carnival	147
Mark J. Mitchell	Musical Chairs	150
Ralph Monday	Ophelia's Flowers	151
Jude Neale	New York, New York	152

BZ Niditch	An Environmental Poet	153
Cristina M.R. Norcross	Just One Chocolate Slowly	154
	Death By Turtle	155
Vincent O'Connor	First Kiss	157
Coco Owen	Downward-Facing Lotus	158
Mangal Patel	Time's Up	159
Simon Perchik	Untitled	162
Richard King Perkins II	Café Epitaph	163
Jendi Reiter	Mis Numeros	164
henry 7. reneau, jr.	Selective Recall	166
Brad Rose	Old Dirk Savors the Prospect of Honeymoon Bliss with His Second Teen Bride	168
	Pink Candy Hearts	169
Sy Roth	The Wallflower	170
John W. Sexton	Through Her	172
Bobbi Sinha-Morey	Missing	173
Smita Sriwastav	Candy Foil Memories . . .	174
	Anecdotes of the Defunct Ferris Wheel	175
Tom Sterner	& the stone man said	178

Kevin Strong	Musical Lives	182
Fanni Sütő	The Shadow Girl	184
Anne Swannell	Keeping Time	185
	Bellis Perennis Imitates Narcissus	186
Marianne Szlyk	Augusta, Maine	187
	Listening to No Other, Thinking of Takoma Park	189
Yermiyahu Ahron Taub	A Knight Shining, Without Armor	191
Judith Terzi	The Anchorwoman	193
Talaia Thomas	After the Before	195
Sarah Thursday	Not Sleeping	196
David Turnbull	I Want Candy	198
Jessica Van de Kemp	The Last of the Old Gods	200
Tamara K. Walker	I'll Show You Sunshine	202
Mercedes Webb-Pullman	Sunday at the Gallery	204
	Stirring Sugar	205
	Reading Shadows	206
Emma Whitehall	Love Letter	207
Ron Yazinski	Placebo	209

	Class at Disney's Animal Kingdom	211
Dana Yost	Among Old Graves	213
Changming Yuan	Natural Confrontations	214

From the Journals

Jonel Aballanosa	While the Crickets are Mating	219
Carol Amato	In the Distance, Crows	220
Janet Shell Anderson	Wolf Cry	221
Steve Ausherman	Untitled	222
Mary Jo Balistreri	Untitled	223
Amy Barry	Candy Colours	224
Karen Berry	Disassembly Required	225
Byron Beynon	The Furnace Quarry, Llanelli	226
Jane Blanchard	Untitled	227
Sam Bockover	Untitled	228
Andrew M. Bowen	Chattlebury Park	229
Alan S. Bridges	Untitled	231
Michael H. Brownstein	Participles of Speech	232
J.J. Campbell	Open Swing	233

	Reflection	234
Theresa A. Cancro	Metamorphosis (A Triptych)	235
	Berceuse In Terra	237
	Glower Scrapings	238
Seamas Carraher	The Spoon in My Eye	239
John Casquarelli	plug into confetti ballroom	242
Alan Catlin	Light Through	243
	Untitled	244
David Chorlton	The Fading	246
	A Rattlesnake in Summer	247
Daniel Clausen	Memoir	248
Mike Cluff	Pieces	251
Kelly Cressio-Moeller	Haiku Noir	253
Betsy Cullen	At Cheever	254
Peter Dabbene	Scratching	255
Dah	Solo Flight	257
Susan Dale	The Song Is Gone	259
	A Fierce Winter Night	260
	Us	261

Cassandra Dallett	*In a Video Today Two Small Deer Ran Across the Golden Gate Bridge Behind Them an Idling Line of Migratory Animals in Plexi-Glass Boxes*	262
J.P. Dancing Bear	*All Soul's Day*	263
	Caked	265
William G. Davies, Jr.	*The Sunflower Chronicles (A Triptych)*	266
Pijush Kanti Deb	*Untitled*	267
Darren C. Demaree	*Wednesday Morning #137*	268
	We Are Arrows #195	269
James Diaz	*Fences Do Not Mend Each Other*	271
	Mountain Never in the Gutter Belly	272
Melissa Duclos	*I Never Told Anyone About That Trip to Serendipity*	274
J.K. Durick	*Inventory*	275
Liz Egan	*When He Leaves You*	277
Neil Ellman	*Woods (2)*	279
Eric Evans	*Survey*	280
Alexis Rhone Fancher	*Bad Apple*	282

Daniel N. Flanagan	Mental Illness	283
Ryan Quinn Flanagan	Everyone Loves a Motorcycle	285
Sarah Flint	Perfume	286
	The Book	287
Vernon Frazer	Fun and Prophet	288
Patricia L. Goodman	All That Remains	289
	When Winter Stayed	290
Taylor Graham	Bird I Never Saw in Daylight	291
	Wild	292
Allison Grayhurst	Complete, but	293
John Grey	Regarding the Hawk	294
	I Have My Own Importance to Attend to	295
Carl James Grindley	Television	297
	Weapons	299
Cristine A. Gruber	Split	300
	Untitled	301
	Standing Room Only	302
Ahab Hamza	Psyche	303

Patricia Hanahoe-Dosch	*Driving Through Utah*	304
Margery Hauser	*Silence*	306
Heather Heyns	*The Chicken Dance*	308
Wendy Elizabeth Ingersoll	*Appellation*	309
	Fear Itself	311
Bill Jansen	*Chinese Take-Away Sky*	312
Ivan Jenson	*Ambulance Chaser*	314
Michael Lee Johnson	*Cut Grass in Snow*	316
	Untitled I Walk	317
Ken L. Jones	*Appears to Be Rimbaud Speaking*	319
	A Few Choice Lines About the Deities of the Mad Tea Party	320
	The Minotaur in the Dime Store	321
	Unicorn Hunt	322
Larry Jones	*Dear Mother*	323
B.T. Joy	*Escaping Criticism*	324
	Cat Energy on the Dog Walk	325
	Reading Jinzhu Ridge	326

	Grampians	327
Steve Klepetar	*The Winter Shadow*	328
	Staff Meeting	329
John Kross	*All That I Have Felt*	330
Martha Landman	*Your Skin*	335
	Back Then	336
Ron. Lavalette	*Haiku Stupid*	338
Lyn Lifshin	*Some Afternnons When Nobody was Fighting*	339
Duane Locke	*Terrestrial Illuminations (2014) No. 380*	340
Jack e Lorts	*Ephram Pratt Exhales the Bliss of Light*	344
Chad W. Lutz	*A Breeze She Hardly Knew*	346
Iain Macdonald	*Already Broken*	347
Stacy Lynn Mar	*Hanging the Stars*	348
Denny E. Marshall	*Untitled*	349
Grace Maselli	*The Twinkies Are Gone*	350
Anna McCluskey	*Found*	352
Joan McNerney	*Where the Lost Gather*	353
Bruce McRae	*Night Train*	355

	Less Than a Single Breath	356
Jim Meirose	As It Is	357
	Harpies	360
Karla Linn Merrifield	Ménage à Trois	363
Les Merton	By the By	364
	Untitled	366
Ralph Monday	Dinner with the Ghost of Marilyn Monroe	367
	Love the Fiber Optics	368
	Limbs Like Dark Branches	369
Jude Neale	Unbutton the Night	370
	We Sing Ourselves Back	371
ayaz daryl nielsen	Eleven Things About Wet Noodles That Everyone Should Know	372
	Untitled	373
Agholor Leonard Obiaderi	Body Language	374
Mary Orovan	Untitled	376
	Reverse Haiku	377
Scott Thomas Outlar	Ballerina of the Sky	378
Simon Perchik	Untitled	380

Kushal Poddar	Am I Awake	381
	Autumn	382
henry 7. reneau, jr.	anaphase	383
Walter Ruhlmann	A Bowling Ball in My Stomach	384
Fain Rutherford	After Rendition	385
	Winter Ops	386
Richard Schnap	Encounter	387
John W. Sexton	World Without Bees Amen	388
	Migrants	389
	Mouth to Sky	391
Sunil Sharma	Raven	392
Lance Sheridan	Of a Run Aground Ship and Winged Crows	393
Judith Skillman	Thinking of Limes in the North	394
Felino A. Soriano	parallel as fixation	395
Brandon C. Spalletta	Passing	396
Smita Sriwastav	See-Saw Dialogue	397
David Subacchi	Mist	399
	Horse Frightened by a Lion	400

Fanni Sütő	*Greening*	401
Ag Synclair	*When the Writer Decided to Share Relationship Advice*	402
	Untitled	403
Marianne Szlyk	*Looking Out to Spectacle Island in April*	404
	It's For You	405
Grant Tarbard	*The Song of the Mean Eyed Cat and the One Eyed Fox*	406
Sarah Thursday	*Honey*	408
Paul Tristram	*She Has a Body Like My Spirit*	409
	Doubtful	410
	She was Insensitive to My Sensitivity	411
	A Naïve Trap for Love-Sick Souls	412
Matthew Valdespino	*Untitled*	413
Michelle Villanueva	*expansion*	414
Anne Richmond Wakefield	*Untitled*	415
Nadine Waltman-Harmon	*The Wolf's Trail*	416
Nells Wasilewski	*Untitled*	418

Diane Webster	Wedding Vision	419
	Soul Mates	420
	Puddle Passage	421
Catherine Weiss	Deflation	422
Jon Wesick	Monica Wanted to B 2-D	424
Joanna M. Weston	I Have Seen These Stones Rise	425
	Held in Forever	426
	Never Again Hand in Hand	427
	On Bad Days	428
Kelley White	Untitled	429
Martin Willitts, Jr.	God Visits Michelangelo at the Sistine Chapel	430
Mark Young	Inanimate	431
Changming Yuan	Chronometry	432
	Chinese Gentility: Four Confucian Haiku	433
Jeffrey Zable	A Hemingway Day	434

From The Editors

A.J. Huffman	Life is Like a Bag of Cheetos	439
	Toes in the Wind	440

	Twinkle Twinkle	441
	Dawn Breaks	442
	Your Penis Made You Do It	443
	Desire	444
	With Iron	445
	I Wish I Had a Donut	446
	Three Winter Haiku	447
	Game of the Gods	448
April Salzano	*Referential Mania*	451
	Garden Hoe	452
	Weeping Willow	453
	Running Dead	454
	If Love Can Be Put on a Shelf	455
	He Loved Me Like a Whore	456
	Out of Thin Air	457
	The Girl of My Dreams	458
	Four Autism Haiku	459
	Days of Our Lives	460

Author Bios 463

About the Editors 509

Thank You From The Editors

In lieu of an introduction, we wanted to take a moment to thank all of our brilliant authors from 2014. We have been blessed with an amazing amount of extraordinarily talented authors who deemed our journals and anthologies worthy of their wonderful work. This thank you extends not just to the authors who made the pages of this anthology, or even to the authors that made the pages of our other anthologies and online journals, but rather to all the authors who submitted their work to us. Accepted, rejected, chosen as standouts, at the end of the day without any of you, none of our hard work would matter at all. Without the diligent work of these struggling artists, we would be a blank page on a screen or a book. So, for saving us from that horrific fate, we thank you. We hope to continue our relationship with all of you, and any and all new additions we can muster. We have an amazing year of projects planned for 2015. Hopefully, we will see you all again in the years to come.

From The 2014
Editor's Choice Contest Winners

Scavenger Hunt

                              The boy was devising a game for his father
                          who might soon wake from a nap, his third that day.

He called his son *the boy* since the surgeon's
knife had sliced most names from his memory. The boy
called his father *Mr. Gus* when they were playing pirates.

                      In his best first-grade printing, he wrote instructions on
                small squares of paper for Mr. Gus to find the treasure chest:
                    "Number 1: Go to the Bathroom." He smiled at his joke
and placed a second note on the toilet tank: "Go to the Bedroom."
                    a third: "Living Room." Yes. "Go to the Living Room"

                He knew his mother would help Mr. Gus read the clues.
                                Number 4: "Kitchen."
                         Number 5: "Tree House Ladder."
Number 6: "Ship," – the derelict porch at the back of the house,
            loaded with all that a seagoing scalawag could hope for.

In time, Mr. Gus found the boy's cherished booty: bits of sea glass,
polished stones, foreign coins, and his great-aunt Jane's
discarded pearls and brooches.

                          They're yours, Mr. Gus. All for you!

Mr. Gus loved the boy with all his heart and soul. He knew
where his heart was and could even find his pulse points,
but wondered obsessively about his soul: Was it there

behind his eyes, floating in the reservoir of tears?
Perhaps in his throat that clutched when the boy piped
sea chanteys they'd sung together. Maybe in his gut,
where he would shit it out as a last angry act. Or his lungs
where it could leave in the death rattle he knew was approaching.
He tried to picture it hovering somewhere in a never-never-land

until it was joined by the boy's, decades hence.

He heard the boy calling and found him standing on the toilet lid, rummaging through the medicine cabinet above, pulling out bottles and tubes and vials.

This is what the doctor will do, the boy shouted. *She'll go through all the pills in her closet and way at the back, she'll find the ones that will fix your sickness,* his voice bounding from the walls

Their blue eyes met in a gaze of longing and possibility. The boy touched his father's grizzled face, then he jumped to the floor.

Wanna play swordfight, Mr. Gus? he asked. *I'll find the cutlass,* and he ran from the room.

-- Donna Barkman
(First Place Prize Winner)

Visitation Tuesday

Women in tattered sweat pants,
swallowed by thread-bare t-shirts nest
outside the visitor entrance
waiting to see their papis,
                      babies,
                      better halves,
                      soul-inmates.
The chica beside me tosses her brass blonde
feathered hair, grabs the spaghetti
strap of my cerulean dress, *This ain't a ball sister.*
                      Don't look at our men.
Her doorknocker earrings swing,
a caged bird's empty

perch. There are no windows inside.
No way for them to see airplanes
soar, with vultures and families
escaping this dried up town.

To the left a mother, her son
no longer legally a child, confined
behind 2 inches of Plexiglas,
cries, picks up the phone, toys
with the cord that links them.
He is the only detainee
unable to hold his visitor.
Her hand flutters, grazing the cage
that took 20 years

to build. In Colorado, guards shoot
crows during target practice
then serve them for dinner to inmates.
Visitors are ruffled, frisked,
then released to an open room of their men—
the well-behaved, in white jumpsuits.
He is in orange

Baby I have missed you so much.
You drop off some cash at intake?
When I'm sprung, we're taking off for Cali.
We got 30 minutes baby, talk.
Black wings rip through my shoulder
blades the color of desire
that cannot be contained in a state
issue plastic chair.
I glide above the prisoners
beak first against Plexiglas.
I snap, chirp a misunderstood subsong,
the guards ignore my caws
take aim.

-- Denise Weuve
(Second Place Prize Winner)

Mathematics

The distance traveled
on the plane
had value
for the crew
as far as
fuel consumption,
wear on the aircraft,
and the mood
of the passengers.

> In row E, window seats,
> two fingers to the lips
> meant shh,
> surrender
> to the captured time,
> absorb the turbulence
> and remember
> it will end some day.

The hotel
was ten miles
from the airport
on a road built
with ruts,
and held together by
dust and stones.

> Midnight crowed
> like a rooster
> insane from the heat,
> row E, window seats,
> shed their skin
> reborn as room 235,
> two fingers to the lips
> meant shh,
> this is all we have.

Time travels
at a fixed speed
and cannot be altered,
you can pray
to the father, son,
or holy variable
of the long lost
algorithms,
time will not
respond.

    Sun-heated
    blue-green water
    carrying bodies
    on dappled waves,
    buoyant layers
    of indirection,
    two fingers to the lips
    meant shh,
    we're almost done.

Air speed is something
you don't feel
when you're in the air,
during flight
no one thinks about
flight altitude
or the precise combustion
of the modern
jet engine.

    Real world math
    feels leaden,
    time reversing
    through fluid
    thick with
    sleepless thoughts
    and fissures in

the new blood,
two fingers to the lips
meant shh,
   we have to start over.

> *-- Christopher Hivner*
> *(Third Place Prize Winner)*

The Traffic in Old Ladies

I'm crossing traffic on 8th and 34th
Looking for the cross-town bus,
confused by the numerous vectors.

Leaning against a rail
casual, one leg bent,
a bright-eyed cocoa-toned young man
croons solicitous:
"What's bothering you?
 Hey, cum'ere ..."
I don't remember what he called me
but he called, again.
 Suspecting him a player in
the traffic in old ladies,
I didn't answer. But his solicitation
propelled me to the mirror back at home.

Twilight softens the contours,
not the intensity.

Face

Not the woman who twice rebuilt a crumbling life
courageous and persistent
(some would say stubborn)
Nor the adventurer friends tap for vicarious trips
(some would say reckless)
Not the bitterness that sometimes thins my optimist smile,
the worry that tightens my jaw
(some would say tense),
Nor the laugh old friends can recognize
across a teeming room

 no...

the shocked look of the curly-locked girl in amber silk
staring confused
through undulating water
wondering why
her lover
is holding her
under

> *-- Mary Newell*
> *(Honorable Mention)*

this small rain

this small rain sambas on San Vicente
wanders through Whittier
mambos past Montebello
and East LA

this small rain moves like a Latina
over-plucks her eyebrows
drinks Tequila shooters
fronts a girl-band

this small rain works two jobs
dawdles in downpours
this small rain seeds clouds

this small rain drives to Vegas in a tormenta
has a friend in Jesus
needs boots and a winter coat

in this drought-wracked city,
this small rain dreams of flash floods,
depósitos, indigo lakes,
cisterns, high water,
Big Gulps, endless refills

in this drought-wracked city,
this small rain settles on the hierba seca
sleeps under freeways
plays the lotto
is unlucky in love

this small rain longs to hose down the highways
this small rain chases storms

this small rain has a tsunami in her heart

this small rain kamikaze's
in the gutter
suicides on summer sidewalks
dreams of a deluge
that overflows the river banks
washes L.A. clean

in this drought-wracked city,
this small rain scans the heavens,
looking for a monsoon,
searching for su salvador in the
reclaimed desert sky.

-- Alexis Rhone Fancher
(Honorable Mention)

yerba seca: dry grass
tormenta: rainstorm
su salvador: her savior
deposito: reservoir

Signs of the Apocalypse

Last night, everyone on the planet
had a good night's sleep.
This morning, everyone used their turn signals
and were gleefully allowed to merge.
No one used racial slurs,
sex was not warfare,
and warfare, finally,
was declared illegal.
The ridiculously rich
fed the poor, voluntarily,
and even fast-food chains
decided to pay a living wage.
Zeus and the Pope
sat down to tea.
And I opened up my hands
and let go.

-- Terri Simon
(Honorable Mention)

*From The 2014
Pushcart Prize Nominees*

Before the Winter Storm Drifted East

As day changed color to color
and the great light went out in the chamber,
someone gathered straw to bury the earth.

Let the frozen fire of ice and snow collect its belongings,
let it settle into seed and burrow, weed and grass,
the tumbledown mesa over to the east.

This is a suicide land, a rock and pictograph,
a grape for encouragement and a grape for the downfall,
a green apple for the rest of us.

-- Michael H. Brownstein
(January Jellyfish Whispers)

Another Departure

Only a week ago
the ice was melting
I was driving home

watching white ground slip
into black – mud everywhere
shining wet, black shimmer of crow

in motion and the slapping
sound of wings whipping
my speeding car, windows down

on the radio
someone was singing
mournfully long and slow

about love and letting go
along the road
dead deer were set free

winter – cold lover
holding tightly
forced to let go

only a moment
a week ago I thought
we were finally thawing.

-- Theresa Darling
(January Napalm and Novocain)

Common Grounds

A friend, the most modern of modern women, was rattled with the realization that romantic breakups and hookups worked as the natural boundaries of her existence. As we tiptoed around the corner between our twenties and thirties, this type of categorizing self-reflection echoed around me. Hair, apartment, job, car. Cataloging their lives brought out my friends' inner anthropologists. They marked trends, measured patterns. They itemized gestures and peeled back layers of mating ritual.

But I thought about coffee. Although coffee was not addiction or love affair, it was a mahogany river of continuity through scene after scene of my memory. It was the mostly empty mug of my best high-school friend chilling on the linoleum of the third floor hallway, banned from the slate lab benches of junior-year biology. It was the smell of epic college conversations at The Grindular Sensation, just off campus and open all hours, that meandered in and out of topics with the same loose fluidity as our drinks. It was the oh-thank-you-God of early mornings when sleeping in and skipping class were no longer options and opening eyes to another endless day of bottom-rung drudgery was made possible only by caffeine.

My parents drank instant, but that didn't stop my mother and her thick sludge and cigarette from laughing at my cream-and-sugar, my starter coffee sweet and innocuous like my heart. Every year I took half a sugar less, one non-dairy creamer fewer. Until one morning, one Christmas, she looked across the table and noticed the French press I'd dragged home, the black bottomlessness of my own mug holding down a corner of the Sunday paper. "Well well well," she coughed. "Look who's all grown up." She was dying, and we both knew it. But we just sat and sipped and read in silence.

At some point, coffee became—to me and everyone else—anything but coffee. It became coffee draped in finger quotes, an overture to possible passion without making intentions clear. It was wine without overt snobbery, fragrance and body and flavor tones. My mom turned in her grave as we derided Folgers and paid way, way too much for hand-roasted, free-trade Columbian at that independent coffee shop down the street. We had great distrust for people who thought coffee too bitter or too unhealthy or too anything but perfect.

Some weekend afternoons, I sit in the window of that shop, still down the street and still with the outrageous prices, and I sip my witch-black brew and read the paper around watching foot traffic and counter traffic and taxis and cars and buses slide in and out of view. Despite the anchor of my mug, the engulfing smell of my coffee, change is all around me, our lives the unending processes of becoming who we are. Strangers, jobs, hair, loves come and go, and we are here to witness it all, all that living and dying and talking and drinking.

-- Amanda Kabak
(Something's Brewing Anthology)

Twenty-Eight Seconds

It took 28 seconds, but it was months in the making. I had been following the reviews about the ride since it debuted last summer. I bought the tickets to King's Dominion when my company announced the outing in December. I organized a group to rent a car, so we could arrive at the gates as they opened.

It wasn't without compromise. Two group members made us go on a water ride first since they were convinced it would be too disgusting after people had time to eat. Despite my thorough research showing a low incidence of riders throwing up and the high dilution factor of the water, this was non-negotiable.

It is frustrating to feel like an amateur going to the lower demand rides. There was no line because no one wanted to ride in a log. Everyone knew that Kingda Ka was THE attraction.

By the time we arrived at it 45 minutes later, the line was already two hours long. It was as if they didn't understand the unique properties of theme park time. The waiting included periods when the ride shut down whenever the tracks got too hot. And there were several restarts when the hydraulics did not propel the train high enough.

Three of our group dropped out after the first time they saw a complete cycle. Not sure what they expected since the ride was billed as the tallest and fastest ride in the country. Four more people talked themselves out of it over the next 90 minutes. Betty actually left in tears. "Humans were not meant to go that high!" she exclaimed with her typical drama. A more relevant thought was that humans were not meant to wear that much mascara before 8 pm, but that was for another day.

It was down to Patty and me, finally boarding the train after 126 minutes in line. We were in the second car, one row behind prime roller coaster seating. Patty gave me a long look, probing my face for signs I wanted to get off. But I was committed.

A moment of stillness fell after the ride was cleared to leave. A sixteen-year-old yelled to keep our hands inside with unexpected authority. The car moved backward, somewhat slowly, to lock into position. My brain finally registered that it was really happening.

And then blastoff! Unlike roller coasters based on gravitational pull, those with hydraulic launches have an abrupt start. The first three seconds took us from zero to over 100 miles an hour. We propelled in a straight line as my stomach pulled my body forward while the safety bar kept me braced in my seat. I literally felt stretched. Another ten seconds took us up the tower in a 90 degree angle towards the heavens, 450 feet above the earth.

And then we stopped. For a second or two I experienced the sensation of floating at the same time I had the sinking knowledge that I was about to fall. I looked over at Patty, somewhat surprised to see her smiling, looking thrilled by the experience.

As the drop started, I felt weightless. Going up was exhilarating. Falling brought fear triggered by a completely natural survival instinct. It made it even better! At the bottom, we abruptly stopped before our train slowly returned to the unloading section.

Patty and I laughed uncontrollably. Maybe it was the adrenaline. But we were warriors back from battle. And as they helped me out of the train back into my wheelchair, I wondered if any 28 seconds would ever feel that good again.

-- Marla Kessler
(Life is a Roller Coaster Anthology)

Signs

In the interval between
an open door and a closed heart lies

a secret rustling like
dried leaves in the wind.

I ask for patience.
Tomorrow comes
before today.

I ask
for truth.
The paper boy
stops writing
advice columns.

I ask for remembrance.
My pen cuts
the hero before
writing the ending.

And there are signs
and signs of signs

and the wind runs
naked in the grass

speaks of nothing

and the new world
grows lightly over the old.

-- Emily Pittman Newberry
(Tic Toc Anthology)

Until Next Time

I feel safest when I am held
by the corner of the kitchen counter
where I tuck myself in
with the sink at my left
and the stovetop at my back.

It feels like warmth,
like coffee brewing and bread toasting,
clean like plates just out of the dishwasher,
like onions sweetening on the hot skillet.

I stare at the broken door
of the refrigerator. My hands
still shake with adrenaline
from pulling him away
before he tore off the whole door.

I stand in the corner
calming down and girding up
for next time.

-- Leland Seese
(May Pyrokinection)

From The 2014
Best of the Net Nominees

Urban Still Life

"A 23-year-old female was shot in the head tonight outside of a flower and card shop. She died a short time later."

Splashes of rain
tattoo neon pools
of pitted concrete.

Pulse of random gunfire
startles the quiet,
flashes revolving sirens

in wreathes
of splattered crimson
and shattered glass.

The 10 o'clock News
punctuates the day's
events—violent and pointless;

irreconcilable episodes
between unbearable
silences.

-- Ben Rasnic
(April Pyrokinection)

Spooning

Dog hairs and lover's laundry lint,
Two things not easily gotten rid of,
And a third, images of love making.

He is the words brick and testosterone;
I am the word confused --
He makes me take vacations from myself.

-- Deborah L. Wymbs
(March Pyrokinection)

Walking Past Mt. Calvary Cemetery in Winter

The last snow (for now) melts under soft gray skies.
Even now it clings, like cobwebs, to corners.

The holly hedge's red berries and sharp leaves
hold the eye until the next snowfall.

Gees graze for grubs on the hillside.
The size of toy ponies, they do not fly.

Just like the waxy magnolia, the spiky cypress,
the leafless, last black locust,

they persist.

Somewhere in the city a woman on a patio
spoons sorbet. The nearby quince blooms.

Somewhere else a bronze nude on a tabletop confronts
the indoor birds of paradise, the bittersweet.

They too persist.

-- Marianne Szlyk
(May Jellyfish Whispers)

I Meant to Tell You

in my last letter
about the downy woodpecker
that hit the window
and lay stunned
on the door-step
wings outspread
each marking clear

how we stood
behind the window
hoped and prayed
that wings would stir

we returned to the window
again and again

the fourth time
there was a movement
a lift   a whirr
into flight

I meant to tell you
but I'm too late
- you have gone

-- Joanna M. Weston
(February Jellyfish Whispers)

A Postindustrial Romance

> . . . *we live in a society that is both competitive and in which we are incessantly evaluated (school, university, performance as writer, poet or businessman or sportsman). The only place where you hope to stop that evaluation is in love.*
>
> -- Eva Illouz

Donna married my paycheck
on an unseasonably warm autumn day.
Bridesmaids in antebellum gowns fanned themselves
and congratulated her on her good catch.
I still have the postcard she sent
from their honeymoon in New Zealand.

I wanted them to be happy.
Even when pricing helium futures
at the zeppelin factory,
I'd set down my slide rule
and imagined her moaning with pleasure,
my paycheck between her thighs.

When the downsizing began,
she sat at my paycheck's bedside
holding its hand   telling it not to give up.
At the funeral pallbearers had to restrain her.
In her grief she began to live for her job
staying at the office long after dark
and subsisting on frozen dinners.

To console her I explained that in today's economy
love depends on the trade balance with China
as well as myriad decisions by executives
in large corporations.   Now she's dating again.

If you're interested, forward your resume
along with a copy of your tax return.

-- Jon Wesick
(January Napalm and Novocain)

Domestic Dispute

His storm trooper voice
Bellowed downstairs
As she meekly cried out
For some miracle of mercy

I cowered in my room
As outside the sky
Filled with the darkness
of black-hearted clouds

His anger seemed endless
As I heard the dull thud
Of something thrown against
The thin, brittle wall

While the frail, little nest
In the tree near my window
Was seized by the wind
And helplessly blown away

-- Richard Schnap
(February Napalm and Novocain)

From the Anthologies

Alzheimer's

Across visible facets of a lofty winter,
I am late. For the turning sun at day
has been skipping in wider strides
over possibilities of a blossoming,
where little sprigs of cleaving self-
adhering rationalities brown into nights
of an unsolicited humidity presaging
a fall into a calloused summer. Call
the winter weak, meddled into twines
of its own brittle verbosity or colour
palette not agreeing to normal turns
of a solstice – an unfolding trap
of ambivalence; call me depleted,
my snow has run its course of use
for the garden soil; call me disposed,
my trees bear no more use for labour;
I am, indeed, late by a full turn
of seasons' luminous vagaries
but I am lucid in this ephemerality:
Now.

-- Sheikha A
(Switch the Difference Anthology)

Half Past

We are hypocrites about the past,
clinging to dead things, resurrecting
some memories like avid hoarders
while others are locked in penitentiaries.
We snap stills with our camera phones:
selected poses, stretched truth marketed
to future reminiscences – in them we laugh
and dance, our faces turned to their best angle.
When we flick through them in twenty years
we'll have convinced ourselves
that it was our happiest time,
that we will never be that way again
and our grim acceptance of the lesser
present is justified - we believe
our own propaganda about ourselves;
so busy remaking and remodelling
the past, rereading and reinterpreting
its texts, we never completely live
in the here and now,
making our past a half past
and our present half lived.

-- Amanda Anastasi
(Tic Toc Anthology)

Closing Time

Carpet cigarette-burned and coffee-colored hue.
The light bounces off rows of bottles promising.
Doorless bathroom and urinal filled with bugs.
Pool balls cracking like marriages ripping apart.
Smirnoff and Everclear, Jack Daniels and Wild Turkey.
Bartender dragging a screaming man through the front door.
The guy to girl ration is fifteen to one. No one cares.
Pitchers emptying into sophomore college bellies.
The old drunks swim in loose orbits avoiding the frat boys.
Walking in the front door smelling fried food and despair.
Marty Robbins, Willie Nelson, Johnny Cash, Lefty Frizzell.
The jukebox driving us on rutted roads through time.
In a year, I cannot recall a single, interesting conversation.
Bored men scratching labels off of perspiring bottles.
A man who fought in a war drunk-leans while talking to a girl.
This is part nursing home and part cemetery for hope.
College girls giggle in the corner turning every head.
There is no clock in this room, no phone, no windows.
Budweiser and Schlitz, Coors and Miller Genuine Draft.
This is part epic novel and part trash-reality tv.
I am stuck in the mud knee-deep and struggling.
Pitchers glow golden with backlight warming their amber.
Men moan when light pours in from an opened front door.
This is flypaper for the hovering hopeless.

-- Steve Ausherman
(Switch the Difference Anthology)

The Steaming Cup Café

Subtle as air altered by a wing, Nora Jones threads soft
jazz through random conversation, through the focused
reading I give to a poem by Donald Hall.

French roast and hazelnut cream weave in and out
of the music, scent words both spoken and written,
    flavor images in my head.

Even The Wall Street Journal rustling in the hands of old men,
    augments and diminishes the morning fugue of "The Steaming Cup"

Toward noon, an Indian summer picks up the beat, drives a combo
    of expectation, all hum and vibration, until the place swells

with calypso and steel drums. A man calls "Mary Ann" and a yellow hard hat
    yells "Over here." The door jingles open, closed, and a covey
of orange leaves somersaults over the threshold.

Soon, the relaxed atmosphere fills every table, and the buzz of autumn
warms to a tone-shifting improv with tropical color.

Heads bend over bread and brew as if noon were sacred, as if the Angelus bell
    that once rang in fields had simply moved to the city,
        still tolling respite, unhinging time.

                -- Mary Jo Balistreri
                (Something's Brewing Anthology)

Coffee at the Double Perk

Neither of us is prepared for the curve in conversation.
As my friend struggles with words, the story begins
to emerge. It's as if an aftershock tilts our world.
It was twenty years ago. And it still hurts.

All the time we had mourned privately, got lost
in the questions:
Why our bodies betrayed us
How our boys were dying inside us, quietness
deemed normal because they were small,
with small heart beats
How the doctors were not concerned until it was too late

Fissures crack open. We exchange our boys' names,
say them softly, almost shyly. Swapping stories, we begin
to interrupt each other, eager to share.
    Andrew comes to me when I'm doing laundry,
        sometimes in the garden.
    Danny visits when I'm making dinner or at the pond.

We both agree our boys like quiet and often come at night.

We walk toward the exit, arms around each other's waist.
Halfway out the door my friend stops – Were we the dead ones?

The door bangs shut behind us and we start to laugh. The reservoir
we thought empty begins to bubble like a fresh water spring.

                -- Mary Jo Balistreri
                (Something's Brewing Anthology)

The Truth About Dahlias

Oh those dahlias!
A drill sergeant's dream of puffball perfection,
they fold out in lemony layers,
salute orange, stand straight,
face the sun, size to coffee cups
and line up in a platoon of primary colors.

I cannot resist all this symmetry.
I push through the inch wide rows,
palpate their raspberry-red flesh,
touch their purple pulse.

Just beyond the reach of my eyelash
looms an arigope spider bigger
than the eye of my center, shredding
any Van Gogh color-soaked reverie.

You need to know say the dahlias *finger caresses*
and moony eyes are nothing to us.
The spider nestles in the cups of our petals,
we lick the silk from their spindled legs.

-- Pattie Palmer-Baker
(Petals in the Pan Anthology)

Recurrents

There we are by the shore again—well, me
by the shore, you out there, bobbing in the waves
once more, eyes bugged out, lips ice-blue,

arms flailing. Desperate to keep your head
above the white caps, you've somehow managed
to grasp a fallen branch. "Are you okay?"

The classic stupid question, but what am I to say?
"I'm sorry," you sputter-shout
as you spit a school of minnows from your teeth.

"I'm always drowning when we're here together."
Yet just last week we enjoyed a day here, dangling
foaming feet, skipping little stones, but now

is not the time to argue. I throw the rope,
always looped to my belt in anticipation
of times like this, but you miss it every toss.

All the while your enormous eyes convey a bevy
of emotions; fear of the current, rage at the waves
and sympathy for my own failings. My rope is too short.

In a frenzy now I fumble through my pockets, and toss
their contents to you—a marble, a feather, a rubber
chicken, hoping you'll know how to use them. "Don't worry

about me," you gurgle. And I am touched; I know
how you hate it when your moods affect me. Too late
I dive and plunge into the icy flow, as you lose

your slippery grip and begin to drift
around the bend, waving kind assurances
as your head sinks beneath the surface. You're always

thoughtful like that. Resigned, I crawl back
up the bank, and find my favorite rock. I check my watch—
it could be hours yet, before you're washed ashore.

-- David J. Bauman
(Tic Toc Anthology)

DSM-V

Do trees hurt when they grow new roots?
The earth feels too tight for them.
When the leaves shift red,
dangle, you pluck one off,
fat and whole.
The tree flinches, either wind or
it hurt like a pulled tooth.
An empty socket, copper.

      Sometimes I tear myself apart

You admit to the benches,
the gravel, the becoming
of October.
Tear the red leaf down its veins
      because it's daylight
because your wrists ache
      because it's just a symptom
of a mistake in your blood
      because a tree doesn't have the gift
of tearing itself apart.

Because this season rips apart the world
and it's diagnosed as beautiful.

      -- Sarah Bence
      (Petals in the Pan Anthology)

Sestina Omerta

       No muttered soul in the dark,
left worn with frayed ages and ragged.
No song for a ferryman who never
takes coin if the payment is screaming.
No virtue in smoke when all we want is fire,
for none love the moment before a kiss.

       What loud soul drinks a moment's kiss
fearing Time's long embrace in the dark?
Paradise is the last ember of a forgotten fire
when all else has burned so cold and ragged.
A mountain's pride bears the wind's screaming,
its grand secret written on the pages of never.

       Drink, terrible soul, which never
hunted the dusk's silken kiss.
A thousand bright dawns all left screaming
in envy of one night's sinless dark.
The robes of the secretless man look so ragged
in the light of precious silence's fire.

       What final soul will set to fire
that simple pearl valued yet never
given price? Once fine, now ragged,
days hunger for a lost mute kiss
in the heartless roaring dark, and
turn away from tomorrow's screaming.

       Endure, patient soul, all of Now's screaming
that brings naught but trials for the fire.
No quiet day gone by will comfort it in the dark.
What soundless symphony for it to never
know beyond a forgotten kiss,
when confused for a thunder so ragged?

Cherish the serene soul that, while ragged,
is placid where others tread screaming.
The constant void bends low to kiss
it, its faith a relentless fire.
The finer gems sang of shall never
shine more radiant than stones left dark.

So come, tattered soul, rest by my fire.
Forget the World's screaming, that we may never
forsake her secret kiss in the dark.

-- Aaron Besson
(Switch the Difference Anthology)

Vintage Vinyl

This is the conversation they never had.

He is sitting on one side of a large, brick wall. It's cold against his back, but he rests his head against the brick anyway. His eyes are closed. He can almost feel her.

She is on the other side of the wall. She's sitting cross-legged, facing it. When she hears him breathing, she looks up. Her hair falls away from her face and in a rush, the emotions paint her expression. She fancies herself stone, immune to everything and impenetrable, but he knows better. In moments like this, he knows exactly how her face looks.

He wants to reach through the stone, touch her cheek. He wants to hold her hands because he knows that she is shaking.

She is scared. She is always scared. And he is so far away.

How it really happens is like this. She stays there, for a few minutes. He begs her to say something. She doesn't. She reaches up and presses her palm against the stone. Then, lips sealed shut, imagining her heart to be stone, she climbs unsteadily to her feet and walks away. The next time he sees her, she is dead.

That's how it really goes.

After, he rewrites it.

He is still sitting on the ground by the brick wall. His knees are drawn up to his chin. He is looking at the sky and, almost too softly to be heard, he is speaking. He is singing. It's a song they both know, from when they were children. She stays, on her side of the wall, and listens to it. Her gloved hands are pressed to the brick. It hurts, especially where the skin has died at the tips of her fingers, but she pushes as hard as she can. She wants to leave a mark.

She says, "We should have never met."

He stops singing, but doesn't move. He says, "I'm glad we did."

Her dead fingers are just the beginning. There are other parts of her that are dying too. There are parts of her that have been dead since before he knew her. She is just pieces--always has been. Pieces that are alive. Pieces that fight. Pieces that are stone. And pieces that were buried a long time ago.

"You're going to ask me why," he says.

She doesn't, because she doesn't want to sound needy.

But he tells her, because she doesn't say anything else. "You changed me too."

"Not enough." Not the way that he had changed her. She'd been so different when they'd first met. She'd been only one piece then. Just the dead one. The buried one. Something terrible had happened to her--like terrible things always happen to people and turn them into something they never were before--and she had become nothing.

Stone, she'd said.

But he had made her more.

"How did I change you?" she asks.

He closes his eyes and breathes her in. It's almost as if she's right next to him. He says, "You made me."

She was two-sided. She had side A, before. She had side B, after. She had the incident that defined her.

But she was the incident that defined him. She was the before and the after. She had turned him from ordinary into extraordinary. She had made him brave.

On the other side of the wall, she hesitates. He can hear the smile in her voice. "You'd have been you anyway, without me."

"I wouldn't have," he says. Then, "And I wouldn't have wanted to be."

She understands, because of her two sides. The first side, from before, understands that he doesn't want to be what he is without her. The second side, the one that is forever, understands that she was the one that made him strong enough to do just that.

Side B says, "I'm glad you came."

Side A says, "I have to go. It's time."

He listens to both sides of her--the stone and the fire--and he understand that this is all they get. This last conversation.

"It's time," he agrees.

The next time he sees her, she's dead.

He wishes he'd said goodbye.

-- Ali Carey Billedeaux
(Tic Toc Anthology)

Morning Goes Down to Night: A Progression of Tanka

The sun steps up the
sky on pancake clouds
buttered yellow on scalloped
edges as mist haunts the big
pond. A horse munches breakfast.

Sun on sheet metal
reflects from a barn roof. Spring's
last storm lollygags
in lazing clouds above ponds
and puddles left by melting snow.

Window slats divide
into jail bars the sunlight
falling on upswept
lion-colored hair. How I long
to kiss the nape of your neck.

Coral and cobalt clouds
loom over lush trees and red
stoplights like great beasts
too lazy to stampede. One
light beckons from dim windows.

Sunset's last clouds, limned
in gold by the vanished sun,
swim above rustling
trees, a sea serpent seeking'
prey beneath the crescent moon.

The light of three towns
casts white underbellies on
cloud salamanders
splaying above the lake while
one light probes the winter night.

Blacksnake roads, egret
banks, black branches scrawl on mist,
lights cast wakes in dark
puddles, stars pinprick the night.
It's a chessboard kind of day.

-- Andrew Bowen
(Switch the Difference Anthology)

Iced Latté

Tall	Mt. Rainier	14,411 feet
Super	Mt. McKinley	20,320 feet
Grande	Mt. Everest	29,035 feet

My massive mocha
comes with a mini-oxygen mask:
coffee with an altitude.

A scoop of sweet snow
captures the summit,
drizzles down the side.

Ice cubes glisten
like tiny glaciers.
I radio for chocolate sprinkles.

No Sherpa guides, I slurp alone
through a tall white straw.
Caffeine attacks my mental clouds.

My brain crackles with adrenaline,
a mountain of chores
disappears and a cold caloric wind
blows my doldrums away.

-- Shirley J. Brewer
(Something's Brewing Anthology)

The Alliterative Assassin

The tabloids labeled him, 'The Solomon Grundy Killer'. He inflicted a sliding scale of harm in a range of locations. He maimed Michael from Malmesbury on Monday. On Tuesday he tortured Tony from Truro. Poor Wendy from Wensleydale was assaulted by a welder's torch on Wednesday. Thirsk residents were already on stand-by on Thursday but it didn't stop Thelma from being throttled. Floral wreaths were left outside Frank's chippy in Frome on Friday. Forensic staff never released to the public which body parts they found in the deep-fat frier.

Many people claimed they were the sole perpetrators and gave reasons for their actions. Scotland Yard received an email at six minutes past six every evening giving details of the latest atrocity. After a few days, the accuracy of the information and specific named location proved the emails to be genuine. Sometimes the emails arrived before the crime had even been reported. Under emergency legislation, facebook pages that glorified 'Solomon's' handiwork, were taken down. Editorials searched for a meaning behind the apparently random acts and locations.

Newsreaders reported with grim faces how an elephant-keeper had been crushed to death by his favorite pachyderm. No connection was made initially as the tragic accident occurred at Whipsnade on the Saturday. When information emerged that the recently deceased keeper was called Satnam and the full name of the establishment was Whipsnade Safari Park. It came as no surprise that the elephant had literally sat on his victim. The daily email to Scotland Yard confirmed what was feared that this was the sixth in a worsening list of crimes.

The more sensationalist of bloggers attributed godlike powers to Solomon. 'He can even control animals!' The Sunday paper headlines were united for once. 'It's a race against time before he strikes again.' Inhabitants of Sunderland with the misfortune to be called Sunny were under self-imposed house arrest.

Speculation mounted over the manner of Solomon's next outrage. Sun-tanning salons were an obvious choice.

At 6.06 the police received a briefer email than usual.

'Like God, I too need a day of rest. Normal business resumes tomorrow.'

-- Andrew Campbell-Kearsey
(Tic Toc Anthology)

Jean Cocteau's Shadow Play of Life
"The Moral Tedium of Immortality."

The blood of the poet is found
in every room, the studio a
tortured chamber experiments in
death are practiced in, creating
living statues, mouths transferred
from pale canvas to the artist's
beleaguered hand, speaking, then
daring the man who paints to
sculpt his life, to travel beyond
self-enclosed rooms contained by
solid objects, presumptive walls,
dropped ceilings, entreating him
to leap through a full length mirror
to the other side wearing the trans-
parent gloves that enable the way,
to avoid the falling glass others
must fall on instead of the unsheathed
sword, to move past the pedestrian
to the ephemeral, rebirthing in uncharted,
subcutaneous passages through a place
outside of Time, a place invisible to
the untutored, the living and inconse-
quential to the dead who hide behind
all the locked doors in otherwise
deserted tenements of the imagination,
drinking spilled blood taken from
the veins of poets as a curative measure
against the fatal disease of living as
half-men, half-shadows, their mummer's
play of being, nothingness enacted
against drawn shades, pulled curtains,
part Afternoon of the Faun, part Guernica,
the transition from Art to mass murder

as seamless as surgery, as a weightless
Orpheus descending, sinking into darkness.

-- Alan Catlin
(Switch the Difference Anthology)

Mapplethorpe's Hand and Flower

The hand that held the flower,
held the whip, held an orchid,

a calla lily, an arrangement of
tulips, held fading roses in black

and white, others in bloom, in
color, held a gun in self-portraits,

made himself a woman in others,
smiling and in multiple disguises,

was a smear in the mirror, a smudge
on the wall; beauty and sadness,

disguised as a shock of the new.

-- Alan Catlin
(Petals in the Pan Anthology)

Going Steady in 2013

You tell me
we're Allison & Cry-Baby,
because I'm your square,
with cherry lips,
you're my grease,
hand cuffs released-
diatonic to each other's keys,
Lucille to BB King.
We hook up
King Khan & BBQ Show,
phone to car stereo,
shoes shuffle against gravel,
silhouettes silk screened to headlights,
bodies pressed,
fret & strings,
sway with melodies & palm trees,
"No Outlet" sign & salty waves,
our own lover's lane.
The scythe moon
reflects in your sun
glasses & they slightly slide
down your nose, passing
off the night
sky to your eyes,
microdot sprinkles
on Snow Caps,
you kiss me with lips
like pink Sweet Tart
candy hearts,
XOXO,
we part & I press
my cheek against
your chest & cry, its

too much Rock N' Roll
for me to handle.

>	*-- Cathleen Chambless*
>	*(A Touch of Saccharine Anthology)*

Revenge of the Flowers

The drunks were always having a go at the flowers,
kicking petals, earth and roots
like litter in the streets.
The flowers held a meeting, distressed
by the thoughtless, the human, the mindless.
Shall we tear down their houses?
A daisy counseled patience,
As sure as the wind tugs at the long grass,
as sure as withering, as sure as falling leaves,
one day we shall dance on their graves.

-- Aidan Clarke
(Petals in the Pan Anthology)

Again

After years of fighting, pointless bickering, we materialize someplace with no walls, no boundaries, it takes in the air effortlessly and produces us as two people in our twenties. I sit in the cafeteria of the university and think--all I have to do is ignore her and this whole thing goes away. Our two trajectories will never touch. Long ago we had stopped communicating in any meaningful way--now we'll just eternalize the arrangement by never communicating in the first place.

Somehow though, I begin to think of life without her. I'm not the man of the future, of pointless fights. I want to live it all again, even as I see the train wreck coming. We'll do it even worse this time. We'll be more joyous in our youth and bitter in our twilight--logic and good sense be damned. We'll be in love, we'll be exasperated. We'll rush where we should slow down, and slow down and wait when opportunity knocks. And in the little garden on the terrace of your favorite Italian restaurant, we'll make magic feel like an everyday experience again and again. All these places and times stop, turn, twist, and there I am again with you, where I should be: miserable, happy, but never lonely.

-- Daniel Clausen
(Tic Toc Anthology)

Writing Poems in Beersaba'h

Mahmood's name contains two mountains.
Modaefa's heart holds his brother and his horse.
I stare out at limestone and rushing roads
which gird this city. His horse?

Nothing alters on him,
Not a smile nor a flicker.
He lives far out and what do I know
of all he knows?
The color of his horse?
How he fares in basalt rains
that pound the desert,
or the dust that streams in from Africa,
choking blue from the sky?
Does he finish his homework by flashlight?
Walk miles to the bus?

February heat blows through windows.
Students climb steps, fill spaces.
They want to learn English and
I yearn to sip this vastness,
to learn why Ameen was named for patience
and Alaa, for a prayer.
I want to sniff the exact bloom
Yasmeen was named for.

-- *Cathleen Cohen*
(Switch the Difference Anthology)

Beehives

"Gramma, what a weird hairdo," said Susan, giggling and pointing to a prom picture in her grandmother's college yearbook.

"That was called the beehive," said Betty, stroking Susan's straight silky hair, "and it was all the rage then. We teased our long hair until it bushed straight out, sprayed lacquer until we almost suffocated, then smoothed and twisted it around and around our heads, until, voila, a beehive. Sometimes we topped it with a flower. We felt very pretty."

Susan looked doubtful.

"Child, girls with short, curly hair were just sick when the fad started. Took them forever to catch up." She paused. "I have a story about that hairdo."

"Tell me."

"It's an old story, maybe the oldest there is. One young man, two young women. . . call them Sally and Sue. Both mad about the man, maybe his bright blue eyes, maybe his athletic body, maybe his natural courtesy. He dated them both without making them enemies, possibly because he made no promises. Some thought he didn't settle on one because he had a girl back home, but perhaps he really couldn't decide. It was spring, and both women hoped for his invitation to a fraternity ball. When he asked Sally, Sue was deeply upset. Someone else asked her—both women were quite pretty and could choose among many who swarmed around them—but she declined.

The morning of the dance, Sue offered to do Sally's hair. Sue had a reputation as a clever, if amateur, hair stylist, especially with the newest, the beehive, so Sally quickly accepted. She shampooed and dried her hair and hurried over to Sue's sorority house. As Sue brushed and teased Sally's hair, Sally began to talk, dreamily and lazily, as women tend to do when having their hair done.

"I know all about that," interrupted Susan. "The things women tell their hairdressers sometimes!"

Sally talked of the evening, her dress, the dinner, the dancing and finally volunteered that she intended to be wearing the young man's ring within the week.

Sue murmured a response and piled Sally's hair higher and higher. When she presented a mirror, Sally laughed happily and jumped up and hugged her.

"You're such a good sport," she said. "'My hair is gorgeous."

"But it's not quite finished. I have a special hairspray guaranteed to hold, no matter what. Afterwards, I want you to sit outside in the sun until the lacquer hardens."

Sue sprayed—Sally thought the heavy, sweet scent somehow familiar—and then settled her into a lawn chair by the sorority garden, draping a towel over her face to protect her complexion.

Daydreaming of the evening, drowsy in the thick sun, Sally dozed off. Bees industrially plunging blossoms nearby, eventually detected an even richer scent arising from the glistening tower of hair. First one, then another, then a dozen flew to investigate, delicately probing the shiny mass. Their activity awakened Sally who shook her head, throwing off the towel.

Threatened, the bees attacked, stinging her forehead, ears, cheeks and even lips, as she screamed and swatted and slapped and finally, too late, covered herself again with the towel and ran for the house.

"Gramma, how horrible," gasped Susan. "Was she allergic? Did she die?"

"No. Sue and the others killed the bees, covered her with ice packs and drove her to the hospital. She recovered but was too swollen to go anywhere for more than a week. Anyway, sweetheart, that's how I went to the spring ball with your grandfather. Honey is a good hair-stiffener, and I swear, that's all I intended to do."

-- SuzAnne C. Cole
(Switch the Difference Anthology)

I Broke into the House of Writing

I had an idea to do it and then did.
The address had changed.
Used to be in a better neighborhood.
In a building, a four story walk-up—4-E.
I knocked for twenty years then kicked the door in.
There were lots of locks but the frame had rotted.
The front room was abandoned.
A type too large to lift sat on a dusty floor.
There were framed pictures on the walls: Mark Twain,
Tolstoy, Dostoyevsky, Hemingway, Steinbeck. . .
staring out from clouded glass; several of these guys
were giving the finger, a strange contrast
to John Updike, smiling, Phillip Roth, scowling.
There was an empty closet with a rusty coat hanger.
A single faucet iron-stained sink in one corner, a window
with a cracked pane and lose caulk, looking down upon a tree
that looked dead. I passed through this room into what looked
like a dining room, empty but for a glass chandelier.
Booger green walls and dark wooden floors
creaked beneath my weight. There was a bar in the corner
with only an ancient bottle of Pernod.
I moved into a gutted out kitchen with vagina pink walls.
There was a window over where a sink had once been.
I looked out and saw a bar with flashing lights: Roy's Place
it said, over and over. I passed into the apartment's
one bedroom. Another door. I opened it. "Goddamn it,
what do you want?" A huge fat guy was inside, lying down.
"I'm a writer." I said. "Did you go through the
submission process? Did you read the guidelines?"
"Fuck you." I said. "Read this." "Poems?" he snarked,
"This'll never sell." "What are you," I asked, "some
kind of agent?" "I'm an independent publisher," he
replied, "and I do it all except for what you're supposed
to do. Here, sign this." "Jesus," I said, "this
is too long." "Just sign it. No ones reads these,
let alone fine print—You're basically agreeing

that I continue doing nothing while you
will do everything." "What kind of contract is this?" I asked.
"Standard." He answered. I took the pen he handed me
and then stabbed him in one of his large pink toes. He
screamed, and began to shoot backward around the room
bouncing off the walls and ceiling, growing smaller
until he collapsed on the floor, the size of a used condom.
I looked around.
The room was filled with manuscripts, most
still in manila envelopes. I could barely see
the room's lone window.
I pushed some envelopes out of the way
they toppled like a tree.
I opened the window. I felt bad for the little publisher
all stretched out and small on the cluttered floor.
I looked out the window. There was a bustling
metropolis, grey, distant, no perspective.
I crawled out onto a fire escape.
The city sang its own praises
as I climbed down and out from the house of writing.
Maybe I'd have better luck on the street again.
Maybe I'd hit Roy's for happy hour.

-- Larry Crist
(Petals in the Pan Anthology)

In Streetlight, His Wet Hair

On the sidewalk standing in the rain
the old man is like a wounded dove.
Longish white hair: wet feathers
grounded in a storm. The rain is heavy
and repeats itself, as if buckets of water
thrown out of windows.

The old man stands there holding
a memory or a wish.
Under the streetlight
his wet hair glistens like tinfoil.
The downpour is a creature
that's eating him up.

Darkness projects
from a three-story deserted
apartment building.
Ground floor windows
and doors are boarded, nailed shut.
It appears dead, like an old disease
or stripped, like a despoiled tomb.
Its bricks cracked and crumbled,
wooden casings dry rotted and helpless.
Painted in bold red
across the boarded front entrance
is a graffiti-message: GIRLS RULE.

Looking back at the old man:
He stands the way a king stands alone
when doubting himself.
Dark crawls around him. The old man stares
at the building. He is motionless,
in memory. Rain gallops over him.

Inside the warmth of a café:
my steaming coffee. Outside, the streets

are laundered clean of everyone
except for the old man who stands and stares
at the apartment building. Time has grown
over his face and body, has grown
over the broken down building.

Now the rain is as heavy as mucus
and with his tiny body
the old man shuffles away
shuffles into the dark
and gradually disappears
like a casket being covered with earth.

-- Dah
(Switch the Difference Anthology)

Spaces Among Spaces

An epilogue to the hours
On a canvas brushed with words
And of the years reflected in a wavy mirror

TS Eliot once peered in and saw lilacs
But I see opaque images
Of spaces among stars
And the clouds that caught wandering winds
To dance aerial ballets

Even today I wander about in dreams turned ashen
And feel a thin tremor of tenacity
Tapping on the door of my soul
Shrunken now to a hollow vessel
To ply the melancholy waters of night
With currents being lit by moonlight
Spreading through the skies like spilled milk

Passions run parallel with time
And swallow the distances
Of spaces within spaces
And fill them with __
Sprays of bygone springs
When violets wore purple capes
And rains fell warm as throats
with memories thick and moist as sixteen
My feet tripping over dreams cluttering my path

Body now ___ all but forgotten
It follows after me like an absent minded apostrophe
Many spaces behind my thoughts
Thoughts I wear in a crown of thorns
to pierce my head
with here and there people
And spaces absent in time, but fastened in my veins

Against my back they brush
In soft breaths of remembrances
Or in sudden shadows falling from trees

And when in a quiet sphere of night
They pass across the moon
In slow-motion wing beats
They whisper "goodbye."

-- Susan Dale
(Switch the Difference Anthology)

Driving To Physical Therapy After Reading Delmore Schwartz

If time is the fire in which we burn
then each day is a slow match of salt-
peter, cord, and ember. What
measures an eternity of ash?

My clock is atomic,
more precise than Swiss,
accurate enough to incinerate cities; geo-
synchronous satellites
tell me exactly when I am.

"Better one hour early than one minute late,"
said Batman to Boy Wonder. I prefer punctual.

-- Tim Dardis
(Tic Toc Anthology)

The Time of My Life

Hot summer afternoon
It's ninety-seven in the shade
And more inside my gear
White paper dust mask
Padded rubber on my ears
To stop some of the noise
A pair of safety glasses
Dark blue coveralls on top my clothing
Heavy leather gloves
Thick socks and steel toed boots.

Holding this powerful electric drill
Eight pounds of heavy metal
Spinning wire-brush wheel
A blur of blue and gray
Against the rust that has accumulated
On eight tons of angle iron
My job.

Eight hours inside a cloud of dark red dust
Fire storm of sparks
Steel bristles flying off
Go through my fabric armor
Into sweating skin
Dust makes it hard to breath
My glasses fogged by body heat
I watch the slow shop clock
Selling the time of my life
Eight-fifty an hour.

-- Bruce Louis Dodson
(Tic Toc Anthology)

*We Hope You Come Again to Funland**

where in lime and melon boats you
circle a spangled blonde mermaid
as your tiny fingers slice water

where you clang bells of fire trucks
and swoop in silver planes

where your bare feet sink into a sea
of red and yellow plastic balls
and you disappear into a jungle maze

where a crescent ship swings
under a plump summer moon
and cars bump like hulky bears

where carousel horses gallop
and even when you're eighty
you will recall its glittering oval mirror
and how you saw yourself inside it

as you clutched the spiraled brass pole
and your father scented with sea air
his brawny arm about your waist
holding you, holding you, holding you.

-- Liz Dolan
(Life is a Roller Coaster Anthology)

*A sign in Funland, Rehoboth Beach, DE

Why I Called So Late

Once, it was stone fruit
halved on a low table.

It had been the backgammon board,
neglected, gathering dust.

It might have been a stack of coins,
could have been creosote from the railroad ties

you cut to make raised beds in the garden,
or maybe just a curry we weren't used to—

that sluiced us into green streams (we'd lost
the enzymes to break down animal flesh).

Someone said time held us, green and dying.
Though we sang like the sea.

Someone else: *it's better to ask forgiveness
than permission*. Love, forgive me—

it would have been
a wilderness of water.

I called because time's a dish
in which fine gold chains get tangled.

                   -- Chiyuma Elliott
                   (Tic Toc Anthology)

Tonight We Will Bloom for One Night Only

Tonight you must plow me a respite between the moonflowers,
mock orange, night phlox, and Epiphyllum Oxypetalum.
You must open me to the summer night like cereus.

You must pick my perversions like petals, allow them for one night
to bloom, frangipani wafting, a concupiscent wind humming at my door.

I've surrendered to your heady sweat of primrose, plumeria,
addicted to your outstretched arms of night-blooming jasmine,
my helicopter buds hard and wanting, reeking of Madagascar vanilla with its
accompanying moral ambiguity.

I am more than a day lily.

We are each bodies, hard-wired for pleasure, destined for momentary blooming,
then extinction.

When the bats swarm and the moths sidle up to this one night of fevered
pollination, let's be ready.

Let's face them, our appetency the headlights they slam into again and again.

We will make our escape at first light. Singing.

-- Alexis Rhone Fancher
(Petals in the Pan Anthology)

Unadulterated

He took me to the coffee shop.
It was almost our first date.
He showed me the his and her espresso cups
on a shelf above the counter.

It was an awkward moment.
They were his
and hers.

And now he'd brought me there
and we played checkers
while we waited for our drinks
and didn't talk about her.

We went back a few times
before it closed for good.
We mentioned it at our wedding.
So she was even part of that.

I make my coffee in her home now.
My tastes have changed and I haven't
had cream in my coffee for years.
I wonder what she liked in hers.

> -- *Cyd Ferree*
> *(Something's Brewing Anthology)*

A Bouquet of Glads

When she moved from Nigeria to the Delta,
the land was so flat that she imagined her
homeland would be seen if she could just
look past the horizon's jealous gaze, its blue
garb no competition for the orange and yellow
wrap she wore.

But what leaned toward her, wrapping her
attention, was a wooden structure part-house,
part-hovel, yet a place she would address home
in time. Kudzu vines had mated on the front
porch steps, their matted irreverence for her
need to walk into her home unencumbered,
disregarded.

Yet when she turned her decorative head to the
sound of a gentle rustle, she saw Nigeria in a
black child's squat hands.

When he handed her his bouquet of gladiolus,
the smells of Nigeria slowly crawled back
inside her, the African irises a petite
introduction to an environment she could
trust to embrace her differences and
teach her, in time, its ways of survival.

-- Claire T. Field
(Petals in the Pan Anthology)

Beggar Lattés

Drowning?
Baby.

I've been drowning
my whole life
and now
the thought of breathing makes me shiver.
we're all in a coffee shop
on laptops in lulls
of latte steam
screams I can hear
everyone singing
under their breath;
here comes the sun,
little darling,
here comes the sun.

No one looks up and no one
remembers
what the words mean when we say them,
I'm so hungry for honesty.
outside I throw pennies down
to give street people
my luck,
I collected too many clovers for myself,
I'm selfish in that way.

a heart surgeon once
couldn't find
the iced heart
in the fridge;
by the time he found his heart it was too late,
it had iced over and turned blue
from the cold;
like the lips I purse over broken
coke bottles,

breathe out,

breathe in,

breathe

out,

breathe

in.

-- Pattie Flint
(Something's Brewing Anthology)

Talk to Me in Marzipan

I want to be covered in
smooth pink. roll up
little balls and cut them
up four ways I'll bloom
bleeding and sugary
monuments sprout
frozen in refrigerated
slices and crumbling
stained saints. spin me
on wooden sticks, paint
me in petaled lapels
pink and rubbed red.

-- Pattie Flint
(A Touch of Saccharine Anthology)

Moon-Fat Moths

Breathing quietly
in the midge massed dusk
moon-fat moths crowd the window.

Pressing against cold glass,
rustling paper wings,
their soft bodies bump and batter

the impenetrable wall.
The thin light they long to own
floods its long fingers onto

the dew thick lawn.
In the musky kitchen
the violence of their passion

is muffled,
their desperation ignored.
On long summer nights

pain can be forgotten
in the throes of infatuation.
We see our heart's desire

but are blinded by
Its luminescence.
Moon-fat moths make dark of light.

*-- Sarah Flint
(Switch the Difference Anthology)*

Weather Hysteria

Hurricane Irene has the eye
for the East Coast and what I do is open
my wooden-sash windows, and doors.
To let the morning air in sweet,
a field of Crayola
"mauvelous" cosmos on the parking strip
in their confusion/profusion
to beguile
as if it's Van Gogh's Provence garden,
eyes squinted, bedazzled
as he seizes the brush,
always going for the devilish
verb, forget about any diluting adjective's addition—
he channeled crux.

It is Saturday.
I have been feral, alone all week,
hunkered with the gerunds and the ferns.
Watering the lazy housewife beans
climbing their tipi of bamboo poles.
Snipping the dying
blooms of dahlia, zinnia, phlox.
Pinching back the window-box geranium,
leggy because it's starved for sun
this northwest summer that lasted all of
six or seven days.

There's a bug with a face, an African mask—
shaman or unremarkable god?—
above my desk between window and screen.
Waving *Hello. Is anybody in there? Does any body see?*
how already the one
burnt sienna leaf is caught,
brittle but unbroken
in the sucker of a climbing rose.

Because, of course, I never got around to
pruning this season, captured instead
by the parts of speech,
stringing them daily,
lexical hankies on the line
across the driveway
where they dry, sometimes sail,
evaporations toward every lie
lifted above my unintelligible
hopscotch chalk.

Because a sidewalk can never
yield the truth, night upon night,
this earth spinning that sun,
reckoning with
earthquake, heat wave,
ice that melts,
and every door in this house
recklessly ajar.

As if I could crayon a sonnet
from whatever makes a hurricane
first category 1, then downgrade
to tropical storm,
these sentences that never storm,
my free-verse floods—
disaster longings that reach
then retreat into the invitation
that is an August shower overnight,
its rooftop serenade. Then poof!
It's this coloring-book poem
with a magic wand to wave.
Oh, look
how painless it is

to change the weather
and the station.

> *-- Nancy Flynn*
> *(Petals in the Pan Anthology)*

Dragonfire

A silent smoldering has shifted
the ground on which we've
laid our track. Each day
a steeper climb, until we

reach the crest.
Words swallowed for weeks
erupt, sting my tongue. I spit
them out, a neon sign 'round your neck.
Your roar thunders through me.
We plunge.
Metallic tarnished moonlight shatters.

Rage condenses into tears,
you reach for me. Momentum pushes
us from the hollow chasm. We level
to an uneasy calm, lean into a curve,
ride on.

-- Linda Gamble
(Life is a Roller Coaster Anthology)

Noir Couture

"Where were you on the night of the crime?"

With a gloved hand, I calmly insert a cigarette into my jeweled holder, shutting my Deitsch handbag with a snap. The detective offers me a light and I lean forward toward the Zippo's flame and notice the 5-barrel hinge on a chrome-plated nickel/silver case.

I cross my legs and inhale. Exhale. My Alice Caviness bracelet dangles from my wrist, making a soft clink. My hair is coiffed with two front victory rolls—the rest hanging down my back in a pageboy.

"I was at the opera," I tell the detective.

"And what were you wearing?" he asks.

"A bias-cut beaded tulle evening dress with matching Ferragamo beaded satin evening sandals," I reply.

"Wedge or stilettos?"

"Wedge."

"What time did you leave?"

"Around midnight."

"And how did you get home?"

"I took a taxi."

"Checker or Yellow?"

"Checker"

"What was the cab driver wearing?"

"Button down shirt, pressed pants, tie, Eisenhower jacket and a hard bill cap."

"And who can verify the time you got back to your apartment?"

"The doorman."

"And what was he wearing?"

"A slate gray overcoat, 100% wool, with button-down tab detailing a dual front flap with welt pockets. Oh, and elongated peaked lapels."

"So, when you entered your apartment, what happened next?"

"I changed into my apricot dressing gown embellished with trapunto stitching and studded with metal brads."

"Then what?"

"I read for a while and went to bed around 2 a.m."

"What were you reading?"

"Vogue."

"The magazine?"

"Yes."

"Who was on the cover?"

"An auburn-haired model in mauve silk tap shorts."

"I'll need to question the witnesses who saw you at the opera, track down the cabbie and interview your doorman."

"Of course. Can I go now?"

"Yes, but don't leave town as the investigation is still ongoing."

I nod and reach for my coat. It's a full-length Nevius Voorhees mink, with burgundy satin lining.

"Let me help you with that," he says.

I walk out the door and take the stairs instead of the elevator.

As I make my descent, I let the mink slide off my shoulders; toss my blond wig on the steps and ditch the purse, bracelet and gloves. I exit through the "employees only" door and disappear into the night in my Oleg Cassini navy wool two-piece suit with matching Henri Flatow patent leather peep-toe pumps.

-- Sue Mayfield Geiger
(Tic Toc Anthology)

Assorted Centers

As a teenager I remember coming home after a night out with my friends
The police would be parked in front of my house

My parents had been fighting again and someone called the cops
Sometimes there would be an empty box of candy strewn all over the lawn

My father's attempts at reconciliation had ended with nougats in the hedges
Butter creams in the magnolias
Dark chocolate caramels decomposing among the perennials

I once found two milk chocolate marshmallows
Still in there brown paper swaddling clothes
Huddled together like a pair of runaways from a Fanny Farmer foster home

Our house had only one center
It was always nuts

Just nuts.

-- Phil Ginsburg
(A Touch of Saccharine Anthology)

Misshapen Adulthood

They remind you when it's time
to disband your
stuffed-animal militia.
To take your imaginary tea and
replace it with an addictive
and acidic
coffee addiction.

And though you're childhood
was confident
sure
with clarity that now
seems
heart-breaking.

They tell you that conformity
is what pays the bills
fills your life
with meaning
and purpose,
something that you didn't
know
was missing
until reality gave
you bruises in places
you'd never even felt before.
And the militia,
sitting in a water-damaged basement--
box,
is sad
silently waiting
with a Care-Bear stare that will
shoot life back
into your lemming
career.

Wishing you'd walk the plank
back into
an existence
that would sustain you
in ways that the 9-5 paycheck
never could.

-- Jessica Gleason
(Tic Toc Anthology)

Coffee Break on the Western Front, 1918

Private Harry Johnson waited in a long line of soldiers for coffee and a doughnut just made by the Salvation Army volunteers. The line snaked around bombed out buildings and under trees. Even though they were miles from the front, they still needed to keep under cover. Harry wiped the sweat from his neck, pushed the strap of his gas mask satchel into a new position, and breathed in the occasional whiff of coffee and fried dough. He had a doughnut three weeks back, and it was the best thing he'd tasted since coming to France four months ago. Worth the wait. Getting a smile from one of the doughnut gals wouldn't hurt either.

Harry's unit had just come off an eight-day stretch in the frontline trenches. He'd pulled guard duty, gone on night patrols into no man's land, dug latrines, cleaned his rifle and gas mask, kicked and swatted at rats climbing over him while he slept, scrambled into dugouts when Jerry sent over an occasional whiz bang or shrapnel shell, and cleaned up the mess afterward, although it seemed like he spent most of his time thinking about his next meal of slumgullion and cold coffee carried by runners to the frontline, and day dreaming about his mother's table filled with pies, sweet breads, and cookies. He always had a sweet tooth.

The coffee smell and freedom to stretch and stand up straight lifted Harry's spirits. He'd been down ever since Lloyd, a soldier in his unit, was killed by a sniper three days ago. Lloyd had stood up on the fire step to take a peek into no man's land one minute, and the next, he was lying on the duckboards, his nose gone, face bloody, and his watery blue eyes staring up at Harry.

Lloyd had been a skinny, pimply-faced kid, not more than seventeen who never should have been allowed to join. "What kind of army would send a silly school boy like that into the fight?" Harry's friend, John, had said after the burial unit took Lloyd away. And that stuck with Harry; it just didn't make sense. At boot camp, Harry was excited about his big adventure. That's what he called going to France to fight the Germans, but he wasn't excited anymore.

Mouth watering from the good smells, Harry moved closer to the doughnut table. He wiped out the dust in his tin cup and tapped his fingers on it in rhythm to *Hinky Dinky Parlez-Vous*, making up a few verses in his head as he did. Nothing he'd repeat to his family, but something he'd share with his squad later.

A dozen men ahead, John waved his doughnut at Harry. Harry waved back, wishing he was up there with John. Just a few more men though. Harry readied his cup and watched the black liquid pour into a soldier's cup a few places in front of him. Then the man's shoulders slumped, and Harry overheard words that made his stomach tighten.

The man walked off, head hung down. Harry moved up, cup in hand, hearing the same words repeated to the others but not believing.

"We're all out of doughnuts," the Salvation Army sister said again when it was Harry's turn.

"Out of doughnuts!" Harry's voice cracked as he spoke. "You don't have just one more hiding back there? Back in the kitchen maybe? Just a broken piece? One little small bite?"

The girl smiled although her eyes had a sad look.

"I'm sorry," she said. "We ran out of flour. We even made the doughnuts smaller so they'd last longer. We'll get a shipment of flour in another week."

"A week?" Harry said which was echoed by the men behind him. Word about the missing doughnuts had filtered back. "A week?"

"I still have plenty of coffee," she said, lifting the big metal pot with two hands. "We just made another batch."

"Well, that's something, I guess."

Harry put out his cup, and the young woman poured out the steamy brew. He moved off, kicked at a stone in his path, and breathed in the bitter aroma. Careful not to burn his lips on the metal rim, he took a tiny sip. It was strong and hot and warmed him inside. He felt a little better. He took another sip and glanced up.

John blocked his way, a smile on his homely face, and a chunk of doughnut in his outstretched hand.

-- Nancy J. Hayden
(Something's Brewing Anthology)

Learning a New Language

A half-caf, double tall, non-fat, whole-milk foam, bone-dry, half-pump mocha, half sugar in the raw, double cup, no lid, cap to go.
Certainly, ma'am. Next, please.
Excuse me luv, a coffee, please.
A what?
A coffee, please luv.
Sorry sir, what kind of coffee would you like?
A mug please with a drop of the white stuff.
Sorry sir. We don't have "A coffee".
But this is a cafe isn't it?
Yes sir, but could you look at the menu, please?
Sorry I don't understand a word. All I want is a simple mug of coffee,
Well how about a cafe latte?
OK, once it's a mug of coffee with a drop of the white stuff.
Would you like a small, medium, large or grande?
A mug, please.
Yes sir, but how big is a mug?
I don't know, I don't work in a cafe, surely you should know that.
Well how about a medium?
OK once it's a mug of coffee with a bit of the white stuff.
And would you like that hot or cold?
Is this a joke? Who wants cold coffee?
So that will be hot, sir.
And would you like that to go?
Would I like what to go?
THE COFFEE.
What do you mean?
Would you like to drink your coffee here or would you like to take it out?
Well I'm not bringing it out on a date, so I'd like to have it here.
And would you like some … Oh don't worry, Is that all sir?
Yes, thank you.
That will be €3.60, please.
Jasus luv, all I wanted was a mug o' coffee with a drop of the white stuff, not with a shot of whiskey.
OK, OK here's a fiver and I'd like the change, please.

Thank you, sir. Enjoy your coffee.
And it's not even in a mug; I don't know what the world is coming to.

-- Damien Healy
(Something's Brewing Anthology)

The Dancer

She twirled her skirt
Free flowing satin
    scalding
My lips came closer
    they touched

Tongue singed on the cup
Taste buds red, awake
I blew on the dancer
The *duende*!
She waved her wispy wings
White, cloud laced
I took another sip
She stomped a synapsis with her heel

That hot brown liquid
Washed down my gullet
Bleeding energy like
A cracked ethereal egg

She clapped her hands, stained with coffee grounds
As continual wafts
Steam sachets
Floated and rested inside my cranial cavities

I stirred the dancer
Watched her elongated steps
My spoon tapped the cup
A tambourine, solemn

I held the cup
With both hands
warming until
    she died

                -- Harmony Hodges
                (Something's Brewing Anthology)

Trash Bag Burial

When I was young, I collected odd things to remind me of moments—snapshots of friends, napkins with signatures and doodles, pieces of ribbon, Roland Orzabal's comb, dried flowers hung upside down by a pushpin, newspaper clippings, mini bottles, candy wrappers, concert ticket stubs, restaurant receipts—mementos that littered the shelves and wall above my Curtis Mathes rent-to-own stereo. I spent many hours mooning the past, the moments that seemed pivotal to existence, the items that made me. Just a blip on the timeline later, what made me became dust collectors, muddied up the little space I had, complicated what I'd become. I didn't think much of it, as I shook the folded trash bag, rushing it with air to create an opening for their burial. I pulled them roughly, tore from beneath pins, raked from shelves, and turned my head as the dust flew and the bag dropped heavy. I paused as I held the comb. It still smelled foolish, like '80's hair mousse.

-- Trish Hopkinson
(Tic Toc Anthology)

Fall Follies

Artificial cattails,
saved from last fall,
prove not so false.

Their fecund fuzz erupts.
I spread it,
a geriatric flower girl
sprinting for the trash.

Over the can
I release a flow
of rippled gold,
an autumnal tumult,
like Rupunzel's hair
let down.

Two stalks explode.
One stays firm.
My mother would toss it,
fearing next year's
fluffy shower.

But I am content with
amber fairy children
at wing in the house.

-- Liz Hufford
(Petals in the Pan Anthology)

BBC Radio Interview

So Mr. Jones, you want to be an egg-timer?
Has the demon of utility
pursued you through life, compelling
you to be useful in death?

No. I just want to be an egg-timer,
to let my ashes drip out the seconds,
pass the carefree time eternally
from one glass world to another.

Mr. Jones, why can't you
be buried decently
like everyone else?

That would be a waste of time.

-- Diane Jackman
(Tic Toc Anthology)

Nine Year Microwave Sky

You thought you could dive through time
as you did the seventh waves
of Cape Conran as a child

You thought the gaping black
was hollow,
except for the odd miracle

languid and creaking, bejeweled
in moons and singing.

But it's a dusty contradicting force,
full of debris and decisions
colliding like chance love.

You didn't realize your ballooning mind
dined on curiosity
at the periodic table,

impossibly expanding in
the belly of a finite law, stuffing

hot stars into your skull
[as much as your pockets
could hold]

You didn't notice your flesh
was blushing,
even as you lay your cooling gaze

on me

I didn't notice
because my newlywed's red dress
had me burning up

on her entry

-- Miguel Jacq
(Tic Toc Anthology)

A Poem of Praise for the Morning

This morning
I woke up early & watched your face
move, tense, relax, watched the skin near your eyes
stretch a little with every breath.

I slid my hand along your waist, hip,
halfway down the leg & then back again
across the hip, waist,
cupping your warm breast.

I traced your lips with my finger,
clockwise, counterclockwise,
trailing down the cheek to the ear,
pushing hair behind & over your shoulder.

This morning, before sunrise,
a dull light drifted in through the curtains
& settled on your cheek like a handful of ashes,
making shadows.

& while my fingers smoothed through your hair,
your face, your soft body,
I watched your eyes float up from a dream,
twirling and spiraling to the surface.

This morning
after you finally woke & kissed me,
I thought of telling you everything I did,
everything I touched while you were sleeping,
but I didn't.
I never do.

                         -- *David James*
                         (Switch (the Difference) Anthology)

In the Church of the Holy Coffee Bean

business plans unfold, spreadsheets
spill off the table. Newspapers migrate
from person to person, a shared offering.
Couples gaze, those who should and those
who shouldn't; tearful mothers, desperate
for stimulation, both chemical and human,
ply toddlers with sippy cups and pastries.

We, the regular parishioners, offer our daily
tithing. We kneel beneath paintings of Latino
saints, who smile and harvest bright red berries.
We breathe in roasty incense, notes of tamari,
smoke, peanut butter. We bow our heads before
high priest baristas, chant *cappuccino, espresso,
macchiato*, reverently sip the hot black heaven.

-- Sonja Johanson
(Something's Brewing Anthology)

Mindful, Mindless, October Date

Mindful of my lover
running late, as common
as tying my shoestrings;
I'm battered as an armadillo shell;
I put my rubber band around my emotional
body, hold tight, armor my manliness,
walk like a stud
in darkness.
I am sealed with dismay.
Though everything in October, has a bright side,
a shade of orange, a hint of witches and goblins.
In the leaves between my naked feet
and toes, I pace my walk feverishly,
trying to avoid adjectives
and soured screams,
in the parking lot.

I count them
color charts, fragments, bites, anything of matter:
hickory leaves golden, sassafras greens and yellows,
maples of scarlet, shades of pink, even purple.
The landscape is turning turf brown.
Barefooted I break into tears, the year-fragmented.
I am male discolored in this relationship,
tested and declared void of my testosterone
no sexual rectification or recharging
of my batteries.
I lie limp, native within myself, my circumstance
mindful of my lover running late.

She finally arrives; I quickly transition myself.

-- Michael Lee Johnson
(Tic Toc Anthology)

She

Somewhere

she has lost
her shadow-

now,

she stands
still…

with nowhere
to go.

> -- *Michael Lee Johnson*
> *(Tic Toc Anthology)*

I Tunneled Out of Bone

You might say I undreamed myself.
Under the swollen moon I found you
half in dust, wingless.

You reached for me
wandering my body
with an ache in your side.

You called me *sparrow, little deer*
all the names you'd already given the world.
But I would not swim in the small pool of your longing.

Now I am ready to haul rock upon rock.

To move muscled and blistered
beyond the clutch of this garden
where roses, dark petalled,

sorrow back each year.
But I cannot hold you in the ruins
of us. And what's more I am afraid

to wake naked in beggar's ticks and tarweed
with night cold on my skin,
and nothing and no-one

to hold onto,
when the beast that sometimes stirs
comes howling, inconsolable, wild mouth filling with rain.

> *-- Babo Kamel*
> *(Petals in the Pan Anthology)*

Spring Sequence

1

All spring I dream about my sister.
She's dancing for rain during a garden drought.
She's at the end of a road, watching dust clouds
tease tractors, every crow haloed in the dust.

There's a dogwood blooming, anthracnose
spotting the leaves, a bluebird perched on a branch,
dropping down for a grasshopper, or a beetle, light
gathered low into its wings, my sister watching.

All spring cancer is riddling my sister's prayers,
marking the house as if soon it sells off heaven.
Two kittens chase something across a rug,
nobody can see it, curtains shaking towards her.

2

I stole from a dream.
Flurries sank into the ground,
found bloodroot, found redbirds.

Trees wrestled the skyline,
looked at my face, tore clouds.
I took their dark branches for my words.

Down where the bobwhites whistled,
you could hear my family mock their songs.
You could nod at moonlight, and shiver.

3

Marsh marigolds have begun to bloom.
Their golden eyes are hypnotized with heaven.
their little swamp pinches against a field.

Thieves might be dancing with a bag of money.
Shape-shifters might be caroling all night with toads.
Swans have twisted high into the stars to fly north.

4

I hide from the April jokesters.
They're my best friends cranked from a dream.
Let's dodge them door to door like medicine.
If you notice their Adam's apples, they giggle
about their deepening voices. I'm still a kid
sneaking a biscuit to the granary for a stray dog.
I dream how lightning kills somebody on the roof.

The real house is burning.
Fire is anchored to the horizon, holds me.
My long dead great grandmother drops a funnel
full of smoke. Flames are curling around me
while she combs my hair, whispers a lullaby,
then winks into a mirror.

I am now awake, I say. I see bluets and moss.
Turkey poults are fluttering across a sorghum field.
They roll in the dust where sorghum should be sprouting.
They roll like baby ghosts. The momma turkey is clucking,
drags her body into a thicket. The poults scurry away.
Our farm is shrinking into their wings. Somebody whispers:
leave here, disappear. I steal from another dream.

5

A ghost is walking across the top of my car.
Dusty boot prints cleave to the windshield
as if glazed into the sky. It grinds the light
into every curve in the road, forces the hills
to strobe away their trees. It helps me swindle
my folks with dreams, with faith, with rain.

My sister is planting amaryllis bulbs.
She prays God will hear the scarlet flowers
whispering for rain. My car is a shadow
she wants to race with. She watches the ghost
walking all over the windshield, tracks,
and more tracks, pressing into the glass.

In April, you can nod at the sun, and shiver.
My sister is shivering towards amaryllis leaves.
My sister has gathered the tracks in the dust.

-- Clyde Kessler
(Petals in the Pan Anthology)

The Job Interview

I was about to retire, so I spent the last few months trying to find my replacement. The first batch of applicants was absolutely awful! I am not sure why kids today don't think they have to work for a living. In my day, we were grateful for any job.

I rewrote the advertisement to improve our candidate pool. We needed someone industrious, a self starter. He would have to be a problem solver since issues came up all the time. The intensity of our factory was extreme at times, so thinking under pressure was a "must have." We also needed a natural leader. I was a shift manager. We couldn't waste time with someone that would take too long to develop. Business training was a plus.

When my last candidate of the day came in, I immediately knew he wouldn't work out. He had a real attitude about high season. He said he didn't see the need to work overtime. I tried to explain that we were in the perishables business.

"You could smooth out demand over the year. Most of your products have a shelf life of 24 months. There is no reason not to pre-pack them."

It sounded like someone who hadn't been on the front line. We spent eleven months of the year accumulating those items. The last month was a combination of production and assembly. Everything was then delivered over a one-day period using thousands of couriers. We scheduled things to the minute.

"And where would we keep the baskets?"

"You could use the advanced storage system that they deploy up North. You collect used baskets in April and have them cleaned and ready to go in May. The baskets could be stacked with packing materials in place by July. And for goodness sakes, stop buying your candy in September and October! Everyone knows you are paying Halloween premiums."

Wow, he had a point. I had been thinking about that for years. But our schedule was developed long before Halloween went commercial. Back then, pagan rituals didn't even involve confectionary items. I was especially intrigued to hear that Santa was using this already. His operations were world-class.

"But what about the eggs? Painting them is a bottleneck. You can't freeze egg whites, so we always have to boil and decorate them at the last minute."

He smiled. He had already thought about it. "We are going to spray paint 50% of them and call it *graffiti eggs*. And the witches, who honestly have nothing to do before Halloween, have agreed to cast a spell over at least 25% of them to just make them look like they are decorated."

I wasn't sure how the Easter Bunny was going to react to all of this, but he only asked one question before hiring the kid. "After the witches do the eggs, is there any way they could make me look like Zac Efron?"

-- Marla Kessler
(A Touch of Saccharine Anthology)

Chance Show

I notice an image of Christ
on the wood floor by the pool table
the image appears byzantine
long nose, oval eyes, orange tones
his beard and thin elongated face
almost visible his invoking hands

oh my god now I'll always notice this image
the waitress says

I try to write while sipping morning
from a small paper cup

what if a war dropped into my paper cup

what about Christ on the floor

-- Irene Koronas
(Something's Brewing Anthology)

Summer Sacrament

Gates are open. Enter
in a reverent

hush—crowds stream through
turnstile gates to the bust
of pipe organ and paper-drum
on the far carousel. The first

coaster pulls me
up, my hands raised
in surrender, the most
evangelical of worships. I spin

in the Scrambler,
until languages unintelligible
pour forth
from my tongue. I rush to the rapture
of the Sky-Lift, taken

up, while those left behind
stare and wonder
but will not dare. I whirl,

the air on my bare feet, spiraling
as the Swings ascend, confess
everything on the Round Up, repent of

all I have done and
all I have failed to do.

Forgiven, I am
splashed in holy waters
and sky-sweat.

A cotton-candy mouth-melt, grape
juice with a curly

straw, this funnel cake
broken for you
to share, pass to the next.

Benediction over the loudspeaker: drive
safely, thank you for coming, go
in peace.

Go in peace.

-- Laura Lovic-Lindsay
(Life is a Roller Coaster Anthology)

Of Pigs & Pizza

I am twenty-nine and, quite literally, a single-mother: sole-supporter and making 100% of the decisions. My son's father is nonexistent. 9/11 hasn't happened yet. My heart has been stepped on, picked up, coddled, dropped, kicked, drop-kicked by my most recent boyfriend. Our relationship was an opossum, least appealing of the rodent family. It played dead. The final ending has occurred, I currently believe. I know he is seeing someone. I heard them having sex. It is the first time I've been butt-dialed, during coitus or otherwise.

I'm out having drinks at my favorite bar with my favorite frenemy. I think I just coined that phrase- I am totally drunk. We sit on stools, chatting with a pretty bartender. Behind us comes a twenty-one-ish guy. I can't hear what he is saying to us but from my friends' reaction, it is sexist and stupid. Pig is hitting on all three of us simultaneously, believing his odds are better. We are giving him the cold shoulder. Pretty Bartender is telling him to move it along.

Conversation resumes as he interlopes on down the line. We are talking about moving on from heartache. Pretty Bartender is telling me that remaining friends isn't something that happens in real life, especially when the breakup takes so long. As she is telling me that it only happens in romantic comedies, I hear Frienemy gasp. She is staring behind me. I look back to see Ex with his arm around his new girlfriend. I think I just pee'd a little. My tongue is a cottonball. I can't breathe and know, already, that my voice will not hold if he comes over to talk to me. He is heading over to talk to me. I see Pig next to me and tap him. I am shouting the first thing I think into his ear. I wish I'd heard myself say it because I already don't remember. He is taking the bait, turning his back on the girl to my left. She looks relieved. He shout-whispers something back and leans in. I see Bartender roll her eyes. Frenemy looks confused. Ex is closing the distance between us. He is saying hello to me and to Frenemy. He is calling to his girlfriend to introduce us but she is taking a seat down the bar, glaring at me while yawning at him. He is telling me that she is bored and her name is Candy. I don't yet know that she is a stripper. I won't be surprised when I learn this fact. I am repeating it to myself, doubting I'll remember her name tomorrow morning. Ex is looking at me as though I've just said her name aloud. I am wondering if maybe I did. She is tall, covered in acne and has ridiculous bangs. She is refusing to wave. Ex is just standing there. I keep drinking, my tongue, still a cotton ball, is stuck to the roof of my mouth. He is waiting for me to introduce Pig, who is now leaning over and onto me. I realize Ex thinks we're dating. I don't know Pig's name. I say nothing. Frenemy breaks the silence with a witty remark about his vintage Pizza Delivery Guy tee-shirt. She is asking him if he gets a collared shirt for his fifteen year anniversary. He is asking *why she gotta be like that* as he is putting his hand out for Pig to shake. Pig is shaking it. They are exchanging friendly words. Probably names. I am leaning in to hear Pig's name. I am a few seconds too late. Bangs appears next to Ex, yelling that she's ready to go. She is wearing Daisy Dukes with pleats (I will later wonder if they were custom made- pleats with short shorts?) Miscellaneous scars are crosshatching her legs. I am trying to say hello. She is refusing to make eye contact.

They're gone and Frenemy is asking me what the fuck. I am telling her I don't know, that everything happened so fast. Pig is fucking off, probably per my request—it is blurry even as it is occurring. Frenemy looks at me with judgment and disgust. I feel ashamed, realizing I used Pig to cast shadow on my insecurity. Frenemy is ditching me (I must pay for my sins.) I somehow make it home.

I am waking up on the hardwood floor. My dog is licking my face. My first thought: shame. Before I am fully conscious. I already know the look on Frienemy's face will haunt me for twenty years, when Ex is a distant memory, long after I've gotten married, had a second child, moved away and left not only my twenties but nearly my thirties behind me.

-- Jacqueline Markowski
(Tic Toc Anthology)

Winter Eulogy

January –
magpies crowd the house
during breakfast.

Two eggs, coffee –
no smile,
or simile.

Rain suffocates the glass,
parlay to Monday morning
mischief.

Outside, kids squash puddles
with their bikes.
You would have been 27 –

children of your own
or grad school.
You were smartest in your lucky sweater.

I drink my coffee monotone.
Magpies flutter at my insides.

-- Bradley McIlwain
(Something's Brewing Anthology)

Making What We Can

He is making stew.
I know because I hear the knocking
of his knife on the steps of the recipe.
He is precise and measured,
counting time on the carrots.
I can hear in the steel's recoil
their vibrant resistance.

This is our together life,
making what we can,
him finding a use for his hands,
spicing a pork to cook slow,
and me, shredding the silence
with the clack of words to savor
or recycle later. Nothing
is wasted that can serve.

-- Jane Miller
(Tic Toc Anthology)

The Shelleys Visit a Twentieth Century Carnival

Percy and Mary Shelley are not dead
They are alive, as Dr. Frankenstein would say
And still under the psychedelic enslavement of their opium buddy/pimp
The immortal Lord Byron, brother of Lucifer
Who is presently the depraved emcee of a carnival
Where our two poets are invited to meander
Like ghosts in breeches and frocks
Infiltrating the sawdusty midway

Lord Byron greets the reluctant Shelleys when they arrive
Donning his leather top hat and steel cane tipped with a carved asp
He introduces his playmates to a myriad of silly exhibits
Mary seems appalled by their fluffiness
She comments, what decay constitutes the twentieth century, the decay of the mind
Mary catches a glimpse of some blubbery Brooklyn broads, sucking on cotton candy
And exclaims, what horrors Percy
Percy passes some muscled queens who finger the drawstrings of his gauzy shirt
And exclaims with an erection, what delights Mary
Meanwhile, Lord Byron is rubbing his cane's snake-crest against Percy's butt
Through a tent-slit, Mary catches a glimpse of the Frankenstein Fashion Show
Where Caesar-banged punks maraud down a runway, wearing combat boots, hulking shoulder pads, and machine screws through the neck
In the background, some alternative band is crooning a song titled, Boris Karloff is dead
Mary exclaims, what transgression Percy, they've eviscerated my masterpiece
She flees hopelessly and takes a suicidal rollercoaster ride

Lord Byron chuckles heartily at Mary's ethereal figure, standing in her speeding car, flapping loosely at the top of neon peaks
Her hands thrown over her head in mercy
She yells through the rickety wood Himalayas
So close to God, I almost feel released from wicked Lord Byron, oh sweet wind of melancholia, take me, and let me not be reborn once again unto his cauldron

Lord Byron chuckles from below
Such melodrama, my sweet
Percy pleads with him
Help her you fiend
Lord Byron responds

The only help I offer, my boy, is this—he pats his cane's tongue against Percy's rapidly
building crotch—Behind the tent, maybe
Percy, that slut, is sold

Mary survives the rollercoaster ride and wanders haphazardly into another attraction
The Tunnel of Womb
A sac-like grotto, ceilinged with blood-stalactites
She rambles through, halting by a flowing spring of estrogen
There, a compressed dead baby in veined marmalade, sits
Undulating in its mahogany egg-barrel with peek-a-boo window
Mary grasps her stretch-marked belly, mourning
Oh, my poor baby, Mumma is here

Soon, the cask shatters, purging its infant
Now, an eggy white gremlin with vulture wings and emerald eyes
The baby attacks Mary, screeching
Destroy thy maker, Destroy thy maker

Mary escapes from its rampage, drenched in slime
In an attempt to eternally expedite this horrid carnival ride, Mary tears off a stalactite from above
And plunges the rosy icicle into her floral heart
Creating a gash that weeps dandelion seeds

As she lies dying in the symbolic cave of her own womb, she whispers
Farewell, my love, my Percy, may my suffering eat itself out and be banished forever

This is wishful thinking
For Lord Byron, Master of Ceremonies, will never permit Mary's absence from his games

Back to Percy
Who is standing behind a tent, pants around his ankles, receiving a blow-job from Lord Byron
His cum is overwrought
Lord Byron drinks it, declaring joyously
You do ferment the sweet cream of life, my boy

Once Percy has revived from pleasure, he inquires
When will you acquit us my lord, how grateful we would be if you freed us from your perpetual nightmare, oh, how us poets yearn to die

Lord Byron chuckles
You will never be released, angel, after all, who else would I play with

He sacrifices Percy again, though still denying him Nirvana
He tosses him into a quicksand ring where De Sadean wrestlers with leather straps and Boris Karloff heads, pound him into a spongy grave
Percy screams before dying an umpteenth time
Not premature burial, not again, not again

Lord Byron chuckles
Yes, again and again my poets, as long as you keep your frail flower-hearts, the pain will never calm
Nor will my games

-- James Mirarchi
(Life is a Roller Coaster Anthology)

Musical Chairs

I constantly move
the violin
risking music and dust.

The house wants
attention:
the toilet sings,
floors applaud.
I pace and smoke.

-- Mark J. Mitchell
(Petals in the Pan Anthology)

Ophelia's Flowers

This rusted wreck, rims coated
by thoughts, words, turned to
dust by actions—by twisted vines
curling through your mind from
the soft voice of another.
We would sit in this metal ruin
like a lost throne where Ophelia's
weeds, royal guardians' broken
spears, spring up through the
rotted floor like your moldered
mind.
A handful of them torn like oxidized,
ancient crucifixial nails, let them be
hammered for you underneath this
blasphemous dome:
Rosemary and pansies for those times
of like thoughts, remembrances when
your sorrow was sucked up like an empath
turning Solomon's key, a lonely grimoire
to shore up your fragments.
Fennel and Columbine for your words, present
for your lover.
Rue for me to taste long after this wreck has
dissolved into Ozymandian dust.
Daisy with a black center for no one
save those who served with innocence.
Plant it beneath the roots of tangled trees.
Violets that do not exist for they withered
before the last day you looked at me.
Life's bouquet for you tied up with
Autumn crocus, Oleander and Belladonna—
sweets for the sweet.

-- Ralph Monday
(Petals in the Pan Anthology)

New York, New York

Jer you were ablaze
with the smear of neon
on the strip
in the hot Nevada night

I didn't want you
to go flying from my sight
on that hotel roller coaster
that flung you past me
and my silent motherly fears

Your face gleamed with shy appeal
so I lifted you from the trappings of safety
giving you up
to the gum chewing kid
who measured your straight backed desire

against the line that separated

the faint gleam of stars
and the shadowed pavement below

You were the dangerous one
tucked under
a torn blue shirt

already to let go of earth
with just one step
and become part of sky

> *-- Jude Neale*
> *(Life is a Roller Coaster Anthology)*

An Environmental Poet

To read other minds
that entwine your own
is to go beyond shadows
of the unfazed bones
in fishing for lost
flesh and bloody fins
which die and regenerate
in a subterranean pink
as a changing lobster
now vanished from the sea
traces nearby a turtle egg
not interfering with nature
in a fetid feverish
tidal basin
spilling over in the sunlight
a relieved whisper
in a lagoon and Laocoon
from a faint wave sinking.

-- BZ Niditch
(Switch (the Difference) Anthology)

Just One Chocolate, Slowly

Lips parted –
to be painted with melted luxury.
Eyes wide to the curve and gloss –
the sheen of velvet brown truffle.

Teeth –
gentle at first touch –
release liquid caramel.
The tongue welcomes a rich river of gold.

The mind knows
this single, round gift –
sun spun into sugar,
love caressed and curled around
a dark, dense center,
the afterglow of chocolate
pointing starward.

-- Cristina M.R. Norcross
(A Touch of Saccharine Anthology)

Death by Turtle

Here, just bury this,
I say.

A plastic wrapped package
with gold letters
contains a milk chocolate-caramel-peanut confection,
also known as widening-of-waist
or –
death by chocolate turtle.

The purple and gold box
sits innocently on the counter.
Calorific enticement stares at me –
a sexy, small box
covered with fancy food photography.

Hiding it on the bottom pantry shelf,
next to the fire extinguisher,
doesn't help one bit.
I know where the turtle lives.
Not the basement either –
there are stairs to navigate,
but I could always waltz down
during a commercial break
and open the cabinet above the bar.

Drastic measures ensue.
Scotch tape,
then wide, packing tape adorn the box,
followed by the dark, plastic stretch of a Hefty bag.
Leave no trace.

Holding my breath, I peak outside the window
where my husband's jacket fades
into the treacherous woods behind our pond.

It's done, he says.
Let's speak no more of it.

There is always the leftover stash
from Halloween.

>   *-- Cristina M.R. Norcross*
>   *(A Touch of Saccharine Anthology)*

First Kiss

I gave her a kiss on
Valentine's Day
that honey-lipped lass
of my just
stirring dreams.

Wordless,
heart weighted,
barely not shaking.
Brazen,
emboldened,
yet painfully shy.

But unlike most girls
who would save such a trinket
a foil-covered taste
to remember me by

she ate it.

-- Vincent O'Connor
(A Touch of Saccharine Anthology)

Downward-Facing Lotus

Downturned my lavender
Face, turned toward the reflecting pool:
My serene nature pressed to
Blue-black water. Krishna makes
A funny flower-face at me.
My thousand-petaled hands pray him
(I'm fuckably vulnerable) not to
Take me from my floating bed.
He pulls me up by the roots
& has me on his watery lap.
It's oceanic for a minute,
But the way he everlastingly
Dandles keeps me fast
In muck I don't understand.

As above, so below.
Namaste's my underwater name;
This pose leaves me open—
Vulva smiling, but taking on water,
While fingerling minnows, tricky
Little phalluses, tickle
Me to little death.
Serenity has its discomforts;
I can't be a happy symbol—
I'm open-minded but getting bogged down.
I turn up my several-petaled face
Too late for the sun's salutation.
Bottom's up—I'm getting a sinking feeling,
Lotus-positioned and going under.

-- Coco Owen
(Petals in the Pan Anthology)

Time's Up

Time and time again the long hand overtook the short one, an eternal movement, round and round, pounding to the rhythmic beat of his heart. Father Time or Tim as his colleagues called him, wondered what would happen if his heart stopped or if for once he took a day off. After all, he hadn't rested since kicking off time, that fatal flick of his toe that had set off the Big Bang.

"I think I'll stay in bed all day today," he announced to his wife who was already dressed and shining brightly in her golden attire.

"As you please dear," she sighed, remembering the other times Time had thrown a strop. Once, when Time had sneezed the whole world had frozen over resulting in the extermination of the dinosaurs amongst other species. Then there was the occasion when Time had slipped and days had merged into one another, a whole decade wiped from living memory. She worried what might happen this time.

* * *

Meanwhile, far away, two inpatients at the local hospice crept along the corridors towards the kitchen in search of a late night snack. After all what was the point of being on a calorie controlled diet of healthy eating if you were soon to pass away?

"Hurry up, time is running out, whispered Bert, then, "Hush" as Sid stubbed his foot.

"I wish I could buy more time," Sid moaned. "I swear the days are getting shorter, I can almost feel Death breathing down my neck."

"Never mind Death, it'll be Matron who'll kill us if we get caught."

"Time's up," Death muttered, silently following the two closely behind, his scythe poised determinedly over Sid. He felt hurt and saddened by the manner in which he was always feared and never ever welcome. It was his unpleasant job to carry away the souls at the appointed time.

Although gravity and magnetic forces would ensure the universe continued with its cycle of perpetual motion, Death needed Time to tell him when the preordained event of spiriting away the souls was to take place. Glancing at his time piece, which lay face upwards across his rotund belly, Death gasped with horror.

"No! Time's standing still, and I've so many expiries to deal with still."

Ahead of him Sid and Bert moved stealthily into the kitchen and gorged on the contents of the fridge. The sound of their crunching and munching drowned out the angry whoosh as Death in a flying rage stormed off to give Father Time a piece of his mind.

* * *

"Wake up you cantankerous old fool," Death burst in on Father Time's sweet slumber. Pulling off the cosy, still warm blanket, he demanded Father Time get back to work.

Father Time, none too pleased at this intrusion flung his staff at Death who batted it off to the left with his scythe. Father Time rushing forward in a rage stumbled on the hem of his nightgown and fell heavily against the sharp edge of Death's deadly weapon. Lying unseeing in a pool of crimson Time passed away.

With a curdling scream frozen in his throat, Death stared wild eyed as it dawned on him that he was now redundant and no longer able to carry out his job. The Devil and Saint Peter too would have a reduced workload unless he worked randomly creating chaos in his wake. Shivers waved down his spine as he mused on how Devil, a stickler for discipline, and Saint Peter, the ultimate bureaucrat, would react to this change? Worse still what would Godfrina, God to all her subjects, do when she found out what he had done to her husband Father Time? Maybe she could reset Time?

* * *

Far away, two elderly gentlemen, Bert and Sid finished their midnight feast and slipping past the snoozing Matron, returned to their beds.

"Funny, that little snack seemed to stretch infinitely!" Sid mused to Bert as he snuggled deeply under his duvet.

-- Mangal Patel
(Tic Toc Anthology)

You grieve as if this shadow
has no sound yet
though once your face is covered

you let more darkness out
and what you hear
stays, clots the way one hand

clings to this dirt made black
by the other, left behind
to hide in the scent from rivers

that move again, keeps you company
years after as the cry
for water and already this crater

gouged from your mouth
stone by stone, caving in
and your lips boiling over.

-- Simon Perchik
(Switch the Difference Anthology)

Café Epitaph

I bleed coffee
conviction
caffeine and certainty

my life is a sip
between cups
of eternity.

-- Richard King Perkins II
(Something's Brewing Anthology)

Mis Numeros

    Inspired by the bilingual picture book *Mis Numeros* by Rebecca Emberley

Una lagartija, one
salamander—son
spun in the vernal womb, you turn
on my lap to gum this page,
dos hojas, two
leaves like your double tree
of names, mothers, she
(me) who waited and she who grew
you, the reason we learn
to try these words on our tongues
like the wet fruit you mash in your fist,
tres fresas, three
strawberries, why is death the color of kisses,
quatros corazones, four
hearts that never banged
against baby ribs like the good ringing
of your spoon on wood,
cinco zanahorias, five
carrots sunrise splattered, scattered
brothers in a fairy tale,
your other father's sons
baptized in Colombian rain—
him salamander again, gone to ground
to work without a name,
paperless, surviving in the cracks, as
seis serpientes, six
snakes of my lean years whispered praise
for quiet rooms, bare cellars, battle-rest
that you laugh at each dawn, silver
rattle crash that shakes
siete estrellas, seven
stars from the sky over two nations,
four ancestors, unnumbered questions

you will bellow, my April ram,
when these words become yours.

-- Jendi Reiter
(Tic Toc Anthology)

Selective Recall

> *"We don't see things as they are; we see them as we are"*
>
> *-- Anaïs Nin*

i remember my daughter's first smile
beneath a maternity ward micky d heating lamp
recall as hauntingly familiar as battery acid
thrown into a public pool filled with black children

i remember wearing levi 501s
raybans
black panther/huelga/power to the people! buttons
to my high school graduation
& the echo of a gunshot as the messiah fell to hate

i remember first love's
tentative carousing puppy love
an emotion so deep i almost perished
like the soldier flogged, lynched & castrated
on the soil he fought to save
hand to heart pledging red whiter blue(s)

i remember signs leading disciplined anger
i am a man!
rocks & bottles flying
&
scalding words like rock salt in open wounds
&
ill-mannered fire hose pushing & shoving
men women & children
&
snarling gestapo hounds keyed on hate

i remember . . .
chewy the pimp at the main motel on union ave.
to live life, you take the bitter with the sweet

i remember . . .
that ear-ringin' beam-me-up boo-yah sizzle
as the gorilla shifted
for better purchase on my back
i remember . . .
things were better yesterday that weren't

-- henry 7. reneau, jr.
(Tic Toc Anthology)

Old Dirk Savors the Prospect of Honeymoon Bliss with His Second Teen Bride

Candy cigarette trembling in her haunted hand,
adorable secrets loosely locked
in that smiling sin vault,
her giddy little-girl laugh track loops,
like a busy signal when you phone
the emergency room.

She's mine now, all mine.

Sweet ghost lounging
beneath the cool avalanche of starched sheets,
she's naked as a cupcake on death's island.
*This isn't the first time
I've shopped for tombstones
at Toys R Us.*

                -- Brad Rose
                (A Touch of Saccharine Anthology)

Pink Candy Hearts

It's just a matter of time
before it's a big legal mess.
I think I know what's happening,
but I don't.
She says, "Sweetheart, you know better
than to try to change the weather in a doll house."
Her skinny scalpel of a smile,
slicing through my life's gray, imperfect fog,
before the lawyers move in,
eat all the little candy hearts.
Some of them, you'd swear, almost beating.

-- Brad Rose
(A Touch of Saccharine Anthology)

The Wallflower

A beauteous garland of flowers, they declare,
Surrounds the garden
Dresses it in colorful saris.
All speak of their pulchritude,
ignoring the others.

But Lacy-leafed ferns,
chided children of the forest floor,
wait in the soil, bide their time,
an artist's monochromatic palette.

Their exiled faces crammed
into overcrowded trains of resplendent flora,
searching for their own earth pockets to plow.

Obdurate roots sprout legs in the moist soil,
their flags unfurl in whipping spring winds
a verdigris sea pushing their popinjay neighbors aside
trumpeting their independence.

Like Alfalfa's cowlick,
mint green leaves emerge erect fans
delicately curlicued arms,
supplicants genuflecting to the heavens
embracing their freedom.

They elbow the others into corners,
their terran-flagged territory anointed.
Nomenclature doesn't truly matter.
Just a Sargasso Sea of whispering leaves
dominate the landscape.

Slow motion time-cameras watch them blanket the others,
colors canopied beneath their green swatches.

others listen for the new garden sounds,
delicate breezes borne carry music in their swaying arms.

-- Sy Roth
(A Touch of Saccharine Anthology)

Through Her

On the first night
of her marriage,
late, late, later into the night,
she found her husband's skin
folded neatly on the bedside locker.

It was folded like a long sheet,
folded over, and folded, and folded,
and folded over onto itself. On the outermost most visible fold,
like the hood of a hoody, was her husband's face;
eyeless, tongueless, as flat as a folded pillowcase.

She shuddered; a chill ran through her,
from her bones out, from her bones in.

From the bathroom she could hear the water
flowing from the shower. The door of the bathroom was ajar,
a thin ribbon of light
cutting over the bed from the opening. She took a step
towards the door.

Through the gap she could see her husband,
a raw inner man of muscle, sinew;
eyes and tongue the only inner-outer parts
that she could now recognise.
He looked out at her from the streaming curtain of water.

He was utterly horrid, sexless,
red as blood but not a drop of blood dripping, every drop of it held in.

"This is the very beginning," she thought.
"This is the very end."

> *-- John W. Sexton*
> *(Switch (the Difference) Anthology)*

Missing

Five days after he disappeared
a Pez dispenser still lay on his
bed, nuggets of candy still left
inside. What good is a desperate
heart when two weeks have
gone by? No sign of my eleven-
year-old son, and every day I
search for him underneath
the uncaring sky. Hours before
sunrise I press my tears with
my fists; his favorite candy,
a box of Junior Minds, near his
picture right by my bedside
where I can see it. On a cold
night I write down a prayer,
weigh it down with a chocolate
Easter egg he once stole.
How difficult parting is as
weeks turn into months
without any hope.

-- Bobbi Sinha-Morey
(A Touch of Saccharine Anthology)

Candy Foil Memories . . .

Memories wrapped in old candy foil,
pasted within pages
yellowed, dogeared and moth-eaten,
are like whispers echoing
from alleys of forgotten minutes,

the lines long scribbled
beneath glued chocolate paper
have a remembrance to revive,
an amnesic story to retell,

they walk me through
long deserted gravel trails
of an adolescence lost
with its giggly reverberations.

wizened fingers caress them
I can taste their long lost sweetness again
while a wistful smile glows
with precious moments relived.

a childish bet won, a silly prank played,
a gift of friendship or a favor repaid,
people forgotten, lost or gone,
faces misted by myopia of preoccupations~

fleet in snippets of recollections
like an old mute movie or a stilted song
from arthritic gramophone,
as I indulge in kaleidoscopic delights
of varied fragments of reverie...

-- Smita Sriwastav
(A Touch of Saccharine Anthology)

Anecdotes of the Defunct Ferris-Wheel

Lying rusted and forgotten,
seemingly within a bubble of time
in abeyance between
yesteryears and nascent morrows,
ignored by selectively amnesic present,
its languid limbs too lazy
to flirt with promiscuous breeze,
it gazes bleary-eyed
at distant periwinkle heights,
where it once chatted
with vagrant, chameleon clouds.

Even a shove of geriatric motor
coughing its bronchitic lung out,
spluttering in pungent, diesel epithets,
fails to make its arthritic stagnancy melt
into whirling fluidity
of concentric revolutions,
while it indulges in anecdote adventures
rifling through sepia glimpses of reverie
within realms of wistful daydream.

It reminiscences about
those gleeful shrieks tinged in fear
and heady anticipation,
now mere faint echoes lost
within the catacombs of memory,
the delight of flight etched
on broadly grinning faces,
it fondly recalls, smirking inwardly
at the pansies wilting
with terror within its embrace,

The air was scented
in sumptuous aromas
of buttered pop-corns, ice-creams,

popsicles, sizzlers and more,
and rarely it would luckily taste a morsel,
due to careless fingers
and gravity's weird idiosyncrasies
~their flavors still revived
as it smacks the lips of memory.

Excited and nervous faces
of menopausal grays stealing a slice,
of that childhood long lost,
dirt smeared faces
and impish grins of mischief,
as adolescence inhaled deeply freedom
from stringent classroom routine,
innocent toddler crying
for milk or sleep least interested
in chaotic rides to nowhere.

The roller coaster and swaying boat
see-saws, sliders and swings,
stand in dazzling splendor performing
to whims of fuel as laughter floats
smearing the visage of moments
like the varied holi hues,
and even the snooty stars,
the hoity-toity moon watch
green with envy at winking fairy lights.

The midnight gossips
amongst the park's inhabitants sharing
funny incidents or heartfelt experiences,
the fickle affections
of soaring helium balloons
emblazoned as air-kisses
on corrugated cheeks while they fly
to horizons unseen
on wings of gypsy, giggling wind,
the hoarse cries of vendors,

allure of magician's tricks,
fortune-teller's round eyed predictions~
premonitions read in the sky,
amounting to mere conjecture,
motorcycle acrobatics to assuage hunger~

The memories are kaleidoscopic,
always seemingly new, multi-faceted,
like beloved folktales read
from a dogeared book,
it munches imaginary peanuts
reliving those lost and still coveted years,
through languid, monotonous days,
and lulls beggar boys to sleep
on insomniac nights of loneliness,
crooning frayed lullabies of tarnished bliss,
and embellished stories of the half-forgotten . . .

-- Smita Sriwastav
(Life is a Roller Coaster Anthology)

& the stone man said

serve me up dirty
filthy & ill-used
I am the cartoon
at the end of dawn

a mother's prayer
quick lips of sorrow
kissed
echo of the new night

god help us
we are slain
by moments of anger
until it hurts
hurts no more

echoes of woe
cry the new city
built upon pastures
flowers of doom

don't cry me down
ye awful lament
scarlet promises
sea of new blood

following empty
you are what lies next
stone heart
eye of moon

fingernail traces
eyelashes weeping
a lone figure
intolerant shadow

maybe she's wicked
lips apart magick
a tongue of flame
passion divides

old soldiers
& new lovers
pretendering peace
a fortune of skin

we are the pale
standing outside you
a misting of star-shine
penumbra undone

don't you dare wake me
with mute invitation
where dragons have flown
mine heart is gone

our cloak becomes
a withering wall
beneath the veil
a hermit resides

she is cooking fish
to feed her man slave
a bit of wine
to hurry him down

he places an ear
on the pit of her navel
a child passes through
the face of a dime
it ain't hitler
it's ike

hurry on singers
watchers impatient
they only came to hear
the end of your song

& so it is father
whose breast is without us
whose heart is within us
whose belt is upon us

& mother stirs the soup
chicken noodle it is
no chicken no noodle
soup nonetheless

a caravan gathers
round an open-mouthed child
he points to their camels
strange alien hump

an hour of madness
must I possess
a vision of angels
heart of the beast

last night I saw you
bare assed naked
bombs made your cities
& titties dissolve

who were you then
with your crack in the sky
who are you now
laying spread before me

there are brave new voices
islands of silence

where cave people dwell
residue of shame

I want a new blanket
to cover my faces
to shield me from the
I want the wind in my home

old man bite your tongue
your gun lies dead in your hand
cover yourself
you are disgusting to the new children

a grave in the city
where geese come to graze
a feast of bones
& hollow moments

pigeon shit in the sand
the mortar of giants
brave deeds spoken
a crumbling wall

visions of paper
pitiful wisdom
the shaman in flames
who laughs the fool

bruised sky of my face
bitter sweet of mine heart
divide the peace of me
make arrows & napalm

-- Tom Sterner
(Switch (the Difference) Anthology)

Musical Lives

Childhood seems to last forever
My days are filled with fun and games
(London Bridge is Falling Down)

I guess it's about time for my youth
I'm growing and learning
This is fun
Can I stay a while?
(Satisfaction)

What do you mean 'responsibilities'?

Oh, I get it...
I'm an adult now
Wow! Big deal.
All work and no play
(Let's Go Crazy)

How can you be moving out of the house already?

Your mother gave birth to you just the other day -
Or was that twenty years ago?
How many children do we have, dear?
Two-and-a-half?
Good, that's normal
(Stand By Me)

Why am I in a personal care home?

I'm not that old
The golden years? HA!
There are so many things left to see and do
I don't want to die yet!
(No One Is To Blame)

Allow me tranquility
And let me make my peace with God
(Stairway To Heaven)

-- Kevin Strong
(Tic Toc Anthology)

The Shadow Girl

Dow lived in an alleyway of crooked bricks and poisonous ivy. It was not much of a home but it was the only place she could call her own. An occasional cat or fox kept her company and every now and again a couple would stumble in to have quick and alcohol soaked love.

They never noticed Dow. She was nothing more than a lingering presence, an uneasy feeling of somebody watching. Dow looked at the girls intensely, creeping so close to them that her nose would be just inches from their kissed mouth and she could even see the teardrop trembling on the eyelashes of some of them.

After a few minutes she always sighed with frustration and retreated to the dimness. None of them was Her. Dow stopped hoping a long time ago but since she had nothing else to do, she continued her search. Day by day, week by week she grew a little thinner and paler, becoming nothing more than an echo of a rain washed afternoon, when the girl she belonged to decided it was time to become a woman. Dow remembered the boy who smelled of overchewed bubblegum and had a pimple next to his left ear. She remembered turning her eyes, trying to melt into the darkness of the alley, she didn't want to see. She huddled behind the shadow of a fat garbage bag and closed her eyes shut. By the time she gathered the strength to come out from her hiding place, her girl and the boy were already gone.

Dow tried to run after them but the shadows of the alleyway were clinging to her and the fingers of poison ivy clutched her ankles. The graffitis overhead were laughing at her in their violent red voice.

In her moment of cowardice, Dow became a disembodied shadow and had to live with the guilt for the rest of her existence. As for the girl, she left the boy on the next corner and ran home; never truly realizing that she left a part of herself in that abandoned alleyway.

-- Fanni Sütő
(Switch (the Difference) Anthology)

Keeping Time

With open palms, relaxed wrists, to loosen congestion
I beat your upper back like a drum—something
—according to your doctor—that must be done
if we want to keep you with us.
This week, it's my turn. I drum. I drum.

How small you've become, how thin!
Your heart beat a rhythm like this one once
when I lay curled, feet upper-most, under your ribs
as your breath nourished me.

"Okay, time to cough," you mutter, and summon
demon mucus from your lungs, spit
fastidiously into a tissue you will later burn.
We begin again. I drum. I drum.

After this session, we'll make tea, peel potatoes,
cut up onions for supper, go on—
as if your lungs were perfectly clear,
as though they were filled with nothing but pure air,
as though this were not a quest but an answer,
as if we were not
keeping time for that clicking rack of bones
who calls himself a dancer.

-- Anne Swannell
(Tic Toc Anthology)

Bellis Perennis Imitates Narcissus

Totally absorbed in the way their long slim petals
radiate from their golden centres,
their myriad tightly-stamen'd rows unfurling
as they contemplate their own intricacy,
they compare themselves to one another;
all exactly alike, yet each the epitome
of its own self-centred glory.

Altering minutely hour by hour
with such light as the window allots them
and whatever nourishment they can manage to ingest,
twisting slowly in their struggle for eternal grace,
these daisies‹day's eyes‹evolve.

More than a few
have committed suicide on this coffee table;
its highly-reflective surface pulls them in.
Obsessed with their own image,
they dive straight at it,
lie there, petals splayed, wedded to glass,
pollen spattered on the shine like dust.

-- Anne Swannell
(Petals in the Pan Anthology)

Augusta, Maine

I was made for the sun,
but here I am in Augusta.
At Christmas, the snow
is as real as ground glass,
and the Three Kings,
are just statues,
less than the live dogs
around St. Patrick's manger.

All summer *mi hijos* played baseball,
and I shivered in the stands,
drinking *café con leche*
from a thermos.
The sun gave no more heat
than a postcard of Florida.
My brown thighs shriveled
like bananas
left on the counter.
I covered them in mom jeans.

All winter I sit, huddled
indoors in a white parka
bought from a catalog.
I drink *Café Bustelo,*
straight, no leche,
my gloved hands around
a thermos from the bank.

Neighbors hike to the ski lift
on the edge of town.
The men balance six-packs
on their shoulders.
No one else winces at the wind,
the snow, the sleet,
the black ice,
the wind and the sleet

that pound at my windows
like someone else's bad lover.

My sons play hockey.
I keep them busy.
They are made for Augusta.

> *-- Marianne Szlyk*
> *(Something's Brewing Anthology)*

Listening to **No Other**, *Thinking of Takoma Park*

Lila remembers
slipping into the storefronts,
the places her parents called
junk stores.

Then the world was a collage
of tinted-blue tinfoil
and broken mirrors (deliciously
bad luck for seven years),
cherry blossoms
against a maroon sky,
the sea-green walls of a
luncheonette (we forget
the cigarettes and grease),
a frayed voice
smothered in sopranos.

But it was not her past.
None of it was.

Then Lila's daughter,
the pink-haired girl
in maroon vegan leather,
a soprano
in the school choir,
slips into the kitchen,
this collage
of magazines, TV shows,
someone else's taste,
not her mother's.

Wishing for an electronic cigarette,
Maddie looks out to the snow
that falls on the cherry blossoms
the shards of mirrors
from Restoration Hardware

and scraps of greasy tinfoil
alike.

> *-- Marianne Szlyk*
> *(Tic Toc Anthology)*

A Knight Shining, Without Armor

As the years did pass so the daffodil did cobble together a survival of sorts.
He buried deep his secrets and endeavored to forget them.
And to reify their remove, to seal their coffin, as it were,
so that the secrets would never reemerge or be faced and so that
such events would not reoccur, the daffodil commenced a new project.
His daffodildom had to be overcome to maximize his survival chances.
In other words, rather than cultivate his inner daffodil, he worked to extinguish it.
And the daffodil did go to the gym and did lift very heavy weights indeed
and study the techniques of lifting in bodybuilding manuals
and he did overload his body with fuel to feed his ever growing muscles
and to bury still further the unspeakability of himself.
And lo was the daffodil transformed into a tank.

And as a tank he did garner glances glad returned on the street
and in the bathhouses and in the kudzu-choked expanses
behind the city park. And the daffodil did find connection,
however fleeting, in this semi-public erotic sphere.
And here he would kiss strangers in the day and in the night
and run his hands over them and entwine himself with them and
sink to his knees and perform that which shall not be named in this poem
for the daffodil does not wish to offend his more modest readers.
And on his knees, with his mouth full, so to speak, the daffodil did pray
that the police would not arrest him for indecency or worse and that he
would not be pummeled and left to rot, for kudzu is rapacious and would
quickly cover the remains of a daffodil, even one transformed into a tank.

And as risky as was his activity—the groping and stroking and beyond—
at least there were others around, and the daffodil thought that perhaps
this was safer than going into a car and entering an apartment
where he would meet a fate even worse than the night so terrible
that it had to be buried and there would be no one around to witness
or help just as there had been no one on said night.
And the daffodil did encounter others truly interested
in more than an encounter of the byway. Only they did grow
impatient for there was much that the daffodil could not bear
and ever did the daffodil deflect and pirouette so as not to

reveal and not to face his secrets. And these others left him to his
dance moves and his evasions, however inadvertent they might have been.

And the daffodil did so yearn for someone less readily deflected.
And he would dream of this figure, as if in daguerrotype, as someone
strong and gentle and patient, someone who would button the
button on the back of his shirt collar in the morning as a gesture
of good tiding for the day and then nuzzle his neck and give his ass
a squeeze as he raced to catch the train. And after yet another
needle-in-the-haystack online date, the daffodil would think of the knight
while staggering towards sleep, this knight on a white horse galloping
towards the tangle of bramble and thorn and kudzu and muscle
that formed the daffodil's carapace. And thus did the daffodil's years pass,
with secrets intact and glances returned (or not) and beds briefly shared
(but mostly empty) and hooves of the knight's horse always within earshot.

-- Yermiyahu Ahron Taub
(Petals in the Pan Anthology)

The Anchorwoman

Bodies in rows like sunflowers.
She wears a yellow suit.
White blouse, collar overlapping
lapels of her jacket.
Too many gone in Gaza. Two
strands of pearls. Think
fifties and teas and silk shifts.
And the trapeze.
Can legerdemain hand us the past?
Reserves of groundwater
evaporating. A hundred sorties
in Iraq. It's like nothing
we've ever seen before, says
Hagel of the red and
blue striped tie. Sleeveless black
dress tonight. She's of
a certain age, but her biceps have
definition. Two lucky living
stiffs fight off ebola. An unlucky
teen left on a "show me"
street to wither, bleed. A flowery
dress, tight around the bust,
short sleeves, mandarin collar up
against subtle make-up.
Refugees leave Bangui, Central
African Republic, for Cameroon.
A hell of a way to learn geography.
Red petals perk on a synthetic
background of solid white. Hunger,
wandering, weariness
replace the djembes of synthesis.
A gold chain with a locket
triangles down a lilac sweater.
A strand of her son's hair
may be inside. Or his first baby tooth.
Or a snapshot of her in those

other times. She wears long sleeves
to keep her blood warm.
We know for sure she's seen
the unimaginable. Who cares
about roots showing if the moon
has forgotten its turn?

-- Judith Terzi
(Switch (the Difference) Anthology)

After the Before

There was a before. Wasn't there?
When new baby blues wobbled for focus
At my breast we gazed into each other.
Wasn't it in the before that he smiled
And we beamed back at him, at each other,
At the amazing art our togetherness bore?

Before he arrived we spoke of every possibility,
A Harvard lawyer, Australian goat farmer and
When we spun the wheel, landing on the
Most amazingly perfect infant, we wept in gratitude.
His first steps? They were before, right?
We were his Pole Stars and he was ours.

When did the after start? Before the before was done?
Reversing falls bewildered, stumbling chaos of
Broken flow, hostaged waters left to work it out.
And when the falls reversed is that when
The before ended? Time's not always so neatly split.

I touched the word as the before receded,
Ran my fingers along the edges, but couldn't
Speak it, until the cicada-stolen silence demanded
Recognition. Who stole our son? Who stole our baby?
And who the hell is Autism anyway?

After the after became the norm, new after-punctuated
Befores began, life measured in past tense befores.
He hasn't bitten anyone or himself in three weeks
And words once learned have been relearned now,
Some of them anyway, but not like before.

-- Talaia Thomas
(Tic Toc Anthology)

Not Sleeping

I can't keep
not sleeping at night
I can't keep
letting all those
    open cupboard doors
pull my shoulder blades
I can't keep
hoping for that miracle
    change black tea
    into coffee and cream
I can't keep
recycling those words
    said and unsaid
replies and responses
never meet resolution
I can't keep
my head full of bees
whispering why
    it doesn't matter
    it never matters
I can't keep
eating the edges of my cuticles
it won't grow flat
I can't keep
my ear to my gut
it's holding on to a secret
    I'm listening
    it's not telling
I can't keep
waiting by the phone
waiting for that email
    to make it right
it will never be right
I can't keep
saying I don't mind
I get it-I understand

     I don't
I can't keep
not surrendering to anything
since the switch flipped
    it got broke
    I can't switch it back
I can't keep
a single person as ideal
as I have loved them
    stop idealizing
I can't keep
all the names off my lips
the push out daily
    hourly I form them
    my mouth aches
I can't keep
this pencil moving
    its eraser is shrinking
there's more mistakes to make
I can't keep
presuming the road's closed
my feet are swelling
    until it hurts to walk
    but I walk anyway
I can't keep
listening to the air in my lungs
rub against my nostrils
    I hear myself living
    I need to be sleeping

-- Sarah Thursday
(Something's Brewing Anthology)

I Want Candy

Candy is dressed all in pink – pink stockings rising to meet the thigh hugging hem of her tight pink dress, vanilla hair puffed and billowing like a cotton cloud, frosted crystals of cheap pick and mix jewelry resting on the plump cleavage of her marshmallow breasts.

There's a vicious little splinter in the hard stick that holds her head high. It will pierce the greedy tongue of anyone who tries to take too much of her in one go. Beneath the orange soda glow of the street lamp she paces in ever-decreasing candy cane spirals, teetering on the caramel constructs of stiletto heels and wafting the irresistible entice of her sickly sweet scent to the night.

A man appears, wide-eyed and drooling, trembling with unfettered desire.

"You look scrumptious," he gasps. "How much to taste your sweetness?"

Candy smiles.

The white peppermint lozenges of her teeth reveal themselves between the cherry-red glossiness of her lips. She whispers a sum and flutters eyelids painted a bubblegum hue. With a jangle from her bangles the syrupy stickiness of her hand melds with the clammy sweat on his palm.

She leads him deep into the liquorice black of the alley.

His will dissolves and liquefies like chocolate become velvet in the intense heat of her embrace. The jellybean lacquer of her fingernails drives into his flesh. She allows him to unwrap her and claim the sticky prizes within.

He simmers a while before she brings him to the boil. She departs the moment he is spent and leaves him a single grain of her sugar. It wedges itself in the cavity of his cold and emotionless heart. In time the lustful cravings that it arouses will bring him back again and again and again.

"You're so sweet," he will whisper. "So, so sweet."

He is not the first and he won't be the last.

Each time he indulges she will leave him with the gift of another granule that will hasten the rot that decays his soul. He will age at alarming rate, becoming wan and haggard and frail. The delicious delight that his torture brings her will help Candy maintain the glow of her sugary sheen. It's all part of the bargain. Enter the candy shop and pay the price.

He will come to view what is left of his life through the peanut brittle fug of some diabolically diabetic coma and will find himself at death's doorstep much sooner than he ever expected. In his final moment the words that ooze like molasses in the last exhalation of his death gasp will be tragic in their inevitability.

"I want Candy."

And she will mourn him in pink - dusting her face in sherbet powders - rouging her cheeks in lollipop red.

-- David Turnbull
(A Touch of Saccharine Anthology)

The Last of the Old Gods

1.

The torsos of women at the bottom
of the ocean—they rush up like moons,

they kick out my eyes like rolling crystal,
like a heartbeat transfixed

on the headless primordial.
I know what it is to feel safe

in a fool-sand darkness.
The dead like cold mothers,

breasts of cut diamond.
I wonder about light in a tunnel.

2.

In time, I won't have limbs.
Hips to neck, I'll be an island

searching for its main.
I'll be a moon

without a body.
When my shadow

barrels like stone, who will
skip me over the bend of Eridanus?

3.

Nothing else but the sound of rushing
light in a conch, dark and endless.

Soon, the earth will speak;
the young will swim

after two days, air and water blended.
The sound of thunder

watering rock: the new gods
shaking from their eggs.

My last thought is of the blind moon
gaining sight of the cranes

spreading their wings at the mountain.
Bog of wild and wicked dreams.

-- Jessica Van de Kemp
(Switch (the Difference) Anthology)

I'll Show You Sunshine

Rebecca adjusts the shocking pink flower on the prosthetic ponytail in her hair and draws dark yellow sidewalk chalk across the driveway. The pavement is wet papier-mâché. The ponytail was a $3.99 special offer, as-seen-on-TV, that aired during one of Rebecca's favorite edutainment shows with promises to 'Make Your Hair Pop!' and 'Bump Your Style!'. Rebecca has abundant flowing hair of her own and isn't usually taken in by faddish infomercials, but she relishes the feeling of having hair that isn't hers intermingled with her smooth straight strands, hair you can take off at night and are actually supposed to. She compassionately adopts the wayward simulation and pretends until she's no longer pretending, brushing it affectionately before bed in a solo show of self-esteem as if it's some kind of vulnerable creature.

The way Rebecca feels when bodily add-ons—jewelry, tie-in hair, a toy plastic claw hand—become part of her is very similar to her excitement when the chalk prints thick, soft lines on the asphalt or concrete, the motion perfectly smooth and buttery with no discordant resonance creating random jarring vibrations in her hand, which she hates. Today every stroke is like that, flawless, her squiggles bold and angles clear. Rebecca's drawings are abstract, unrecognizable, yet distinctly mature. Playful, but they resemble more the idle doodling of a bored adult working at a call center. Now she sketches a warped essence of a hopscotch board, with letters instead of numbers, adrift in a scenescape of astral waves. A blue '4' is eked vividly above the entire drawing.

Rebecca's mom emerges from the beginning of the driveway and places a moist hand unobtrusively on the very top of her daughter's head. Katie acquiescently glides her hip, thick-rimmed glasses up the bridge of her nose for exactly the 40th time this day before gliding the opalescent orbs behind them thoughtfully over the visual network of chaotic intentionality at her feet. She thinks the drawings are projections of Rebecca's subconscious.

Dinner. *We could have this, this, or that, what sounds better?* As Katie presses pride and soft kissing membranes into Rebecca's built-in hair while stroking the ponytail, the final dot is placed onto the limestone painting. The sun has shifted towards imperturbable sleep, and they are now lightly cloaked in shade.

Katie walks away and Rebecca notices the mushrooms growing from her scalp. Three diminutive toadstools with rounded caps at the back of her mother's cranium, little steps, like the pixilated 2nd, 1st, and 3rd place platforms at the end of a Super Mario Kart race. On second thought, she brushes another dark blue line onto the cement canvas and a tiny row of identical mushrooms sprouts instantly from the powdery surface.

-- Tamara K. Walker
(Switch (the Difference) Anthology)

Sunday at the Gallery

"For I have known them all already, known them all—
Have known the evenings, mornings, afternoons,
I have measured out my life with coffee spoons."

    — T.S. Eliot, *The Love Song of J. Alfred Prufrock and Others*

Well-dressed women come
and go; some
speak of Michelangelo.
Time smells of coffee
stirred clockwise. Tinkle
of metal on china makes
the wall clear its throat.
This wall is not a wall
warns Rimbaud's cupboard.
An hallucinate Venus
with spiky chitin vulva
floats by, humming
like an air-conditioner –
it may belong, along
with the violin,
to Chagall.
Quick - duck
back through cracks
while Miro explodes.
Pick Constantinople -
you'll need persistent weapons.
Escher and stairs! Follow, but
no matter where you go
there you are.
Let's do the next room.
They say there's a Magritte...

    -- Mercedes Webb-Pullman
    (Something's Brewing Anthology)

Stirring Sugar

your coffee cup
has left Olympic rings on the
classified columns
of yesterday's newspaper

you stare through the window
eyes fixed on some other place

while I stir sugar
tinkling through the silence
between us
if you could see this impossible
half-melted sugar Fibonacci
on my glass coffee-mug's side -
this diamond feather lace-web delta -
you'd smile, too

-- Mercedes Webb-Pullman
(Something's Brewing Anthology)

Reading Shadows

Breeze-stirred shadows tremble
and tumble down your living-room wall
like electronic blips that reassemble
long forgotten warnings scrawled
to the future; *'judge not by their looks*
but by their behaviour' perhaps
'there is danger in having all the books
in one library' – Alexandria adapts.

Like Pythia's smoke they writhe and curl
with no-one to translate them but you
and you choose what you need, working girl
pimping words, but all of them true.
The universe spent centuries perfecting these
exact transmissions, just for you to read.

-- Mercedes Webb-Pullman
(Switch (the Difference) Anthology)

Love Letter

I leave you messages in the dust. But you never read them. With a hiss of Pledge and a swipe of cloth, you wipe them away.

I line my hands up to match the marks yours make when you press against your bathroom mirror, examining your face for imagined imperfections. They match perfectly, and I think of how your fingers would feel interlocked with mine. Your thumb absently tracing circles over the flesh between forefinger and thumb. But you brush your teeth and leave without a backward glance.

I leave you poetry in the pages of books you got bored of. I scatter the dry petals of long-dead flowers at your feet. See me. Want me. I've waited so, so long.

When you leave the house for the day - all bustling, patting pockets, muttering lists of things you need to remember as you slam the door behind you - I get unsettled by the silence. I never enjoyed silence. I could never get the hang of sitting quietly, of not doing something. Perhaps that's why I'm still here. So I drift, making up stories for the people you drape around, grinning, in photographs. Trying not to feel sick that they know the weight of you, and I do not.

I follow behind you, lovesick - sick of love - as you potter from room to room; just close enough so the wisp of your scent passes between my outstretched fingers. I curl at your feet like a lapdog while you watch TV and pretend you know I'm there.

I adore the vitality, the reality of you. The way your blood blooms in your cheeks, the delicacy of each eyelash. The ease with which you laugh. The grace in your limbs as you fold your laundry. I long to be the breath which fills your lungs. You remind me of things about myself that I thought were long since lost.

Sometimes, I almost reach you. Some madness overtakes my mind and I begin to call your name, to touch your shoulder, you turn -- and then your eyes cloud over with confusion. You laugh under your breath.

You shrug, and get back to your book. Nothing there. Silly you. Jumping at nothing. Next you'll be believing in ghosts.

Perhaps...perhaps, so many years from now, your heart will cease to beat, and everything will change. Your world will shift, the shade of the darkness will tilt, and there I'll be. Where I've always been. You'll see me, at long last. And you'll smile. We will drift together for all time, so close our atoms will merge and there will be no space between your lips and mine.

Or perhaps you'll leave this world as you live in it; happy, strong, busy, ever looking forward. Your loved ones will call you, and you will answer, running into eternity unafraid, unattached. And I will shrink into the cold sheets and try to remember the songs you sang under your breath. I would not hate you for that. We never met in life. My name was well-worn on my stone when you moved in here. Why would my smile make you weak, the way yours makes me weak?

But I do long for you, so.

I was never good at resting. Now, I cannot sleep, even when I am desperate for the oblivion of it. So I fill the secret places of your room - the top of a cupboard, the space between your drawers and the wall - and listen to your deepening breaths, imagining my heart beating in time as we drift into dreamless, contented slumber together. And I wait for the dust to settle in the stillness, so I can write to you again.

-- Emma Whithall
(Petals in the Pan Anthology)

Placebo

As an artifact of Catholic schools,
I accepted half-truths,
As long as they served the purpose of a good story,
Like some that are in the Bible.
So I had no trouble believing
My friend sitting next to me at lunch.

Even when I knew he was manipulating me to share my M&M's,
The ones the nun gave me for scoring highest on a beatitude test.
He didn't come right out and ask;
He had heard her warning me against charity,
That if I shared them I was just encouraging laziness.

Rather, he took the approach that I would reward him for his tale:
How his Dad's uncle, before World War II,
First came up with the idea of coating bits of chocolate in hard candy.
He had bet that since children love to mimic their parents
They too would love to take pills.

Pharmaceutical firms had recently developed the technology
Of compressing remedies, which had until then been dispensed in packets, into pills.
Why not give kids their own version,
A sign they were growing up, just like candy cigarettes?
But that approach never caught on.

It wasn't until the Army Air Corps
Were supplied with candies in cardboard tubes shaped like bombs,
That the product became successful.
The military wanted its crews to have an extra burst of energy
On their extended missions to bomb and burn
The last cities of the German Empire,
Those left with nobody but children and the infirm.

When the pilots returned home,
And this he heard from his father who was one of them,
They brought with them an appetite for his uncle's invention.

Except for his father.
He once heard his father tell his uncle
It also brought back the flash and smoke of crumbled cities,

That the sound of the candy coating cracking
Reminded him of bones breaking.
Which was why this candy was never allowed in his house.

Feeling sorry for the way his parents were treating him,
I passed him my last three.

-- Ron Yazinski
(A Touch of Saccharine Anthology)

Class at Disney's Animal Kingdom

After we had tired of watching the silver-back gorillas
Chase each other like kids on the playground,
And then the tiger fall asleep
Like the misplaced student who found long-division,
Even with a calculator, too difficult,

We ran into a pleasant old cast member
Who guessed we were either teachers or nurses.
Teachers, how did you know?
"I noticed you were paying attention to other people.
"The only kinds of folk who do that are either teachers or nurses.

"I myself am a retired teacher from New Hampshire.
"After thirty-five years of killing Romeo and Juliet,
"One-hundred-and-seventy-five death scenes,
"I had had enough.
"When I first started, I tried to make the kids feel that we were in it together.

"But I was only kidding myself.
"During my career, my students went from Cliff Notes,
"To movies, to Internet summaries, to "I bet you can't fail all of us."
"My last year, I took them up on the bet, and failed all of them.
"That's when I came down here.

"But it wasn't all wasted.
"Since Disney doesn't give out the names of the apes,
"I'm free to call the immature ones Benvolio, Tybalt, and Mercutio.
"Of course, the dominant male is Romeo,
"And all of his females are Juliet.

"If anybody, ever asks me what I know about them,
"I tell them that silverbacks speak to each other in sonnets.
"They think it's a type of ape-language
"That Disney came up with,
"And I let it go at that."

-- Ron Yazinski
(Life is a Roller Coaster Anthology)

Among Old Graves

Among old graves, you do this:
you think about the dead,
you leave small gifts, talismans upon their limestone
markers. You brush crumbs of dirt out of the barely-there
grooves of a grave-maker's etchings: numbers and letters,
swirled stems of flowers.
Some of the dead, here and always,
will be remembered.
Many more forgotten, even their names
glazed to smooth oblivion by time, rain, wind, cold.

Which of the dead would I want to be?
I ask this of myself, kneeling beside a young girl's headstone,
cattails' white explosion of cotton drifting through my gaze.
Forgotten, or leaving a legacy?
I don't know, I say to the girl buried here.
What should I answer?
She is quiet, of course, as they all are,
as I soon will be. I am middle aged but old,
mind slower, legs like those of the miserable:
bowed, knees in a dragging sort of ache.
Maybe it matters, maybe it does not.
My son says there is a cardinal in the gold leaves of a maple,
although I cannot see it.

-- Dana Yost
(Petals in the Pan Anthology)

Natural Confrontations

1/ Orchid

Far on the hillside
Alone on a shady spot
The orchid blooms aloud, albeit
There are neither eyes
Nor ears open nearby
Paying the slightest attention
To its shape or melody
Be it ever so fragrant
So fulfilling

2/ Plum Blossom

Without a single leaf
Grass-dyed or sun-painted
To highlight it
But on a skeletal twig
Glazed with dark elegies
A bud is blooming, bold and blatant
Like a drop of blood
As if to show off, to challenge
The entire season
When whims and wishes
Are all frozen like the landscape

3/ Lotus Flower

From foul, decayed silt
At the very bottom
Of a big lake of dirty murk
You shoot clean
Against the morning sun

Always pure
Crystal
Unpollutable

> *-- Changming Yuan*
> *(Petals in the Pan Anthology)*

From the Journals

While the Crickets are Mating

The moon thinks the crow is firewood
So it splits the bird's shadow from its sneaking.

The bird thinks the moon is the fruit
Of contention that splintered the flock
So it tries to return its fullness
In the thickest crown it found.

In the right tree, the owl might be laughing
If it hasn't swallowed the wrong snake.
The frogs have stopped complaining.
The boy scribbling under omniscient stars,
Tending his mind's earliest fire, Albert,
Who decades later will confound skeptics
With three letters and a number: e, m, c and 2.

-- Jonel Abellanosa
(April Jellyfish Whispers)

In the Distance, Crows

Heading to the roost
the way they do with
single-minded determination
flying alone or with others,

she sees them from the window.
On the table the steam from each
bowl rises to meet the faces of
silent strangers.

The salt is passed and spoons
clink against the Delft-blue scenes
into the shimmering broth.

She imagines the crows stopping
at staging areas to gather forces.
They sound their clarion calls and
then, at dusk, hundreds meet in the
silhouettes of trees greeting one another
with a cacophony of welcomes!

Fussing and preening, fluttering
leaves darker than night, they
finally settle into their joined warmth

-- Carol Amato
(June Jellyfish)

Wolf Cry

"You keep the children." Jason disposes of them just like that as the aurora burns over the Vermilion River. Witchlight. We've been married nine years. "I'll keep the dog," he adds.

Across the river, a wolf edges out of the forest to drink. Our sons, Jeremy, eight, and Kevin, six, sleep in our tent, unaware. Upriver, wolves cry, a pack. Jason doesn't explain, but I know it's Sharon, honey haired, golden, one of those twenty-somethings in the Montana Café in town, charming as otters, smooth and quick. Jason saw her, wants her. Her father's rich.

In a sudden wolf silence, the river talks, chugs over hydraulic potholes. Our fire snaps. Jason's throat works as he drinks cold beer, sits firelighted, honey gold as Sharon. I can almost hear the thunder of the falls, south of us. I can imagine the deep pool at the cliff foot, black water there, or maybe gilded by the streamers in the sky, running down the magnetic lines, like a script, like a written language of gods.

Ten miles north is the border. I've crossed it a hundred times. A lot of us from up here are very good at border crossings. Late at night. In any weather. Summer or winter. Private business. Nothing ever stops us. Jason has forgotten that. He's from the Cities, from Minneapolis, not really like us.

The wolf drinks, looks at me, a knowing look. Wolves cry like humans sometimes, late, late at night on the Vermilion when the aurora shines. Things happen in the forests, at the border. The terrible witchlight of the aurora flickers green, white.

"So Medea," Jason asks, "you gonna be all right with this?"

-- Janet Shell Anderson
(June Pound of Flash)

Chalky limestone cliffs
Lug upon their fossil backs
Shadows of clattering birds.

> *-- Steve Ausherman*
> *(November High Coupe)*

muted smoke-peach blends
daughter watches gulf sunset
mother's ghost painting

> *-- Mary Jo Balistreri*
> *(February High Coupe)*

Candy Colours

Sunset paints the room
pink, red, yellow and gold.

A pleasant numbness
settles in my bones.
It dances
inside my head.
You bring the same
dedication
to your seduction
as you do to your music.
Eyes shut,
I smell the leather
of your coat,
the cigarettes on your lips.
Almost fearful,
I kiss you
Risking my life
with that kiss.
Like a fool.
Like an animal-
Desperately in love.
Shaken
by a current
of wild happiness
that is dangerous,
but strangely-
Pure.

-- Amy Barry
(June Pyrokinection)

Disassembly Required

It was an unbuilding,
more deliberate than a demolition
a deconstruction accomplished over time
a plank-by-plank denuding
of our most basic structure
as patient, planned, and organized
as the original architecture.

Remember, this was a decision,
this prizing-out of driven nails,
this breaking away of all supports,
these careful taps to dislodge mortar
from every dusted brick. Lifting the planks,
pulling down the ceiling, unhanging the doors,
the windows not shattered, but closed, latched,
then unshimmed, unsashed, uninstalled.
You did it all on purpose.

The house is down. I hardly remember
what it looked like, standing.
It's been counted, divided, shared-out.
But now you stand between the stacks
with a list, gesturing here and there,
along among the beams and braces,
the shingles, fittings, screws and steps,
smiling your encouragement,
speaking words of salvage.

-- Karen Berry
(October Napalm and Novocain)

The Furnace Quarry, Llanelli

after the painting by J.D. Innes (1887-1914)

The industrial juggernaut
has continued
into a new century.
A background of stacks and smoke
in a town by the sea.
A primal wound,
the cleft made on the shocked land.
The quarrying goes on,
filling the world elsewhere
with promises of progress,
remembering too
that nature's mind,
in all her eternal guises,
will observe undaunted
the pillaged scene.

-- Byron Beynon
(April Pyrokinection)

midwestern landscape
patchwork quilt of green and gold
best seen from above

-- Jane Blanchard
(November High Coupe)

Chords rising through air
Harmonica and guitar
Naming human pains

> *-- Sam Bockover*
> *(February High Coupe)*

Chattlebury Park

A rising wind flicks ripples
from the sun-flecked river.
Kites float in the air
and clouds laze far away.
Grass fresh mown sends you off in time and space.
The day beholds everything,
wine and beads and smoke,
love waits just around the corner,
and happiness is just to live
in Chattlebury Park.

A lady waits there;
Mystery is her name.
Straw hair flows down Venus' back
she smiles with turquoise cat's eyes
and her body flows like a river.
Wine-sweet kisses make you drunk
and lying within her arms
you come to know eternity.
You take her where the blossoms fall like rain
in Chattlebury Park.

Tomorrow beams a million years away.
Life says: live for now
and feel the rush of this moment
because all time stretches ahead
and nothing seems vital
in Chattlebury Park.

But phantoms rush from every corner
and laugh inside the blushing ear:
"Tomorrow is here and you've still got nothing done."
The sky turns gray, the wine to sour lemonade,

and a dustdevil scatters the blossoms
in Chattlebury Park.

-- Andrew M. Bowen
(September Pyrokinection)

the iridescent flash
off a dark wing
roadkill

                -- Alan S. Bridges
                (November High Coupe)

Participles of Speech

midnight in the old saloon
and we're tired and we're upset,
the world's growing old
and we're tired and we're upset.

wounded healer as shaman,
the shade is the man,
climb the valley,
sink into the mountain

a good death rises
from one spot of imperfection,
blood-gates open:
in the wind, the pull of backfire.

-- Michael H. Brownstein
(January Pyrokinection)

Open Swing

a wonderful sunny
day spent indoors

trapped with the
sick and children
that just want to
go out and play

they couldn't
give two shits
that grandma's
on the verge of
death

not when there's
an open swing
right outside
the window

-- J.J. Campbell
(June Pyrokinection)

Reflection

when i pour
water into the
bowl for the
oldest cat out
here on the
farm

she sees her
reflection and
gets ready to
attack

the other day
she actually
threw a punch
at the water

i patted her on
the head and
said good girl

that's the kind
of self-hate i
can admire

-- J.J. Campbell
(August Jellyfish Whispers)

Metamorphosis -- A Triptych

metamorphosis 1

stretched butterfly seems to know too much
about us as it pumps its wings,
then tiptoes around the grass
where family once met,
can no longer grasp
why it should cleave
to the grub cave,
long soft beats
roil astray
now.

metamorphosis 2

small tadpoles wriggling no knowledge
of the miscreant tattered footfalls
muddled on the bank dropped underneath,
in slick form, cropped without water.

bull frogs taunt at the end of the rock-strewn
ledge, recoil legs and bulging throats
that rumble; I watch them destroy numb flies
of decked love with the tips of their tongues.

metamorphosis 3

katydid mythology takes me into
its folded wings, a panoply
of leafy bits, remnant pupae
loam flicks an acrid odor
while new summer arrives
at the top of the trees.

tsunami song engulfs last light,
ever glib and dipping over
the deep night breeze, a wonder
grip I want to see as
well as hear; nature would rather
simper under the cloying vine.

-- Theresa A. Cancro
(March Jellyfish Whispers)

Berceuse In Terra

Each rumble of the 'quake
holds in its grip last gasps,
babies' first breaths, end tucked in
at the beginning, a heart tremor,
lost as it falls.

Blue sky catatonic soon folds
with swells off the reef, isn't truly
shaken. Cloud eyes dim, brighten
when pressed to the sea,
taken to cradle.

Long striations on the horizon
mimic uneven lengths of energy
fingers clawing thin crusts
through scree, pumice,
plied clay and rocking beds.

Earth crack elongated by sun's glare
carries bright songs birds continue
to warble, while it rends the selvage of
sateen hours: in complacence,
gaping wide, it exhales.

-- Theresa A. Cancro
(August Jellyfish Whispers)

Glower Scrapings

Your malcontent mixes
with ennui in the morning, just
watch it cast mortal slices among
minced words until we fall
into the basin under the sink,
bits of shaved lead, sexy-less
yet still druzy, sparks beneath
flannel, loose and shifty.

Shall we break the edges
of that wilted rose, never notice
where its soft petals land,
slink away while walls crumble
around us as a moth slips
off chipped piano keys, those
dirty teeth grinning at
our final demise?

-- Theresa A. Cancro
(August Napalm and Novocain)

The Spoon in My Eye

for Cesar Vallejo

"I want to be free no matter what sacrifices I must make. In being free, I sometimes feel surrounded by the most frightening ridicule, like a child who mistakenly lifts his spoon up to his nose."

-- Cesar Vallejo
<u>Epistolario General</u>

The spoon in my eye
now sparkling with sense, i reverse!
daywards, weeping worlds
with their shoulders
that stutter into storms.
My morning all mist
raises these walls to my head.
In this dull space i have been abolished.
In this dull space i come back again.
Unfreeing my debts i call out.
Such sorrow to be human
to beg in our being, cramped
into thin air
like a world blank.
In this place words eat themselves
with my hunger.
Permanent, cyclical, my unruling
now in its bones and syntheses.
Here, dialogically, and written in economies,
ripped to shreds and savaged by lovers
our growing with abundance and
convulsing in riots,
here, erased in my vomiting and wounded
by weather
i throw the dog, my last friend in the temporary,

on my shoulders,
and enter the rain.

Rooms fill in my beautiful abolition.
"i have not been here," they say,
(like the end of a vendetta, or a civil war.)
"I have not seen him," she grieves, solemnly.
(Her eyes black with the daylight.)
In here life limps in wires and personalities.
There is no one home to collect my longing.
i am not, yet. In lungs filled to choking.
In fingers whose funerals are wreathed
in cigarette smoke.
In armies denouncing the rights of man.
In shovels heaping their criticism with friendliness.
This spoon shakes my eye
in its instinct to be born.
My walls fall in their clocks and calendars.
Such war!
in my disarming, mouth disembodied,
my meaning now matters!

This child is my little man, stunning in escapes.
He eats, with solitude, the wind
of my whistling.
We are stilling the day to cement our dead.
My debts pile up, in courtcases and laws.
In waiting and endlessness.
We are dying by radio, in newspapers,
in secrets
struggling
to cross the universe of our feet,
red and raw with their agitating.
Our secret history and its life full of louts!
i call out, to the spoon in my eye,
let me go. Let me go!
(in this war filled with skeletons).
Only the dog

shows me his nose in my crippled friendships.
i cannot eat the silence.
i am shouting at my self, as large as an abattoir.
In this way, with coffee and cigarette, with
all the dead
dancing on my tongue,
and the living littering my life with their dying,
i denounce my friends crippled with icepicks,
i denounce all enemies with the price of my hate.

i see him born rolling in an unceasing complexity
and in all my grim abolitions,
my denouncements,
and intrigues,
in all this whipping weather, and
the depth of my dog in depressions,
in all these governments and juntas,
and my funerals in bed,
(in all these lithe women with their masks made up with air)
and in this spring of a new year,
and with the spoon in my eye, loosening its syllables,
in all our fleeing, among reflections,
in our history, their hunting, and our shapelessness,
my daylight calls out its mourning:

now here is his incorporation in chestfulls,
witness like a resurrection, all
springtime to my easters,
my exploding corpses. Both self, and you,
and our othering.

-- Seamas Carraher
(October The Mind[less] Muse)

Plug into Confetti Ballroom

cross the tropical galaxy threshold
               my hair in knots
you said you loved me
but those were old threads
the champagne   the mussels
like birds are distant in flight
               they melt into
        moonlight static energy
        on dusty interstate
        searching for a new equinox

each curve that embraced
        the morning splendor
        on the back of your neck
along the crest of the moving sea
trembled and fluttered in distant breeze
over fence   onto countryside road

where jasmine whispered and muse cried
these words were never hobbies
or listless daydreams
they're midnight blues
with a million quivers of glitter dust
               welcoming yesterday's page
            the hidden story
      the smile's echo

                    -- John Casquarelli
                    (April The Mind[less] Muse)

Light through

a cracked window

All the things
we once loved

lie broken
on the floor;

only the bed
still standing

-- Alan Catlin
(March Napalm and Novocain)

The stillness of the bar after last call. All the bodies at rest. Some with their arms tilting back that last frothing pint. Others holding their hands about the glass, considering what lies inside: the dissolving head, the melting ice, the dregs, the hours lost.

Above the bar, tract lighting's reclusive glow amid dissipating clouds of cigarette smoke, blackening ashes spread across the dulled sheen of the bar top, so many times resurfaced by forgotten butts rolled from their glass moorings onto the wood. Or scratched by ashtrays sliding across scuffed surfaces pushed by a careless, drunken hand. Or gouged by broken bottles, glassware struck against wood in anger, jagged ends thrust in fury into an unsuspecting face, an equally as aggressive drinker, bearing his own weapon. Blood stains no longer visible beneath the daily wear and tear, the cursory repair.

But the impact scars remain.

The ghosts of wars fought, contained in the very stillness of the colored by pollutants, air, wrapping the drinkers tightly into a hypnotic state where dreaming, and living and drinking are all one frozen motion; a thought about to be blinked away into nothingness, drained away in the stainless wash sinks or the spill plates where the loose beer taps leak and the dead soldiers spit there, thick as mucous, remains.

Neon beer signs harsh bright lights reflected in the tarnished backbar mirrors, their unnatural red and green aura a glowing pit in the eyes of the drinkers, a flash of artificial life covered by a patina of not yet completely dry, tears. Gradually hardening, sealing the heat source, the heliotropic bouquet of plastic flowers tight against the ungiving surface where light meets tissue leaving only the bright afterimage of the killing tracer rounds inside.

The immovable clock hands pinned against the worn-to-almost-nothing, facing; glass front panel scratched and grime encrusted, shellacked with an impenetrable coating of nicotine; years of chemical infusions, a useless ornamentation at last call and beyond.

All the spaces between the sound of incessant, dripping faucets. The dull metallic ring of water on stainless steel, once shiny, now a collective of black mold, indeterminate growths: fading grey on a mound of black, on a living surface where the once rinsed glasses wait.

Hands collected in their individual suspensions: pressed against the dull shine of the smeared jukebox facing, liver spotted, ravaged, arthritic, not part of the selective process of sound but propping up the misused, diseased body of man in his formal, last decline. Others used for propping up the all-too-heavy head, paused in the futile signaling for what may never be delivered after the end, others reaching out in the night for what will never be there, still others grasping at the invisible fabric that separates them from what lies beyond, the evanescent place, the not to be avoided, compelling call that summons all to bars for the reckoning; to be fulfilled or denied in turn.

As the spirit wills.

As the silence fills stilled lives, the picture window facing the deserted street, the trees burdened with a weight of dark leaves and spread shadows, as the false dawn reconfigures the pavement and the glass and what lies within and without; a smear of light on glass disfigured by elective signs, the stillness more alive, more animated than the bar life trapped inside.

Last call an unnecessary formality, nothing is moving.

Nothing at all.

-- Alan Catlin
(April Pound of Flash)

The Fading

The paint flakes away from the letters
spelling Christ is the Answer
along the tall white side on a trailer
left in a yard beside the Interstate
to stand before all weathers
while traffic on its way to Tucson
passes by. The message is paler
at each journey taken; in winter
when a chill runs inside the metal,
and in summer when the heat
burns right through it. Years ago
the words stood out, their letters
had crisp edges, and the black was blacker
than any black before it. Nobody
could pretend not to have seen it;
there was no way around
considering the possibility that here
was the truth. Now the bold assertion
has become shabby as graffiti
after too much exposure
to merciless light.

-- David Chorlton
(May Pyrokinection)

A Rattlesnake in Summer

In her place on warm concrete
where a board has come loose
from the house,
a rattlesnake wound tight
has come from the dark space
to soak in morning sun.
                    She's golden
with brown angled all
along her body, and her eyes
look out from a current of scales
when she shifts to accommodate
the light, sliding
                    against a metal tube
lying on the ground to mark
how close is safe
for anyone approaching,
until hunger leads her
to the grass,
                    and she stutters forward
to where it slopes
toward the road winding through
the mountains that cut
into the sky's every storm
                    and settle back
in place when the universe
at night flows overhead
after lightning has passed,
                  in the calm
that follows a bite.

-- David Chorlton
(August Jellyfish Whispers)

Memoir

On a quiet evening in my upscale apartment in Tokyo, I start typing these words. I pour myself a cup of green tea, take off my suit, and without even understanding why, I sit down and begin to type something. Not sure what these words are at first, I suddenly realize that they are memories of my arrival in Nagasaki four years ago.

As thoughts work their way through tiny neurons, electrical pulses turn into movements and I find myself punching away at my laptop keys. I begin to see myself as I was: twenty-two, I might as well have been some kid on the verge of puberty—pimples, awkwardness, and all—except that my face had the ornery expression of a coal miner, or no, maybe a tired insurance salesman.

At the age of twenty-two, I was traveling across the world for reasons only half-understood, or not understood at all—my insurance salesman face took care not to register this fact too loudly. I was convinced that an English language school was bringing me there, some company, branded and marketed, active and thriving with power and money behind it, when really it was her.

Jet-lagged and hung-over, I came by bullet train to the steep slopes and regenerative soil of Nagasaki. Nagasaki—the not-birthplace of atomic warfare, but instead its brother, second cousin—was a radioactively peace-loving city. Though I was a foreigner, in a foreign land, I had not come alone. The vague presence of a disgruntled girl gnawed at the deep well where my heart had been. Not yet aware of the ghosts surrounding me or of the perils of my situation, I was compelled to think of it all in terms of a great adventure, like a Hemingway or Fitzgerald expatriate story. But she and the others were deceptively close, waiting for the romance to wear off.

In retrospect, I came to Nagasaki for the regenerative properties. The second atomic bomb blast so many years ago, which had swept up most of the city in a plutonium cloud, had made the city radioactively peace-loving. Reversing the usual cycle that turns victim into perpetrator, the people who stepped from the rubble filled their hearts with a fervent devotion to peace in all its forms.

In my mind's eye I see them: wounded and dying, their lungs filled with ash and smoke. The ash sits there for some time, and when they exhale, miraculously, something akin to love comes out. From all those bitter seeds that usually grow hate, something emerged in Nagasaki's soil-spirit that could heal and grow hearts. Beyond scientific innovation, beyond administrative decision making, the power of a city to heal itself and others lay in something less tangible than the splitting of an atom. And there I was: awkward, tired, a nasty emptiness in my center that was filling itself with something unbearably sad and heavy.

I look on, and I see part of me, perhaps the part of me that is dying or perhaps the part that drinks and practices business analysis and dances with Apollo and Dionysus on the mountain top with the spirits. Or maybe it's the part of me that died the day I left her.

*

In my Tokyo apartment, these observations pour out and exhaust me. I get up and stretch. Tea? What am I thinking? I need coffee. My mind wanders, I check my email, surf the Internet, look over some papers for work. As someone who has lived a great deal of his life in the pages of biography and autobiography, I know that self-revelation can be both the cure and the disease.

These memoirs. These bad news memoirs. They stand in the way of the serious work of beating back the past. Best to let the past lie, if it's willing. And the spirits that brought me to Nagasaki so many years ago? They were gone. They vanished the moment I left her. I should leave them where they rest. In the soil of half-formed hearts, buried in history books, in the collective consciousness of the Japanese spirit—waiting for another historian-novelist to find.

-- Daniel Clausen
(April Pound of Flash)

Pieces

    I.

bonsai tree
centered in mid-museum
grows alone.

    II.

main thoroughfare
a tennis shoe equilateral
to staring headlights

    III.

a bit of brick
embedded in tire tread
and burqa now slightly moist.

    IV.

a pepper switch
behind the diploma
Junior never displays

    V.

jacaranda shits down its flowers
onto my freshly pressed suit, cleaned car,
I will chop it down with relish.

VI.

plywood tree house
draped in flag
confederate in nature.

> *-- Mike Cluff*
> *(March Jellyfish Whispers)*

Haiku Noir

I did not want to
burn the bridge, only remove
a few of the planks

sometimes we have to
throw ourselves off the cliff in
order not to drown

lampblack raindrops fall
from the nib of my fountain
pen, a vein punctured

black widow spider
mother protecting her young
still, the hourglass drains

inhaling paint fumes
the sigh of brush on canvas
never been higher

-- Kelly Cressio-Moeller
(May High Coupe)

At Cheever

time moves
as slowly
as paint
peels from
clapboards,
as slowly
as barn spiders
dress monarchs
in silken thread,
as slowly
as White Mountains
shrug off ages past,
so slowly
I become
a wood thrush
at dusk

-- Betsy Cullen
(July Jellyfish Whispers)

Scratching

A quick swipe of fingernails—
digging vigorously, like dogs on the scent,
flaking skin from these legs, as if they could be sanded
to perfection, rosy and ruby-studded, from imperfect marble.
Blood erupts from volcanic scabs roused from dormancy
and collects in red rings above ankle-length socks
—at least the carpet won't get stained.

"Leave it alone" sounds simple, but my body's not my own.
I inhabit, slave of impulse, a dog without a lampshade cuffed;
I am choking on my long leash.

scratching at an itch...

and when the urge comes again, it's impossible to resist, it's inconceivable to resist—
taking it in, sucking it down, shooting it up, shooting it out, letting it wash over you, seeking satisfaction and hiding in the flawless moment because it's easier than waiting for life

to brush against you like poison ivy, or alight upon you like a mosquito, or find a way into your body like *varicella zoster*

this is easy...

easier than applying creams and third-rate folk remedies

easier than wondering if there's something under the skin that needs to be torn out

or if some missing key component could tie it all together

and make it work

the way it was supposed to

A lucid pause turns cloudy
and I crave clarity once more...

Looking down at bleeding scabs and welts that will not heal,
my hand prepares to sin again. I think to myself, just before it takes me:
there's so much more; this is only scratching the surface.

-- Peter Dabbene
(March Pyrokinection)

Solo Flight

In this valley of earth
the wind
comes with the same gift
the same solitary wind
that carries
faith without speaking

with the same sightless purity
that sees everything
as it is
that causes the same quiver of branches
that have pulled their skins
out of the soil and rocks

The wind's long horn blows
into this valley's earthen jug
and applies its wisdom
as thin as
this silver hair that holds the heat
to my bones

this wisdom that assembles and
stirs above me watching and
me standing
below
in this valley as cold as heaven

where there has always been
and even now a river's
unsaid oath and lyrics
where birds drop feathers
where birds balance the wind
even in sleep

even when nothing moves
even when knowing that

each feather dropped
can fly

alone

each one
gifted with the wind's wisdom

-- Dah
(June Jellyfish Whispers)

The Song is Gone

A 60's waltz
Ephemeral as a dream,
   the song
      slipped into quietus
The dancers gone too
Their footprints washed away
by the heartbeat of a lake, persistent,
      ever flowing onwards
We danced our days into Lake Erie's currents

Rainbow seashells, driftwood sculptures
Broken glass scrubbed gentle

Behind this rock, that
water chants
answered with a song of remembering
Walking across the thin sands of seaweed and bloated fish
to work our way into rocky waters
And further
past a broken pier
Into a sunset horizon
rising into twilight falling

Slivers of shadows creeping thin
The soul of remembering
Wrapped tight in tides of yesteryear

-- Susan Dale
(November Pyrokinection)

A Fierce Winter Night

The wind roars with polar bear breath
And cuts with silver rapiers

Hoof beats thunder
Across the mountain of night

Shuddering atop the pole
A flag wildly furls
Unfurls
Wind swoops down the chimney
And shouts imprecations to the fire
In the stove___
blazing
to greedily gobble up logs, cringing

In the basement the sub pump
Gurgles and swallows

Scratching at the windows,
Steel nails of sleets' white-bone fingers

Ah, we shiver inside, for we know
we are held hostage
by the blinding white wrath
of a fierce winter night

     -- Susan Dale
     (January Jellyfish Whispers)

Us

A barb wire
    hour
        around us
A ragged tear
  Beyond repair
      Arrow piercing
   this bloodless vein

                -- Susan Dale
                (September Napalm and Novocain)

In a Video Today Two Small Deer Ran Across the Golden Gate Bridge
Behind Them an Idling Line of Migratory Animals in Plexi-Glass Boxes

when I was growing up we saw deer dart across country roads
big brown eyes stealthy on pavement
sometimes they didn't make it splattered windshield glass
leaving meat inside the grill
the whole car often crushed in around the body
and there was trouble to get into if it wasn't hunting season
so you quickly stuffed him in your trunk so as not to waste them
washed the blood from your hood
butchered him in your kitchen
tables running red
head staring sad eyes off the countertop
hooves and soft hide a savage decoration

in season it was free reign and the hunters came by truck load
dressed in their orange day glow vests their camouflage pants
little pouches of hot rocks to warm bottoms and cases and cases of beer
it is somewhat terrifying to wake up to armed men in your yard
their hunger not for the venison, too gamey for suburban taste buds
but for the kill the outsmarting of the spry animal
the satisfaction of tying him to the front of their car
prone legs splayed helpless
I always felt compelled to cover them
close eyes untie roped legs
lay him buck or her doe down with dignity
something those drunk and murderous bastards never had.

-- Cassandra Dallett
(October Pyrokinection)

All Souls' Day

1.

Here I shall lay a wreath
of sugar skulls
in hopes that a prayer can
release my dead.

The candle flame lunges back and forth
to a music only heard
between the breaths of the living.

In my quiet making,
the shrine rises up out of needful things
that miss their place in a hand
as a (dare I say this word:) possession.

Offerings of wine, of smoke, of favorites.
The morsels I forego
on this day of my dead.

How do I begin to say the words
of the tiniest remembrances
I have of them?
The shard that cannot
remake a complete image.

2.

Yes, I too have a shimmery thing
within me, a body of water,
a fog that rolls in each morning
and out each afternoon—a thing I call my soul.

And who do I believe would pray for it
when I won't? Who do I think will
bother an offering on its behalf?

It will go back to the collective pool
of eternal waiting. Eventually forgetting
everything for the repetitive motion
of a ripple.

3.

There is no one way to build a altar, like the many dead, each remains a life that was served individually. The ornate cloth of one altar attracts its intended while repulsing others. Each spirit makes its way. The candled pumpkin and marigold light the way. We summon these dead to us to embrace. Here all the words that bond one person to the next are offered on the altar. What was shared is reconnected again.

I do not know what happens after life. It does not even matter what I believe or cannot. The dead know but stay silent. Good for them. I take this day to remember my dead and thank them.

4.

If the naked soul travels
then let them see what is offered.

It is in their memory that I am here.

I leave all my words on the altar
beneath those things that made a life so memorable.

-- J.P. Dancing Bear
(June Pyrokinection)

Caked

> *I just ate my feelings. They were equal to a sizable portion of cheesecake.*
>   -- Dyana Bagby

What I saw in the cake was the silver reflection
the cold eye I hate the most about myself

calculating the cut and then adjusting for a selfish portion
that would slide down and disappear

like a collapsed star in my gut—
eventually pulling in everything, but not

at first, and not for a long time...
thousands of slices later, in fact.

All the while whatever was there that I saw
within myself, real or imagined, regenerated—

like something fresh from hell's oven.
I rode the pastry cart like one of the four horsemen.

Each new sweetness a misery, a pang,
a feeling I had forgotten, refused, denied;

until something escaped the gravity well within me,
something sparking, alive, and angry,

the little imp of self-improvement,
ready to phoenix me, right after I blazed down to ashes.

                     -- J.P. Dancing Bear
                     (June Pyrokinection)

The Sunflower Chronicles (A Triptych)

Straphangers

Sunflowers cram into the morning bus,
they unfold yellow newspapers
and droop their heads reading over
each other's shoulder.

Sunflowers

They crowd about me
as I open to the Gospel,
their yellow heads
wait for that moment
when Jesus speaks
and only as they can,
bow their heads
in prolonged adoration.

The Countenance of a Sunflower

She leans towards the Virgin Mary
her yellow Stole swept back,
two Queens in an earthly garden,
one hastening to the other
in a peaceful acquiescence to radiance.

-- William G. Davies, Jr.
(September Jellyfish Whispers)

The flying flowers—
fairies of reality—
ignored as insects.

> *-- Pijush Kanti Deb*
> *(January High Coupe)*

Wednesday Morning #137

Then it wasn't about above
or below, it was about forward
& stasis, which consumes us.

to
be alone with you

-- Darren C. Demaree
(May Pyrokinection)

We Are Arrows #195

Segmented
fruit, we have
arrived in
stages, we
have entered
with a
piercing
action,
without sound,
without regret
for the
minimalist
thwack of our
descent.
    We have
no existence
until we
acknowledge
the width of
our own
shoulders.
    We have
no existence
until we
reassemble the
great path
that crumpled
to deliver us.
    We are
heart-
stopping, as
in our hearts
can stop at
any moment,
and this is
why we are so

desperate to prove that we have existed at all.
    If you trip near the edge of this problem, shed your weight, and it could be flight you have found.

-- Darren C. Demaree
(December The Mind[less] Muse)

Fences Do Not Mend Each Other

Time
said, sea needs
you, immediate light
or curved
word
to break like bread
in the insular atmosphere.
Lend me quarters-
spare me politics,
specify on the door
and your body
if I wasn't suppose to enter.

-- James Diaz
(March Pyrokinection)

Mountain Never in the Gutter Belly

There
you are
spread like an animal
small talk

composition of seriousness
below the primal want

wed to painting
mother mouth
mourning in a time of laughter

day or sea
lit from the inner flower
bowing to lover
in Arabic
proximity

the nearness
of the invisible dead
falling asleep under
the door.

Here; I threw myself-
I took the Occident
under my tongue
and bowled out the earth
from which the wound name
lived
pouring blessing
into the honey lung of hell.

Eye-

the double olive

pin prick

present
under a skirt
where the law cracks

to pieces
inside you.

> *-- James Diaz*
> *(October The Mind[less] Muse)*

I Never Told Anyone About That Trip to Serendipity

I was seven, and thought my father and I were going into the city for a special date. I'd gotten dressed up and had wanted only to order a fruit tart because it looked delicate and grown up inside the glass case. My father pushed for the hot fudge sundae, perhaps wanting something he knew would take me a long time to finish.

He started up with his ums and ahs when I was just a few bites in, and as he continued talking I began shoveling larger and larger bites into my mouth, barely stopping to taste the ice cream or the chocolate sauce, feeling only the sticky film on my hand and the end of my spoon and around my mouth.

When he finished talking, finally, we both sat staring at the cherry I'd left in the bowl, so red it was almost obscene, though that couldn't have been what I thought at the time. He asked me then if I was going to eat it, as though it had been any other day and any other dessert and I leaned over and threw up beside the table. My vomit looked like some lunatic's idea of happiness, just like my parents' marriage.

-- Melissa Duclos
(June Pound of Flash)

Inventory

We have set aside too many things
As if supply and demand had little
To do with everyday use, as if our
Demands could ever be satisfied
As if supply was the easy answer
We bought and brought, selected
And collected, this and that and yet
More to store away, let's just say
Until today, our day of reckoning
Of tabulating, getting the measure
Of our time spent, of our hoarding;

Here we have several shelves of
Canned goods, without opposing
Selves of canned evils, an obvious
Metaphysical flaw, a balance lacking
Like this explains the unread books
The recordings and tapes no one
Plays, like the tree falling way out
Somewhere with no one to hear it
Fall or call, and over here we have
Paper products, all useful things
Waiting us out, enough tissues to
Sneeze at, to wipe tears and noses
Soothe and suffer, paper plates and
Plastic cups, enough plastic knives
And forks to feed the troops, and
There are toys and games minus any
Children or anyone playful enough
Any more to find the sense in them;

There are cobwebs enough here too
And dust, as parts of our collection
Reminders of where all this is going
This supply and demand, our certainty
Our caution, our planning, inventory

Surrounded by cobwebs, turning to
Dust, as we sit here counting it all.

-- J.K. Durick
(August Pyrokinection)

When He Leaves You

I.

When he leaves you, he will say, "It's not you, it's me." He will say it is all his fault. He will say he has changed, there's nothing you can do, things are not the same anymore. He will say he knows it hurts you now but this will make you happy later.

> (You will say, out loud, "Can we please just talk about this?")

>> He will say his mind is made up. He will say he still loves you. He will say I hope we can still be friends.

II.

When he leaves you, he will say, "Of course it's you, you crazy bitch!" He will say it is all your fault. He will say you changed. He will say you are not the girl he married.

> (You will say, to yourself, "Well, no. Mostly because I am no longer a girl.")

>> He will say none of his friends ever liked you. He will say you were a mistake. He will say he doesn't love you, not anymore.

>> He will say he is keeping the television, by the way.

> He will say don't call me. He will say I don't want to see you again.

>>> Ever.

III.

When he leaves you, he will say nothing. No explanation, no reason why. When you scream and cry and thrash on the ground shouting, "Just talk to me!" he will only blink and say, "I don't know what you want me to say." He will be gone by the time you come home from the grocery store, arms loaded with the apple juice and Little Debbie snacks and rack of lamb you know he loves. He will leave you in the bed that smells like him, alone in a hurricane with the wind rattling the windows and a leak sprung overhead.

-- Liz Egan
(October Napalm and Novocain)

Woods (2)

after the painting by Gerhard Richter

In the woods a lexicon's
concentric rings
speak ancient dialects

of seasons come and gone
broken promises
civilizations' rise and fall

liaisons in the shade
of twisted limbs
names carved in weathered bark

of the forgiven and unforgiving
confessions and lies
the birth and death of gods

straining to the light
trees endure, survive
to teach the earth its past.

-- Neil Ellman
(December Jellyfish Whispers)

Survey

> *". . . hell doesn't want you,*
> *and heaven is too full . . ."*
>
> *-- Tom Waits*
> *"Earth Died Screaming"*

And the survey of the selected
says there is no justice for
the trafficker, no sufficient
retribution for the salesman
of a seven-year-old's still-forming
sex, just a businessman, he'll
claim, matching service to clientele,
finding a market and making it known.

The survey of the selected offered
suggestions of the second bunk
in a rapists quarters, of incarceration
and the burial of an ocean-bound
key, of torture and colonization
and the chance to prey on one
another, of a metal chair and
a slowly flipped switch.

The survey of the selected fell
silent *en masse* with a thoughtful
pause before a voice rose over
here and a murmur issued from
somewhere there, words measured
for weight and handled with care
as I asked with the certainty
of genetic disease if hell, in
all its permutations, could be too
good for such an enterprising soul,

the punishment grotesque enough
for the incomprehensible crime.

>	*-- Eric Evans*
>	*(August Pyrokinection)*

Bad Apple

he's a bad apple.
the kind you hope kills himself,
saves you the trouble.

says there's a gun in
the garage, but won't say where.
in clutter it hides.

she sees she was blind.
now that it's too late, two young
boys to feed and clothe.

protection order?
get real. if he wants you, he'll
find you, anyway.

at your mother's house.
your girlfriend's. some cheap motel.
there's no money left.

he's ruined your credit.
destroyed your self-esteem. now
you can only wait.

he's a bad apple.
the kind you hope kills himself,
before he kills you.

-- Alexis Rhone Fancher
(April High Coupe)

Mental Illness

Ahh . . .
I love the idea of
Reading.
The author.
I've only read half of
The Bell Jar, but yet
I love Sylvia Plath.
The more you read of someone
The less you can romanticize about them;
Except for Bud Light & Bukowski,
I'd rather keep their words inked to page.

And editor said, "It would be more interesting to read about the
Origin of, not the present state of,
Suicidal depression."
Well . . .
I'd like to understand the root of it
Too.
But until you pick apart and
Buy my beauties from me,
I cannot fund such analysis.

\#

How narcissistic is mental illness . . .
Hours of therapy, premium drugs, and
Thousands to find out
How badly Mother & Father
Damaged you. While there are
Beaten prostitutes, like my sister Desiree.
Single alcoholic mothers, like my sister Marie.

\#

And it's amazing what the mind is capable of
How much it will repress.
Freud said our conscious mind is like the
Tip of an iceberg. While the subconscious mind is
The other 80%, buried deep down
And it is the forgotten memories which haunt,
Causing anxiety daily, without you knowing.
And that's what my family is.
Knowing your own sister sucks dick, gets beaten by pimps in order to
Smoke crack &
Shoot dope in order to
Escape her own life, disables mine
Subconsciously. Thousands I must spend on my
Pompous mind just to feel real, while there are
Starving children and
Pretty girls on tv telling me
I should donate to save the crying animals as well,
Well, 10/10 I will choose me because
I cannot control the kittens or the whores
My family is blood but the river steadily streams,
Fleeting.
Hopefully I can fix me before I
Implode.

-- Daniel N. Flanagan
(February Pyrokinection)

Everyone Loves a Motorcycle

Everyone loves a motorcycle,
and here it was
cleaned and polished
and set to the curb,
the *for sale* sign staked
into the lawn
with firing squad finality,
and the neighbourhood kids came
from all around;
the boys climbing on
and playing the outlaw,
the starry-eyed girls
dreaming of something their fathers
wouldn't like -
60 years after Brando,
the Wild One
in black and white -
this motorbike for sale
in a world
long sold away;
the silver swanlike handlebars
like some strange chrome god
straight out of
Egypt.

-- *Ryan Quinn Flanagan*
(February Pyrokinection)

Perfume

I will make a box.
A box that comes from the dirt,
that is molded by crackling frost and parching sun
and that smells of wet soil after rain.

I will make my box from
the bark of Eucalyptus
with a lid of quilted hosta.
It will be lined with satin magnolia
and have hinges of antirrhinum.

I will embellish my box with
the eye of viola
the tooth of sumach
the claw of pyracantha and
the tongue of digitalis

I will put in my box
a drop of the blood of euphorbia
the heartbeat of helianthus
the sigh of gypsophila and
the breath of Daphne

I will keep the box in a dark and cool place
for several weeks until
it rots and withers away
And then I shall press it between my hands
until the sap runs
and from this liquid
I will make a perfume that only I understand.

-- Sarah Flint
(November Jellyfish Whispers)

The Book

He's a closed book.
A hard back cover of control
Hides his story
Until a grin flashes across his face
Like lightening
And I hear the pages rustle.
A deep salty kiss lets me taste
The text with my tongue.
Later
In the sweet sweat of bed sheets
I gently prize open the cover and
Start to unstick the pages
His gift:
He lies wide open for me to read.
But it's a short story:
I hear the slap of the book closing
Before I reach the end.

-- Sarah Flint
(February Napalm and Novocain)

Fun and Prophet

The linear
met retrospective entities
previously hidden

where the chiseled glyph curves

Cassandra
her message a twisting
inventory

meaning shifts its moment

a vacuum away
from tiding the breath events
cresting over

the wrath of uncomprehending seas

-- Vernon Frazer
(February Pyrokinection)

All That Remains

In startling desiccation,
    he lies
      beneath a pink peony
in my garden,
      no smell of death,
      no weight in my hands,
      only bones
and feathers,
black starling wings
      extended stiffly,
   dark feet
clasping emptiness,
      beak crookedly agape
from the impact
      that broke his neck.

Above him,
    the window
   to my studio,
cruel cause
    of a simple error,
real reason
    to question
    why we create
such fatal illusions,
    how man fits
   in this world.

        -- Patricia L. Goodman
        (April Jellyfish Whispers)

When Winter Stayed

The geese look
like decoys, asleep
on the ice, not praying,
yet all facing west. You say
it is because
they are heading the wind.
I have other questions,
but I watch a hawk
land in a bare maple,
and when I turn
you are gone.

-- Patricia L. Goodman
(April Jellyfish Whispers)

Bird I Never Saw in Daylight

It hit the windshield, changed parabola
of flight.   You braked the car,
ran back.
            Great Horned Owl broken
in the ditch. Quite dead.

How gently you cradled it
to the trunk. How many lambs like ours

disappeared to its talons.
            Such a beauty,
you said, folding it in plastic;
placed it in the freezer, prepared
to ship to the museum.

            Now our windshield
begins its fine-calligraphy fault-
            line, a glass

trajectory of dawn-dim into bright.
            Inside the Hall of Ornithology

            Owl stares down
from its beaked   mask,
            fixed forever-eyes, its voided
breast and fluted bones
    immobilized in flight.

            -- Taylor Graham
            (July Jellyfish Whispers)

Wild

Mini-cougar in domestic guise,
the cat assumes his Crescent Moon pose,

a motionless dance. You hardly notice
how he segues into Extended Sphinx:

claws retracted, energy uncharted. Never
mistake it for giving up the more than possible,

though he radiates indifference, a mime
of Consciousness Exhaust. Now

the dog, who's journeyed farther with you
from the wild, lies down facing him.

Palms reaching. Dog touches finger-tips
with Cat. Silence gaze-to-gaze.

Do you dare lie down with them,
speak to them as friends--

you with your load of expectations
in a language they don't share?

-- Taylor Graham
(November The Mind[less] Muse)

Complete, but

to no avail. Sitting as a new house sits
on its lot, needing occupants.
Sewer sludge, soiled napkins, anthills
too late underfoot. Held up by restlessness
in the many gardens of Mount Sisyphus, heave-hoe
to the point of rudimentary madness.
Windows I look through, birch trees I stop at
to collect nuances, rest like the sparrow in hopeful
camouflage, wearing myself down with unrealizable dreams.

If I had claimed myself a calling as a chaplain -
ritualized pacing in university halls, my arm
around youth, accompanying my affection
with a spiritual smile, then I would have
the certainty of some kind of career,
not be a carved body on fire, totem
of tripwires and aftershocks.

If I was a young starling neck deep in uncut grass,
pecking at exposed roots, I would be
sky, downspout, bush, tip of a cross on a steeple,
cured of isolation, taking flight and landing when I choose
and
I would choose a fenced-in backyard
where a boy's imagination owns the splintered bench, weeds
and a dug-up secret hole. I would watch that boy plot his
course
and leap, knowing no separation,
I would spread, sing
and fold.

-- Allison Grayhurst
(February Pyrokinection)

Regarding the Hawk

The hawk plunges
into the crowd at the bird feeder,
grabs a mourning dove
in a wild flurry of feather and blood.

It had been waiting for just this moment:
the convergence of
my generosity with seed,
the hunger of the small birds,
the even greater hunger of the raptor.

I watch the hawk lift off,
the flapping gray bird in its talons,
shifting to another gear for uplift,
then settling on a wind draft
to calm its racing blood,
before alighting on the top
of a telephone pole,
to devour its catch
in full view of the neighborhood.

How can this sight not stay with me,
aiding and abetting death as I do.

The hawk will return to its aerie in the high oaks,
sparrows, finches, retreat to their nests in the thick brush.
mourning doves batten down in their loose bed
of leaves and twigs in forks of maples.

And I will fill the empty feeders, pick up the feathers,
hose away the stains.
That's as close to nature as I get.

-- John Grey
(April Jellyfish Whispers)

I Have My Own Importance to Attend to

I break the plane of your surface,
as my lips on your lips,
holy upon holy,
moon, light, couch, zipper--
this will have ramifications
like world war three starting.

Look at that guy in the photograph.
Your father is it?
He most certainly would not . . .
He would not try to . . .
He would not say or do anything.

But I'm tired of living like
I'm the only one that matters,
the only one loving
at any given time.

Responsibility . . . how about a rain check?

I should drown myself,
leave it to a morgue attendant
to identify this man--
not your fingers,
not your yearning.
Lots of water in the lungs
and let's let see if I take
all feelings down with me.

Yes, sex is what the stars
would be doing if they weren't stars.
And I do twinkle and shine a lot.

Outside, there's traffic,
people watering their gardens—
bad choices on their part.

They leave it all up to me.

Well, of course, you have a say,
a role, in this.
What I mean is,
who's writing this poem?
me or you?

-- John Grey
(November Napalm and Novocain)

Television

No one on television is ever going to live
My life for me--and it is both
Disgusting and disappointing
That it took so long for me
To figure this out.

Notate bene, you people of the cold Pacific:
I have been repeatedly woken up
By all sorts of irritating
Noises: rusting buses idle interminably
Outside my apartment in Little India;
Nearly ask and my laundry room
Window, a thin woman with brown, rotting
Teeth slurpily sucks cocks in the alleyway; George
Bowering angrily writes shitty poems
In rathole that passes for Kelowna;
My downstairs neighbors actually stay
Drunk for weeks on end. The guy who got
Evicted rather than break
Up with his girlfriend, returns
Every other Friday to sell me
Illegally-caught sockeye
For five bucks a fish. Virtually worthless
Knowledge continuously washes
Down on me like fire. It no longer
As much as stings and I miss
That sting in much the same
Manner that I miss the cold
Ocean and all those dank
Mats of stinking cedar needles.

If Floyd showed up, by God,
I would wave away the flies

And buy a fish--the Crown
Be damned.

-- Carl James Grindley
(August Pyrokinection)

Weapons

Sterile weapons, dead and yoked
To a horsey mist of regret: this poem is a meat.
Missile, one you cannot possibly
Recall--recall, by the way, meaning
That a) you cannot take any of it
Back and b) in a few years, you will
Not remember any of it, even
If you wanted.

Life is a salad of doubt
And fate and as everyone grows old
And misshapen, a whole
Bunch of ruthlessly random
Maladies conspire
To crop the edges away
Until everyone is either content with
Everyone else or too miserable
And too drunk to care.

No amount of arugula is ever
Going to change
Anything. *Frisee avec lardoons* is ultimately
Pointless with or
Without Southern Ontario *chevre*.

Ballcocks and razorblades and
Two young people screwing
Every single chance they get--
If there is more to life than that
You are going to have to work much
Much harder than I did and even if you
Do, you are never going to convince me
That I should care.

-- Carl James Grindley
(August Pyrokinection)

Split

The headboard
has a crack in it, five inches
from the top, nine inches across.

I've no idea
how it happened, nor
any clue how long it's been there.

When the movers
arrive to pack up the house,
one of them notices the fissure

in the marital bed,
asking how long it's
been damaged in that way.

Presumptuous,
I'd say, though I'm
sure he means no harm.

I shrug
and say I've no idea
when the split first occurred,

but it's
clearly grown
to unbearable dimensions.

I pack the rest
of my things, then call
the Salvation Army to pick up the bed.

-- Cristine A. Gruber
(October Napalm and Novocain)

Bright constellations
form a nocturnal map
lead the cat back home

> -- *Cristine A. Gruber*
> *(October High Coupe)*

Standing Room Only

Like a scene from a hospital show from the 90s, I stand in the hallway, one hand on the wall, fingers splayed, not so much to hold myself up, as much as to simply have someplace to put them, something to do with my quivering digits, the other trembling set wrapped firmly around my waist. I'm polite as you give me the news, nodding slowly, my eyes never leaving your face, focused on your mouth, possibly believing if I stare hard enough, I'll be able to rearrange the words spilling forth, thus altering the news, changing the course of the landscape. You apologize more than once for the lack of privacy as you tell me the MRI shows an undetermined mass at the base of my brain. I think I ask you for a more precise explanation of what I'm supposed to do with that information, but the effects of the morphine rushing through my system make me question whether I speak at all, or merely hear the words inside my head, false niceties alongside vicious curses I'd only heard in movies I'd never admit to watching. Tears well up, but not for me. Surely, they're nothing more than tears of empathy for the look of pain on your troubled face as you graciously conclude by telling me it will be another three hours before the Attending on Duty will have the time to get to my chart, review my paperwork, and find me a bloody room.

-- Cristine A. Gruber
(September Pound of Flash)

Psyche

Fear is septic
and reeks of something evil. Sharp
rusty claws scratch in the night.
Joy and despair quite
fine and sweet.
About a lonely peak.
Love is fond in the tales
on a white knight's shield.
Pride has thin and
lovely feathers. Hate is
incessant inferno almost ready
to die. The seeds
of righteous anger are easily poisoned;
a snake oil salesman
rapist and murderer. Uncle
Sam meat packing quickly. A
hell-fire missile, two
degrees, a brown family
sees the cup empty, ignorant
the office worker sits
quietly, in his cell, tired.
His co-worker hidden
behind a luminescent screen
a message pops up again and again
irritating, infuriating. Guilt
is the strongest, hate is
most torrid, apathy
is man's poison of choice.

-- Ahab Hamza
(November Pyrokinection)

Driving through Utah

Cracks and wrinkles in blue skin
sliver across the desert sky
like streaks of clouds.
The left and right horizons
are fractured jaw lines and coffee stained teeth.
The desert seems flat
but beyond the asphalt
lumps of sand spotted with tufts of grass
rise and fall: the moles and pores
of Utah's skin. Then a butte
and ridges, a wall
like shards of dark glass slicing into a brown back
bent forward at the waist from hard labor.

The acrid air abrades even human skin.
Funnels of wind
rise and dissipate
in the distance: rust red,
burnt orange sand and gravel. The turn
to Moab and the National Park
promises fossilized dunes, like layers of stretch marks
and cellulite across the belly,
and geologic fractures,
beauty framing the blue,
leaking sky and tears of sunlight
between round windows and arches
of granite and sandstone,

formations like ogres, like trolls,
like abstract sculptures and sand paintings
defying the world's evil spirits,
to balance the spirits
of breathing creatures.
Tourists' car radios, cameras,
caravans of RV's and plastic water bottles
leak the world into this space,

a hot wind billowing out of the horizon,
a haze that distorts the landscape
into photos and family vacations.

We are all guilty of anthropomorphism.
The arches continue to stretch and lean
despite the humans hiking and posing around them.
Snakes, lizards and scorpions, ravens
rabbits, yucca, pinion pines, prickly pear cactus,
live despite us. The sands burn and cool, shift
and erode, despite us.
The asphalt road circles back to the entrance of the park.
The desert and mountains
stretch and streak and wind and drop and rise
despite us.

-- Patricia Hanahoe-Dosch
(September Jellyfish Whispers)

Silence

We lay together
I twined around you like ivy on oak.
Warm and dark
a soft blanket of silence
comforted and carried us
together into a single dream.

> *Morning came*
> *dreams dissolved.*
> *Light shone in the space*
> *between you and my idea of you.*

We faced each other
you a wall against which
I flung myself.
Silence cold and gray
froze and shattered
strewing the ground with
fractured passion.

> *no I wish no I can't*
> *no I meant no I should*
> *no but you no you wouldn't*
> *no you didn't no you never*

> *Shards of us pierced my soul*
> *desire catalyzed memory*
> *memory blurred and grew*
> *soft at the edges.*

I sit alone in silence.
Our last words hang
in the empty air.
I breathe them in

like toxic fog
and my heart
implodes.

    -- Margery Hauser
    (October Napalm and Novocain)

The Chicken Dance

When it came down to it, I slept with him because Mom made a dead chicken dance. She hefted it up under its wings as if presenting a child. A trail of pink slime dripped on the counter as it kicked and shimmied its way across. A dead thing, a used-up thing, a pitiable thing, but for two minutes it danced and soaked up a little admiration.

I met him at the park, behind a line of shrubs, when my friends and I shared a single cigarette I'd stolen from Mom. I tried to smoke the one he gave me without coughing as he played with the strap of my dress. His skin cracked over his knuckles, like a road map of a hard life. His hair had started to recede, and lines creased the corners of his lips. The years that sat behind his eyes doubled my own, but the way he watched me made me forget to care.

He drove me to the end of a dirt road. I stared at the frayed hem of my dress, pulling at a wayward thread when I couldn't bring myself to look at him. The shadows cast by the light of the dashboard made his face dangerous. The anticipation eluded me as it always had. Shame scrubbed away any excitement, leaving me covered in welts like road rash.

The weight of the night smothered me like his body did. His calloused hands felt rough and his shadow of a beard scratched my neck. I felt no pleasure, and swallowed down the complaints and refusals that always crawled up my throat like bile. Instead, I closed my eyes and clung to his shoulders as he made me dance, a dead and used up and pitiable thing soaking up a little admiration.

-- Heather Heyns
(December Pound of Flash)

Appellation

I. In June I Changed My Name

It happened during my wedding, right at the very end,
    when I was being kissed.

Then the two of us and our nine grandchildren
    clambered and scrambled

into the wagon and my son started the tractor,
    drove us by river and cove.

After eating cake we swam and sailed
    all sunny afternoon.

It's so different this second time – different river, wagon, us.

II. Switchbacks

For our honeymoon we're climbing a mountain—
    me with a pacemaker, him

arthritic knees. It's his first crack
    at this crest, my third,

each time lugging a different
    name. At our trailhead

the forest is lovely, leafy. But
    why didn't we check

the forecast, memorize the maps, why did we choose
    this track of many stones? Midway,

I'm thinking we're drinking
    too much too quickly from our canteen; late,

we argue but cannot resolve:
why is it all so steep?

III. Precaution at the DMV

This is the third name I've driven
and it feels

like I'm grinding my gears.
After the cake and tossing

of flowers, it only took a week
for our first fight, "minor tiff"

his terminology, though I asked myself
just what my name is anyway.

First time around I threw my birthname
out without a second glance, rubbernecked

the new one like grass
on the far side of a fence.

This time maybe I should stow that old friend
in the glove compartment—

keep it close
just in case.

-- Wendy Elizabeth Ingersoll
(April Pyrokinection)

Fear Itself

At the Museum of Natural History my granddaughters and I seek dinosaurs
but chance upon the tarantulas --

Goliath Birdeaters, Curly Hairs,
Greenbottle Blues, Chilean Fires --
in an attempt to minimize horror
I read the poster:

a tarantula's too big to dwell on his web but will spin
a trip line to lead to his warren,
where he waits,
            speed
enabling him to catch and eat.
My granddaughters are enthralled

though I'm appalled. But -- yet another sign on the wall:
Though frightful, tarantula bites are not lethal
to people.

Saving grace! When venom strikes, just proceed down the wall
to the dinosaur hall.

                -- Wendy Elizabeth Ingersoll
                (February Jellyfish Whispers)

Chinese Take-Away Sky

Muttering something from Shakespeare,
perhaps "Woe, alas, time calls upon us!"
the nuthatch pokes sunflower seeds
into a cranny of the psychiatrist's palm.

The shrink asks him again how many followers
he has on Twitter...

--Over a million, he replies,
including the Boston symphony Orchestra.

--and how does that make you..

--feel?

_ I don't feel, Doc, I fly..

The psychiatrist makes a cage with her fingers,
and starts over:

--in our last session you were checking the pulse
of a Hawthorne
in the 12 thousand block of Martinazzi Avenue..

--that's right.

--tell me again exactly what happened or did not happen.

-- well, Doc, there were these two hearts
carved into the bark, old hearts,
stuffed with micro jitter and boneless parades,
twerking mites smarter than Pascal,
but unintentionally funny like Sid Caesar..

--and how does that make you.

But the nuthatch had hidden himself
in a Bonsai tree
on the left edge of her enormous desk.

When his hour is up
the psychiatrist takes a carton of Chinese takeaway sky
out of her backpack
and stares at the sun inside.

-- Bill Jansen
(March The Mind[less] Muse)

Ambulance Chaser

bypass the heart attack
and don't go out
in that broad stroke
of genius
known as
sleeping through
your own death
instead go out
surrounded by
jugglers who go
for your jugular
or go out
on a limb
limber as a gymnast
until the branch
breaks then
fall with the
autumn leaves
and land with a thud
on the auburn crud
or better yet
lose a game
of strip poker
slash
Russian roulette
and die in a
naked
bloody
Peckinpah
pirouette
then writhe
on the floor
only to extinguish
your existential
anguish
with one

silver
bullet more

> *-- Ivan Jenson*
> *(September Pyrokinection)*

Cut Grass in Snow

All daylong
night is my storm lantern.
I carry it into the farmland
cutting into my harvest emotions
covered by snow
edge them in half
in front of me
see me open, bleeding.
I am seed like a small orange
pit me out and devour me
spit pulp and seed
I step on jagged edges
of my feelings, sense my pain
cut stretched skin with glass shavings
torture under toes hurt bad with pain.
Pitch that stuff with dark
black top tar if it makes
you feel relief.
Do not laugh at me, a circus clown down,
I am 66; my dimples show smiles, ripples, age.
This day is a lawn mower
even in Canadian December.
Machinery is shacked-up, covered.
I plow beneath the white surface
cut rotten leaves beneath settled snow.
The aggravation,
cultivation nonsense hell with my runny nose.
In spring, the grass never pops up right.
All day, night is my storm lantern.

-- Michael Lee Johnson
(February Jellyfish Whispers)

Untitled I Walk

Untitled I walk
through life
with a shrink
from Yugoslavia,
who is as large as Bigfoot.
With a novel in one hand,
and shaking his fingers at me
with the other,
he wants to control me with a shovel,
tie me in knot balls, emotional twisters,
and squeeze the emotional pages
out of my life like a twisted sponge.
I retaliate, control him back,
wage war in a vicarious cycle
squeeze his testicles like electrical wires
inside my mind's eye,
cut his tongue with razors,
dull his clinical words.
Play his game, only better.
He picks up the play phone,
threatens to call the police,
leashing me in my corner
like a trapped dog
forces me to bark
into submission
like a beagle basset bitch.
He treats me with word babble.
I tell him he is a damn Ukrainian idiot.
Peeved off I race
to the parking lot, head to the bushes,
like a blue racer snake threatened,
hop bunny rabbit into my S-10
Chevy pick-up truck,
memo pad in hand,
scribbling ruminating notes

I surrender naked until my next prescription,
untitled I walk.

-- Michael Lee Johnson
(January The Mind[less] Muse)

Appears To Be Rimbaud Speaking

My shadowy wraith like goldfish pond is only bones and gristle
An ominous childhood collage of fairy lands
That causes my living room to speak in a gravelly whisper
And here where you first have to descend into Kurt Schwitter's Prelude
Of nasty red welts to where the railroad tracks beat their wings
Near a city that has become a touchable phantom
As its asphalt comes awake and the lost jazz
Of Ezra Pound is played upon a punctured saxophone most red
Till it becomes a key turned in the lock of that egg spoon hour
When poetry pulls my strings till my hands do ache
Before it releases me from its power once more
Until later it once again lights my powder keg.

-- Ken L. Jones
(April Pyrokinection)

A Few Choice Lines About the Deities of the Mad Tea Party

Green husks everywhere
Bamboo like stalks
Now divested of their
Ripe golden roasting ears
Filaments of silk
Blow on the wind like manna
The most wonderful and yet neutral
Smells of the kernels themselves
The ruts in the cultivated earth
Dark and brown
And moist and fertile
And all beneath a painfully
China blue sky
Agog with chicken and dumpling symmetried clouds
On this most perfect of harvest afternoons.

-- Ken L. Jones
(January Jellyfish Whispers)

The Minotaur in the Dime Store

My thoughts they are a puppet show
Where sour apple paper dolls
Act out candlestick lit bedtime stories
As ashen as Emily Dickenson's
Purple shadow songs
And in the sweet, sweet lilac
Of my afternoon nap
Where tumbleweeds like spinning wheels
Perform a rusted symphony
As I dream of the silver dust of your kiss
Now an apparition in the mist
A warm whisper of indigo
Because though we still live together
You left me long ago.

-- Ken L. Jones
(June Napalm and Novocain)

Unicorn Hunt

The mind drinks up the highway straight ahead
Dogs and cats in slow motion
On a night full of the evil thoughts of typewriters
Drowning in the dish water of comic books
The image is a loaded gun that must be burned
A well read stomach that must be fed
It lights such a candle that it tapes up your mouth
Like delirium in a red brocade smoking jacket
Inching across your lawn like a snail
Then down the streets of fever in the morning
In a vertigo of top forty song lyrics
Gathering dust on the lips of millions of women
In the navel of a love manual
That can't be purchased at any store.

-- Ken L. Jones
(January The Mind[less] Muse)

Dear Mother

my mother died yesterday
she was 95 years old and
a mean bitter woman

she hated my father
she hated me

she swore she would haunt me
after she died.

bring it on
bitch.

-- Larry Jones
(May Pyrokinection)

Escaping Criticism

Last night I dreamed a zen monk was writing
a description of paper by dipping his dry brush
into an empty inkwell; then letting the bristles splay
for a few seconds on each square-inch of pulp.

Most of us can't, of course. We stage a play
called *Nothingness*; but can't resist, at least once,
coming out onto the dark stage
bowing from the hinge of our waists,
whether we expect rancor or applause.

The best is not to lay a single finger on the strings;
to say the sound most natural to *violin*
is what it does in the corner of a quiet room,
responding to woodlice and small currents in the air.

The best is not to paint at all. Just ask del Caso
who should have left his critics with an empty frame;
who couldn't help but render the boy's fleshy toes,
two fingers and a thumb; hair lit and eyes overawed
by a light no artist ever caught.

-- B.T. Joy
(November Pyrokinection)

Cat Energy on the Dog Walk

    While walking the dead I woke the dog.
Their small bodies are audible at 60,000 hertz.
Every link in the choke-chain is another poem
that John Keats never wrote. Every photo album
is a catalog of human strivings.
    The streets are watermelon red.
The experts of the cold seas say
the seesaw of the tide has gone off kilter
by a quarter of a degree. Somewhere
the Beaufort scale is hitting twelve and a hundred million
pairs of sweatshop trainers are irredeemably lost.
    While walking the dead I saw two pools,
their freckled water was the colour of unwashed jade
and somehow they resembled your eyes before leukemia.
Mystic tunnels in a pine-nut shell. How every pistachio
longs to visit the cave of silver doves.
    I'm a penniless student outside the dancehall at 3AM.
I'm a mother of three, turning fifty now,
and already unseen among the mangoes' sweat.
I'm a terrapin's legs and the chalky night and all
the young hopes Augustine must have had.
I'm walking a dog
    while walking the dead.
The morning moon is the color of an artichoke's heart.
The hedges smell like the heat of July
and the linden, like a moody child, throws the puzzle
of faint shade across the grass.

                    -- B.T. Joy
                (November Pyrokinection)

Reading Jinzhu Ridge

Dry blooms are shivering in the varnish trees.
Lines of white daffodils bend on greenish hills.
Wang Wei is up on Jinzhu Ridge again,
not a buddhist yet, but writing buddhist poems.
I imagine this as some time before the war.
The spring wind tugs childishly on his grey robes.
Out of the sharp grief he felt, thin as a bird,
under the shade of his dead mother's shrine
I see him smiling beneath his thinning facial hair.
Never one to write about the things people do
he has found the most direct road over mountains;
a path that even the woodcutter doesn't know.

-- B.T. Joy
(February Jellyfish Whispers)

Grampians

The hills spill with light
interminably along the landscape's endless lines.
Standing in these highlands: their enormity,
and their rivered roots rolling in gentle tides,
give you the impression of being
very weak and very small.

On each extremity
the furthest mountains in the range
are blue clouds wilting, partially-unseen,
against the blue sky.

You have no idea where the river is flowing
or where the mountain raven will perch
among the upper-stones.
Sometimes it seems
not even to matter.

So you cried with joy in the silence above the town.
So the electric burn of your constant mental questioning
died away in the tireless answer of terrain that steeped
its forested body in geological time.
What does any of that matter?
The wide Grampians are still as impassable to you.
Nowhere did you solve the puzzle of your life.

-- B.T. Joy
(April Jellyfish Whispers)

The Winter Shadow

on the wall
has no eyes but it sees
every grain of grit
pushed and anguished
by snow

it has hands like dark
webs shooting out
from thin wrists
it has legs like stilts
stalking a cold land

Tonight the shadow will shrink
to a frozen
spot

which cold night
will swallow
the shadow is
not lost
but wandering far
in the moon's restless dream

-- Steve Klepetar
(March Pyrokinection)

Staff Meeting

The girl to my right is wearing three shirts,
gray over black over white. Her nails are clear;
her friend's are painted black. Each has driven

a thin spike through the flesh of her ear.
This room is cold. Some people are eating
banana cake; white icing clings to yellow plates.

Wall clock lurches forward, one minute at a time.
Somewhere, green snakes wind their twisting way
beneath the blasts, deep through undulating earth.

-- Steve Klepetar
(March Pyrokinection)

All That I Have Felt
(In some semblance of order)

(1967 to 1975)

kittens
carpet burns
fear
WGN presents "One-Eyed Jacks" starring Marlon Brando
my grandmother's basement
slaps from my mother
fear
kicks from my father
fear
Nerf basketball
10CC "I'm Not in Love"
fear

(1976 to 1980)

sunny, cool, fall days
the woods on Sundays
tall green grass
raised red seams on a baseball
fear
Tickle Pink wine
the smell of hashish
the buzz of high tension wires
Stroh's beer, pull tab tall boys
the woods at night
the breeze through the car window
her breath in my ear
fear

(1981 to 1988)

"Footloose" starring Kevin Bacon
Michelob Light in bottles

extra spicy guacamole
fear
"Members Only" black jacket
    para mutual wagering
    fellatio
4 seam fastball
fear
the garlic taste of Dimethyl Sulfoxide (DMSO)
a 91 mph fastball
Feldene dissolved in Dimethyl Sulfoxide and applied to my skin
via tongue depressor
my 93.5 mph fastball
The roar of the crowd
fear
October
the swirling light and sound of a west Texas freight train at night
in the fog
Jesus Christ
    Fear

(1989 to 1999)

the anticipation of child #1
the birth of child #2
6 hours of uninterrupted sleep after child #3
an 8mm obstructed kidney stone
fear
morphine
fear
Vicodin
fear
sunny, cool, fall days
"The Road Less Traveled" by M Scott Peck
hydrocodone
fear
the woods in fall
thunder
Valium

fear
the woods in winter
the rumble of Niagara Falls
Valium
fear
Oxycontin
shame
Valium
fear
"Ruthless Trust" by Brennan Manning
the woods in spring
The Stanley Cup
fear

(2000 to 2004)

detox
nostalgia of my youth
photos of my children as children
hydrocodone
detox
fear
Jose Cuervo silver tequila
sunny, cool, spring days
Major League Baseball opening day
Jose Cuervo Gold tequila
fear
Chinaco Reposado tequila
the stench of pavement
Gran Patron tequila
the heat of pavement
Herradura Anejo tequila
detox
hydrocodone
fear
Marca Negra Mezcal
detox
AA meetings

Oxycontin
fear
Alice in Chains "Down in a Hole"
detox
nostalgia for opiates
fear

(2005 to 2007)

AA meetings
Camel 99's
her infidelity
fear
photos of my children as children
Camel 99's
the sweet, sweet voice of Martin Sexton
AA meetings
shame
regret
fear
Suboxone
regret
shame
fear

(2008 to 2010)

the tenderness of your touch
a king size memory foam mattress
the tenderness of your touch
Amerique Verte Absinthe
fear
discussions with the dead
the tenderness of your touch
Ray Lamontagne "Winter Birds"
the tenderness of your touch
ablution by Amerique Verte Absinthe
fear

visions of the dead
fear
visits from the dead

(2011 to 2014)

their forgiveness
AA meetings
Camel 99's
my inability to sleep
fear
www.hellopoetry.com
the tenderness of your touch
the tenderness of your touch
the tenderness of your touch
the tenderness of your touch
fear
Centenario Reposado tequila
regret
Tramadol in large amounts
regret
thoughts of you leaving me
thoughts of me being left alone
thoughts of you being left alone
regret

nothing
nothing
nothing

the words I have just written

darkness

fear

-- John Kross
(June The Mind[less] Muse)

Your Skin

You cannot travel within and stand still without.

-- James Allen

To be drunk from the color of your skin
Wrapped around you in biscuity ash-white,
Flawless like a prayer-shawl
I think albatross, or even something bigger,
More severe, but I do not know why
My thoughts are analytical, like clear blue sky
The smell of wild animal, of wild
                       of animal
The taste of you, reckless like chili
Con carne, travels inward along my spine

I pause—blue; like a sign of punctuation
Standing patiently on the bitumen's edge,
The smell of your skin's karri-tree aroma
Spreads faster than any train of thought
Tucked away in the shade
I think little leather miniskirt or naked flesh
The sacredness of spider's silk, of spider
                       and of silk
Reassembled into a silhouette honest as
Skin on skin in the slit between dark and light.

-- Martha Landman
(The Mind[less] Muse)

Back Then

Just because it happened a long
time before my imagination's
eyesight, my retina's perfection,
Just because it now all seems blurry
and memorably impaired . . .

When I relax the I and see the full
stop and let my mind loop from
thought to thought, I find symbolism
in the ulcers bursting in my stomach
feeding me organic wisdom.

My soul's windows need a wash
to see my students in the balance
they offer me when they exercise
all the muscles of their mind even
though they don't process the facts

I feed them day by day. They are not
to blame for emotions triggered by
my hypnotic influence, my vision
training, my problem-solving approach
skillfully gazed upon their innocence.

Mother and child bonded on a clean slate
back then, but I've learned to become scared
of dark material clouding my equilibrium.
My ears, my eyes, my orientation have
grown deaf, stress-inhibited, unrecovered.

My preference is to link sound, smell and
taste and indulge in a bowl of chocolate-flaked
ice-cream while I listen to Maria Callas'
frequencies even though some are missing.
It's been a long time since my brain hungered

for otherworldly explorations: the ability to
communicate subtly through the electronic
ear, not shutting down at a baby's cry or
closing my eyes when romantically kissed
—my left stockinged calf elegantly uplifted.

-- Martha Landman
(June The Mind[less] Muse)

Haiku Stupid

1.

sixteen chickens cross
I curse the road for its width
stupid slowpoke birds

2.

they roll themselves down
stupid Pakistani socks
blame it on Wal-Mart

3.

stupid galaxy
we have nowhere else to go
stay home in the pits

4.

deadly golden arch
America malnourished
stupid plastic food

5.

turn the damned thing off
stupid reality shows
big ol' bunch of dopes

-- Ron. Lavalette
(June High Coupe)

Some Afternoons When Nobody Was Fighting

my mother took out
walnuts and chocolate
chips. My sister and
I plunged our fingers
in flour and butter
smoother than clay.
Pale dough oozing
between our fingers
while the house filled
with blond bars rising
and kisses of fudge
Mother in her pink dress
with black ballerinas
circling its bottom
turned on the Victrola,
tucked her dress up into
pink nylon bloomer pants,
kicked her legs up in the
air and my sister and I
pranced thru the living
room, a bracelet around
her. She was our Pied
Piper and we were
the children of Hamlin,
circling her as close as the
dancers on her hem

-- Lyn Lifshin
(July Pyrokinection)

Terrestrial Illumination No. 380 (2014)

I.

The garden ticket booth wet by rain.
Minute stone chips
Loosened from old asphalt
Rolled from roof

To fall on slabs of cement,
To fall on
A fallen world

As the world has been libeled for over two thousand years.

A string quartet was to play in gazebo postmodern music.

II.

It was as if the downpour was a new flood to cleanse the world
Of its past fantasy enchantment and its false beliefs.
For over two thousand years the people had misled themselves
By mistakes, and lived by lies.
The had lived by illusions
Of the theological and the scientific circus and sideshows, and now
With the transvaluations of mostmodern people were on the threshold
Of salvation and finally, a relationship with reality.

The music would celebrate the new dispensation of postmodernism.

III.

The rain was the heaviest of the year,
But the people not having read the program was to be postmodernism, set
As it dry, awaiting the usual trivial and petty amusements.
The old beliefs and living according to the old axiology
Had made the people obtuse

And the people could not feel any more natural sensations
Such as the wetness of rain.

But they were told by the TV set that it was raining. The commentator
Read from a script that outside was a heavy downpour.
The report resulted in everyone putting on raincoats.
Over their unnoticed soaked tuxedoes and evening dresses.

IV.

For over two-thousand years the earth had been turned into an insane asylum.
Causation was the theological and the scientific minds
Echolalia was the normal way of communication,
Communication had ceased to exist under the old order before
postmodernism.
The clean and distinct had failed to communicate,
Postmodernism discovered profound and meaningful communication
Came only from poetic opacity.

V.

Now in raincoats, some started to pass the time by reading.

The scraps of paper turned from page to page
Are seen as graphic elementary designs, straight, cursive lines.
Blurred by false memories of their blue blood,
And the curls under the hoods of nuns. Antic,
Their fingers whirl car keys. Some have in bags
For gifts toy replicas of anorexic tiaraed royalties
Posed as the tiny white globes that roll over numbers
On roulette wheels. All eyes spin as do slut machines.
What is there to be read is never read, content chased
Away by vague desires and inherited meta-narratives
Of angels painting their fingernails gold as tattooed
On hairy arms or shaven legs. Books written to be destroyed.

From the shrubbery comes the song of the wren,
What is unconcealed by the wren's song is vaguely heard,

And quickly reheard as something else, as something
That was believed to exist but never existed. And
The current fractured, fragmented, faked life
That began in ancient time with the original lie
And original sin still reigns, comforted by the thermostat.

VI.

Adorno observed how faith in logic and reason by
The Enlighment's white wigs, bows on knee pants,
And white stockings prepares for Auschwitz
And the Marquis De Sade. But the Enlightment
Was already corrupted by attitudes and habits
Implanted from the Middle Ages. Logic and reason
Were the clowns whose acts took the peoples' minds
Off the fact that there were truths.

VII.

The musicians have not arrived, a nightclub comedian is substitute.
Champagne is distributed and the audience is in ecstasy.

The applauded comic weeps as the audience laughs.
The comic has sensed the responses to his stolen jokes
And how these responses will lead to the destruction of humanity.
He knows that the inferior quality
Of his jokes is what makes them such an outstanding success.

VIII.

The wet chairs in the park await the musicians
To play the music that celebrates the return of enchantment
And the return of truth that postmodernism will bring to the world.

The musicians' instruments rest on the chairs,
The musicians have refused to play.
The musicians refused to play
When the musicians learned they were to play a composition
That celebrates postmodernism.

IX.

The comedian was informed, so he had to tell more dirty jokes.

-- Duane Locke
(August The Mind[less] Muse)

Ephram Pratt Exhales the Bliss of Light

The bandage on the clock
fits tightly

like amnesia
leaking into

a dry pool of acid,
into a drift-wood

alabaster ingot
tasting the wares

of insulated daylight.
Crease your fingers

as if they were
on fire,

ignited by
crystals of joy

dripping onto the page
of mismatched

mandalas
clustered in silence

around an enclosed
isothermal blot,

anchored in space
by practiced

and practical
insignias of light.

>	*-- Jack e Lorts*
>	*(October The Mind[less] Muse)*

A Breeze She Hardly Knew

She used to watch the waves crash the breakers
Clutching old love letters like life-strings;
the only things she had left of him.
She stood wishing for times to be as they were,
Despite having moved to the Puget Sound.
Sometimes she would think about the rock facings,
And how high they once stood.
How they had been weathered by surf and time
Yet still remained.

Seagulls used to scour and pick for crab shells.
on the beaches below.
They'd peck
the remains until
they were bored,
and then fly away,
without a care,
on a breeze
they hardly knew,
from the bones they'd never remember.

Staring out over the breakers,
As the waves splashed over and over,
she would read the letters over and over,
searching, as if missing some key element
time or her own blind negligence had somehow overlooked.
She still wore the ring, when she went to the ocean,
She still wore the dress. She still thought of him.
She carried those letters on a breeze to forever,
The seagulls picking away at the remains of everything she
needed to let go.

-- Chad W. Lutz
(April Napalm and Novocain)

Already Broken

As soon as my elbow grazed
the wineglass left carelessly close
to the counter's edge, I was
already reaching for the broom,
knowing that was all she wrote.

Somewhere in the final years,
long after we'd given up
on trying to find the perfect gift,
you came home from a yard sale
with four glass goblets, each one
large enough to hold a good
half-bottle of Sonoma red.

I loved them on sight, while you
grew to loathe that love.
Now, only two remain, and
as I sweep up sharp-edged
shards from the linoleum floor
of my single-room apartment,
I imagine that I hear you laugh.
Sympathetically, I hope.
Enough's been spilled already;
no need for malice now.
Whatever we think we have,
we come to learn, will not endure.

-- Iain Macdonald
(October Napalm and Novocain)

Hanging the Stars

She's not doing much,
Just wrestling a werewolf moon
And hanging silver stars

-- Stacy Lynn Mar
(October High Coupe)

Worn roadside sign says
Unlimited dreams ten bucks
All nightmares are free

> *-- Denny E. Marshall*
> *(May High Coupe)*

The Twinkies Are Gone

But then they came back,
even after Hostess tanked.

Other Big Firms to the rescue,
lest you flip
out and horde, as some did,
the golden sponge,
filled and artificial.
You'll wish you'd had more cream
before The Nuclear
Winter
with only cockroaches left to feast
on the sugary nectar,
the radiated sponge a bygone thing.
Take back the night swinging
on the yellow mini cake like an oblong moon
bounced into open ovens in bakeries.

A skilled workforce pulls down the door
to 425 degrees or so of heat —
slips raw batter into the cooker
open
euphoric
a sugar high
at the Emporia.

Sons, daughters, mothers, fathers,
cranking out sponge cakes for 50 years.

Better than Hungarian cherry pie.

The darling of fake foods:
golden

and glorious,
from which American dreams are made.

> *-- Grace Maselli*
> *(July Pyrokinection)*

Found

As the needle compresses
her bones melt and
she oozes out between the slats of her parents' picket
fence
Her gelatinous form
slinks along the curbs of
dozens of streets
through dozens of
months
Each time she tries to
form an arm from
the liquid she has become
and reach the hovering glow
of satiation just above her
shape diminishes that much more
Until one day someone
stepping in her puddle
leaves a piece behind

Life blooms within her and
she finds herself solidifying
once again
She reaches up and finds
that fullness in another
way and she is
emptied out again and
holds her daughter in
her new-found arms

-- Anna McCluskey
(September Pyrokinection)

Where the Lost Gather

"Maintain your perspective just keep going" she thought while waiting for the bus. The sky resembled an ink blotter drenched in grey and black. People trekked along avenues attempting to cross over mounds of snow. Teenagers ganged up huddling under broad awnings. Their brightly colored jackets spread like rainbow clusters against brick buildings. She twitched her umbrella awkwardly, its handle was cold. Where were her gloves? Would the bus ever come?

Stepping off the curb twisting her head fidgeting . . . "Stay optimistic. Be brave. Everything will work out eventually." The familiar tape played over and over in her brain. Another appointment, another pill pusher . . . another doctor as healthy as a horse. How could he possibly understand? Always the same questions. What about her habits . . . smoking, drinking, taking street drugs, having an active sex life? Was she anxious, depressed? Prying into her life then offering no solutions. A waste of money with so little cash left. And a waste of time. But time stood still now. . . heavy hours pressing down crushing her.

The doctor's office needed a paint job. There was no coat closet or water fountain. An old magazine minus its cover curled up next to the lamp. Lorraine wished she had brought her crossword puzzle. Increasingly annoyed by the long wait, she realized her turn was hours away. Looking over the other patients, wondering what was wrong with them. Finally the doctor had time to see her to listen to complaints about fatigue, shortness of breath, being dizzy. Promising to run some tests, he left. A nurse entered to draw her blood filling three vials with a long needle. The results would be available next week. Handing her check to the receptionist, that was that.

It was so great to get home, she felt so free, so happy after leaving the oppression of the doctor's office. Home now: beating a retreat under lumpy bedclothes where several paperbacks and her eyeglasses were hidden.

Many pages later windowpanes clatter like nervous teeth. Zillions of icicles etch fine line portraits of frost. Snow fell and kept falling.

Unleashed . . . storms overtake darkness . . . making all mute. A storm of light covers the night as she slid to sleep. Dream sliding to a house of mirrors where countless images surrounded her. Where is she? Reflections without number repeat her every gesture. Somehow she must look for her real self. Sifting within these icy sheets of glass, suddenly all her fingers began to burn.

-- Joan McNerney
(November Pound of Flash)

Night Train

A train of thought,
traveling from somewhere to somewhere else,
the engineer dragging on its lonesome whistle
as if a convict his cigarette, the conductor
in two minds, in two opposing quantum states,
existence vying with non-existence.

A train of thought in the long black night,
the passengers inhumanly quiet,
their tickets punched and paid for,
their mouths shut but their eyes open,
stealing a few cursory glances
at the blackened countryside,
that light at the end of the tunnel
receding, coming closer, moving away.

-- Bruce McRae
(May Pyrokinection)

Less Than a Single Breath

On an island in a lake on an island . . .
At sea level. Stranded on morning's beach.
Donning our rough apparel.
The small appearing large. The sleepers weeping.
Yesterday's rain making fools of us all.

Dawn saws a jig on its catgut fiddle,
the wind in an awful and needless hurry,
gravity's barbed hooks dangling provocatively,
the wind beside itself with work and worry.

Pauses couple, birthing an inbred stillness,
each eventual life losing its tiny lottery.
Soon the moments have piled high,
a tower of time, a backlog of grim reckoning.

Soon, the unbearable gifts of winter.

-- Bruce McRae
(May Pyrokinection)

As It Is

The door closes and the round mirror holds her image a moment before she turns away. She looks over the room he has just left. She gets her black suitcase from the closet and puts it on the bed, and begins to pack. She bites her lip.

Well now, she thinks—that is done—

Her hands tremble as she moves the clothes from the drawer to the suitcase.

—and I am glad that it is over.

Outside, he gets into his car and turns the key. The car powers to life. What should I do now, he thinks; what should I do where should I go.

Upstairs, inside, the phone interrupts her. She picks it up.

Yes?

She holds the phone to her ear, but there is no one there. It's funny how phone calls come like that sometimes. They click hanging up. It is just as well. Listening is impossible; she hangs up and resumes her packing. Two tickets are lying on top of the dresser. They were to have gone together but now that's just a ridiculous memory. She thinks what to do with the extra ticket. She takes it and tears it up and throws it in the trash can. One ticket means one person. There is no turning back. She resumes packing.

Outside, in the car he thinks he should have brought his ticket down with him and he half-thinks to go up to get it, but no, that would mean seeing her again. He is done seeing her; he never can see her again. The car backs out of the lot and he drives off into the dark. The street lamps on the poles cast down circular beams of overlapping brightness into the night. It is late and the streets are deserted. Headlights appear in the distance and approach. The black car pulls up before the apartment building's door. It sits idling. Waiting.

She closes her suitcase and puts on her coat. It is cool outside; not cold, but cool. She leaves the room after looking in the mirror again and turning off the light. Outside, she gets into the waiting car. It leaves. It turns off onto the ramp to the Interstate and in a moment is up to seventy, eighty; she sits in the back seat reveling in the speed of it. She reaches two fingers into her purse and the ticket is there. Her ticket.

He drives randomly. He passes Steck's bar—then Solly's—then Mijo's. He wants a drink badly, but is in no mood for company. He cannot speak to anyone tonight. He will go home to drink. It is twelve-thirty.

She is nearing the airport. The black car pulls up the departing flights ramp. The driver helps her with her bag and briskly she walks toward the revolving door of the terminal building after having tipped him, and he drives away. She goes through security—there is hardly anyone there. She goes to the gate; the red-eye flight to Newark is boarding. She has just made it; thank God she had not spent too much time with him before. Thank God it had been quick, and easy.

He gets home and goes in. He takes off his jacket, throws it on the couch, and rips off his tie. The vodka comes down from the shelf. It pours into the glass. It is pure, clear, and honest. He looks through the bottle; everything is distorted. He puts down the bottle and picks up the glass.

She boards the plane after checking her bag at the gate. She enters, finds her seat in first class, sits, wipes her hand down her cheek and after they have rolled and are in flight, she asks the attendant for a drink.

Vodka, she says.

He takes his glass into the living room. He sits in his chair. He drinks one, then another.

She drinks; one, two. She puts her glass in the holder.

Their hands reach out gripping the chair arms as the liquor does its work. With eyes closed, they squeeze the chair arms; it feels as if they are sitting side by side, hands clasped together, as they used to; as if that were not now forever impossible; impossible, as it is.

-- Jim Meirose
(April Pound of Flash)

Harpies

Margaret came in the yellow kitchen and flicked on the light. Centipedes scurried out of sight under the stove and under cracks in the baseboard. Margaret got the big black iron stew pot from the refrigerator, put it on the stove, and lit the gas. Mother Rose came into the room trailing her scarf as Margaret put knives forks and spoons and plates out onto the chrome trimmed table. Mother Rose went to the glass-fronted side cabinet and opened it and reached for the dark brandy bottle. Margaret was quicker--she pushed Mother aside and grabbed the brandy bottle down from the shelf and pressed it to her breast. Rose grasped at it.

Give me that bottle, said Rose--I need it--I want to get out of here--this lousy place--the brandy takes me out of here--give it to me.

No Mom, said Margaret, holding the bottle closer--you're a damned drunk--

No, I'm not, shouted Rose--I need that give it to me--

As she clutched at the brandy bottle, Jeffrey came in the room, open mouthed and haggard.

--give me the bottle--Margaret, I am your Mother--

--No--you're a lush, Mom--you're a damned lush--

God, said Jeffrey, tearing his hair, looking from Rose to Margaret and back again--don't argue--you're always arguing--please don't argue--

Ignoring him, Rose went on, pounding her palm into her own chest, her black eyes bulging.

--I need the brandy for my nerves Margaret--you're a damned prude--a damned prude is what you are—

The stew pot softly simmered.

Margaret held Mother at arm's length.

No Mom--it's bad for your health--it will just make you more nervous--you know how you get when you've had the brandy--

Jeffrey raised his hand and shouted and pushed between them.

No--Me! I have had it with both of you--I will decide who gets the bottle!

No! said Margaret, setting the bottle on the table and pointing into Jeffrey's chest--you have nothing to go by to make that decision--

Oh no? And why not--listen, he said, tearing his shirt--I am the man of the house!

Rose and Margaret froze a second, wide eyed.

--I am the man of the house--and you are mere women!

The stew pot bubbled on the stove.

What do you mean, mere women, barked Margaret.

What I said, yelled Jeffrey--just what I said--

As Margaret and Jeffrey faced off, Rose fumbled for the bottle--

Mom! said Margaret--no--no!

The two women wrestled with the bottle and it slipped from them and smashed to the floor.

Oh real smart Margaret, yelled Rose, kicking at the broken glass--real smart--

Margaret pointed from Rose to Jeffrey, saying If he hadn't said those shitty things bout us being mere women, it would never have happened--it's his fault--

Rose turned to Jeffrey, eyes ablaze.

Yes it is his fault isn't it!

The stew pot boiled harder.

Rose grabbed a kitchen knife from the table, as did Margaret--they advanced on Jeffrey, like two jagged toothed sharp clawed winged creatures, two harpies.

He did it--

Yes! He did it.

Jeffrey fled out the door, ran across the living room to the staircase, and ran up and locked himself in his room.

My God, he yelled as he ran--my God--

In the kitchen, atop the broken glass and brandy puddle on the ground, Margaret and Rose smiled at each other as they waved the knives, and stamped hard on the glass shards on the floor, crushing them smaller and smaller until you'd never have known they had been a bottle. The stew pot boiled up, finally out of control, spattering, spattering, spattering.

-- Jim Meirose
(September Pound of Flash)

Ménage à Trois

for David Richter

Once upon Rimbaud's 1870s time
in a Left Bank gay quartier, as a man
fragmented, saturated, he first wrote,
first recited in public the 100-line poem
of a drunken boat, boat like himself,
drifting, sinking at sea, lost
in the shadowed arrondissement of loss.

Once upon his time, a century later, Richter lived
just around the corner, one steep flight up
at #4 Rue de Canivet, window shutters open
to Saint Sulpice at his back (in case of guilt),
Steinway facing south so he could play nocturnes
for the bronzed, muscled pagan statuary
in Luxumbourg's lush garden of easy liaisons.

Once upon a time this summer in Paris,
just down the street, I stared at gaunt twin ghosts
haunting the worn cobblestone ways of doubt,
the narrow, shadowy paths from pain.
From nearby belfry rings the hour of need,
from apartment window sounds a coda-echo of desire
from marble wall etched with"*Le Bâteau Ivre*—
I read in full— at long last write my *Chanson d' Amour*—
in reply—

                 -- Karla Linn Merrifield
                 (December Pyrokinection)

By the Bye

By chance,
they met
at the bus stop.
The weather,
was the topic
as they waited,
in the rain,
for the bus
that never came.

By choice,
they agreed
to share a taxi.
Their homes
were in the same area.
During the journey
they became better acquainted.

By coincidence,
they met again
later that same night.
As they queued
for a pizza take away.

By mutual consent,
they went Dutch
on a bottle of wine.
Choosing the nearest
of their flats
to dine together.

By the time
they had wined, dined
and enjoyed a smoke,
they realized how

attracted to each other
they were.

By the morning,
they knew it was
an unforgettable experience.

"Bye for now,"
they said in unison.
Knowing
they would never
see each other again.

-- Les Merton
(March Napalm and Novocain)

girl on mobile phone
plaits hair with freehand fingers
her eyes comb escape

> *-- Les Merton*
> *(March High Coupe)*

Dinner with the Ghost of Marilyn Monroe

An odd pair these two,
Marilyn's ghost, Rush
And his cigar, dinner date
For the living and the perished
Though difficult to fathom
Which airwave specter
Truly voices knobs of desire:
A lipstick microphone or a
Golden ass pundit braying.
She didn't discuss Robert
Or Jack.
He never mentioned femi-Nazis,
Obama or Romney.
She dined on ghost bites,
He on filet mignon.
How can one distinguish the
Living from the dead?
Radio or movie dittos
Slaughtered images,
Soundwaves slicing dead air.
Marilyn blonde, unbloodied;
Rush balding, forever eating
Progressives, Marilyn drinking
Presidents, they inhale the
Same group vapors and she
In her dress, he in his tie,
Are removed from the land
Of the living.

-- Ralph Monday
(April Pyrokinection)

Love the Fiber Optics

God may be dead but love is not. The internet has revived romance.
    Strange thing the way that time is not linear or cyclical,

but rather a weird juxtaposition of images, memories, experiences
all jumping about like pieces in a puzzle.
The way surfing works, the dead made living, all fitting into the
living room picture frame, Scotch and sofa, roses and violins,
    a few tapping keys like Poe's raven at the window.

    Here, controlling the screen, and forgotten goddesses of the 40s, 50s

live again, images placed in the mind and they know time and kudos,
but more importantly Kairos, a moment of indeterminate time where
everything happens.

    Like now and Gigi Montaigne, Mollie O'Day sit in this room

drinking Turkish coffee, giggling, alive in death, digital tropes that bring
with them the lost values of another time, stirring romance of creatures
who know that this instant matters.
They love me as I them, the more so for bringing conversation, drink, flowers,
to black and white images snapped decades ago that is the present moment.

    Alas that the relationship ended before it began.

        -- Ralph Monday
        (October Napalm and Novocain)

Limbs Like Dark Branches

That morning your tongue turned to leaves
articulating changing seasons where you
walked with green moss, tangled vine
as hair. In the evening a waning moon
became your pupils, your laugh sound
of an owl among treetops.

By the witching hour your body's heat
forced all the insects absent, a skin-fed
fire that made me turn my eyes away
where it consumed your dress and left
you naked, smooth brown skin belonging
to a Mayan priestess.

At dawn your kiss left forest traces on
my tongue. I knew the stuff of streams
running to the sea. Your limbs, like
dark branches, carried you away to
mate with life. No solace in your passage—
I would not see your kind again.

-- Ralph Monday
(October The Mind[less] Muse)

Unbutton the Night

I breathe in the peppermint moon.
It floods through the valley
and settles over the trees.
onto the frozen ground.
Shadows collect
like sticky pollen
in the icy footpath.
Quickly, quickly,
you come to me .
Your hand, a white dove
suspended by moonlight,
reaches out to touch
my chilled skin.
We lie in silvered meadow,
on a porcelain bed,
unbuttoning the night
with our yearning.

-- Jude Neale
(July Jellyfish Whispers)

We Sing Ourselves Back

We are born singing,
orchid air in freefall beneath our trapeze feet.
We open our jaws wide,
balloon our throats
swinging ancestral anaconda notes down
across the emerald city.
We dance antic swags, ellipses, somersaults,
wound the air
with our bass, treble, bellowing melodies.
The women go first
and the men sing back in waves,
above the recitative.
And later with dusty feet,
we wander like leathery kites
shipwrecked with words.
Wanting again to float above it all,
we drill underground instead
to look for our voice,
deep inside the belly of the whale.
We sing ourselves back
and become once again whole.

-- Jude Neale
(April The Mind[less] Muse)

Eleven Things About Wet Noodles that Everyone Should Know:

-- a six-year-old nicknamed Chuck-a-muck often drapes wet noodles over his ears (when his mother isn't looking)

-- Chuck-a-muck's sister Maria doesn't drape wet noodles over her ears

-- Thor didn't eat wet noodles as a kid (Odin and Elvis did and still do)

-- every wet noodle is first cousin to all other wet noodles

-- wet noodles give boa hugs

-- dry noodles sometimes hesitate before accepting boa hugs from wet noodles (but never regret it afterwards)

-- unintentionally stepping barefoot on a wet noodle means good luck

-- unintentionally stepping barefoot on several wet noodles means a gooey foot (but in a between-the-toes goody sort of gooeyness)

-- wet noodles are allies of wet beeps, drippy faucets and poets with writer's bloc

-- wet noodles -- so cool when hot!

-- and hot because we're always so cooooool!

and we wet noodles (us) of every where/when/how/dampness thank you for reading (and appreciating) eleven things everyone needs to know. . .

about wet noodles!

-- *ayaz daryl nielsen*
(February The Mind[less] Muse)

replacing floorboards
the grey expired strides
of ancestors

> -- *ayaz daryl nielsen*
> *(February High Coupe)*

Body Language

When you came in through the
door,
language followed you.

The way you held your
head,
was in itself more eloquent
than speech, high ,
regal like a queen decked out in

pink petals which decorated
the ruffled neck of your gown
flowing, its own smooth river.

No words tumbled out
of your mouth, or crashing
waterfall, yet your eyes held

a vocabulary more vast
than Shakespeare. You sat
in the window seat to watch
the morning sun
speak
to the gold-coloured curtains in
soothing phrases.

Your presence was meant to calm.
Every time you raised a slender finger
to smooth your hair
each strand
was a personal idiom that admonished
me.

About mother's death? Wipe
away your wretched frown.

In your presence, I flourished in the
flesh
but memory floated higher

and higher
each time you stepped through
the door, language, an epiphany
like a dog at your heels
chewed dead consonants.

> *-- Agholor Leonard Obiaderi*
> *(July Pyrokinection)*

in a few days
spring painted herself
ecstatic

> -- *Mary Orovan*
> *(March High Coupe)*

Reverse Haiku

he was the rainbow
of my life
and the blueberries

                -- Mary Orovan
               (March High Coupe)

Ballerina of the Sky

A Blood Moon
Lunar Eclipse
smiles in the skyline of a predawn morning
with rampant fervor building to a crescendo
of age changing ramifications.
The signs of the times spark with vibrations of
electromagnetic transfiguration
as metamorphosis of the spheres spins in full effect.

Tides shifting . . . pivoting . . . pulsating
with a sideways advance,
crisscrossing in a dizzying twirl
from a high spot in the heavens
downward into my wide open heart;
beating in harmonized accord
with the nexus core
across eternity
and the infinite abyss
one inch at a time
closer to you . . .
closer to me . . .
closer to eternal answers . . .
closer to the truth
of reality's ultimate grasp of reason.

The existential energy source
of perfect Veritas
sparks across the Elysium heights
where I seek solace
in the blue/black canopied sky
which is lit up with pillowed comfort
as the symphonic stars sing out
in an awesome conductive opera
of God's sweet lullaby,
mimicking the initial word
of creation as it was first manifested into form.

A miraculous spontaneous generation
of divinely orchestrated inspiration,
intuitively embedded in the blueprint
of our collective DNA signature,
is woven like a synchronistic web and
sent Earthward to fill our souls with wonder as the
satellite signals play out in a rotating orbital dance.

The ballerina of enlivened rock dust
rolls across the gravitational ether
in astrological intoxication,
smiling out across the vacuumed void
with a Cheshire grin of deeper knowingness.
As within, also without;
as above, so below.
Awed in mesmerized transient grace,
we watch patiently throughout the cycles
as these ageless planetary seeds
take root in dark matter,
mature, sprout wings and grow.

-- Scott Thomas Outlar
(November Jellyfish Whispers)

You are pulled and the same darkness
lifts your arm around these stars
spreads out door to door

knocks so your fist can smell
from blood become your heart again
dragged ahead as if you belong

near distances, end to end
                though this cemetery
has forgotten its dead

holds only the invisible hillsides
                soaking in stone and narrow alleyways
passed along till they close

and what will be your tears
waits as lips, as the sky brought back
crumbling with not a light left on.

                    -- Simon Perchik
                    (December Pyrokinection)

Am I Awake

During winter the shadows
awaken me. I gasp, seek
the faithful glass holding fluid.
Outside some birds fly away
as if once they leave we'll have
a birdless world, inherit
numerous nests, cold, brittle.
Then I seek you and find you.
Why do I feel disheartened?
Do I want to stay alone
and crave for warmth, toil over
finding what I want and know,
I have right here? I swing the shawl
around my shoulders and stand
not doing a thing, not
gathering my body and hauling
it back to sleep.

-- Kushal Poddar
(October Pyrokinection)

Autumn

The crows are murder
this autumn, the finches
nowhere to be seen.
Just when we gave up
on the wind fallen
in the well of rot,
it rescues itself
and knocks on the door.
We brace silence
even harder.
The shadows of the crows
devour the crows.

-- Kukshal Poddar
(October Jellyfish Whispers)

Anaphase

the quantum physics of
attraction solely dependent
upon a singular view

inanimate
still life two enigmatic
now lickety-split

his &
her (lipstick smeared)
cigarettes flattened on the pavement

two impossible
(smashed & torn)
to read the remnants

cleaved two heartbeats
torn asunder
two break apart

or two holding on
across some distance
as cleaving athwart
the distance grown fonder

> -- *henry 7. reneau, jr.*
> *(November Napalm and Novocain)*

A Bowling Ball in My Stomach

A dragon laid an egg inside my corpse;
not a body, nobody sees that I exist,
yet my scales shine in the beams
but an egg lies here inside me.

The hatching is coming,
I can sense strange vibrations,
the ovum was once fertilized,
invaded by white sperm
from an ancient Python,
or some reptilian snake.

-- Walter Ruhlmann
(July Pyrokinection)

After Rendition

He wakes naked on the wet metal chair,
breathing inside the pillowcase hood,
wrists tied with her nonsense-colored scarves.

She wants him to say it.
She wants what she wants.
She wants it all.

He says nothing.

So she jerks off the hood, and he blinks in the light.
Her furrowed forehead concerned at his silence.
She'd rather not hurt him, but she will if she must.

She wants to hear it.
She wants what she wants.
She wants it right now.

Still nothing.

So she throws the switch on that voltaic smile
somehow hooked up to his limbic insides.
From scrotum to scalp his subdural wiring
twitches and hums. Vision tunnels. Belly cramps.

Then, in a sudden incontinent whoosh,
the gut-heated words spill out over his chest,
and puddle embarrassed on the floor. Maybe now
she'll turn off that terrible grin. Now that

She has what she wants.
She has it all.
She has it forever.

-- Fain Rutherford
(December Pyrokinection)

Winter Ops

It's so cold outside, flies
lie along the doorjamb
where a little heat leaks.
They're lined up like fighter jets
de-icing on a vertical runway.
Stealth black fuselages conserve fuel,
vibrating just enough not to freeze.
Bug-eyed cockpit canopies defrost.
When the door opens,
the squadron suddenly scrambles
into the studio's steamy warmth,
flying missions against assigned targets-
coffee grounds, egg shells and toilet lids,
evading all countermeasures until,
one by one, acting on higher insect orders,
they crash into the window glass and die.

-- Fain Rutherford
(May Jellyfish Whispers)

Encounter

A stranger with no shadow
Came to me last night

He offered me a key
That would unlock any door

I asked why he was here
He said "You called for me in your sleep,"

And then I remembered
The dream of a realm of cages

With prisoners who all wore
The exact same mask

And sang the same song
The one with one note

But when he asked me "Well?"
I sent him away

For I recalled the secret
The wise man builds his own cell

-- Richard Schnap
(February Pyrokinection)

World Without Bees Amen

On the sills the bees are dying. Bumbles
fuzzing in their humming. Their furred knitwear
losing lustre; their breathing visible,
their wings crisply stopped. The dustpan will share
them to the hedged garden. I fling them out
against the wind, and they fly one last time,
but just the flight of falling. Who will shout
to stop the dying?
      There just isn't time,
so watch them die in their furry troubles,
fuzzed in their humming, the dying bumbles.

-- John W. Sexton
(October Jellyfish Whispers)

Migrants

Please state your full name?

 seals
 dark blisters

What is your country of origin?

 on the surface
 of the ocean

How long have you been domiciled at your current address?

 fishermen claim
 that they hear them
 barking
 beneath the waves

Have you been actively seeking employment?

 that they lounge
 on the shoreline rocks
 for hours under the sun
 until daylight burns them
 into new shapes

Are you currently in receipt of welfare benefits?

 and then rising
 as plump men or women
 in leather coats
 will wade ashore

 live for months
 the mundane lives
 of villagers

State the number and names of any dependents:

    then take
    to the waters again
    having sired or conceived
    half-human pups
    in their sojourning
    amongst us

Failure to answer these questions truthfully may result in prosecution.

    moonlight leaves its signature equally on all

              -- John W. Sexton
              (November The Mind[less] Muse)

Mouth to the Sky

The speckled thrush stepped onto the sunlight conveyer-belt to the hedge-depth and was gone into shadow. Somewhere in there the thrush became a cat, or was eaten by a cat, or killed the cat and wore it as a coat; but out the far perimeter of the hedge emerged the cat. The cat approached the opened door of the car, the car shining black like a soul, a soul of darkness so pure that the sun turned it white as a flash. Out the other side of the car stepped a woman in black coat, a coat so black it absorbed the sun. She opened her mouth to the sky and out came the song of the speckled thrush.

-- John W. Sexton
(November Pound of Flash)

Raven

A raven drinking
Out of a small puddle
Formed rudely,
On a tar road in the
Suburban Mumbai,
On a rainy afternoon,
Blending well with the
Darkness around;
Its bobbing neck,
Giving a queer kinesis
To the little fractured pool
And the otherwise static scene.

-- Sunil Sharma
(November Jellyfish Whispers)

Of a Run Aground Ship and Winged Crows

marked depth of saltwater by a
yardstick in inches,
storm clouds receding like
playground children
into secret places, oak timber
painted white
painted red
ran aground in a mist,
in a rainy fog, crew abandoned...
fallen sails and
mitered joints left
to rot in mud, on a forgotten
shore, winged crows
to nest in a timbered mast,
reeds grab and choke
the oxygen
out of splintered wood,
last breath taken, gasping,
choking...
a trickle of saltwater,
then a torrent, canvas hoisted
by an updraft,
sets sail, no longer moored,
crows cast adrift
in flight, wings like
oars in clouds.

-- Lance Sheridan
(January Jellyfish Whispers)

Thinking of Limes in the North

The man's changed again, fuse
lit by a scent come into a leaf
so succulent he must've wanted
to eat it whole, and go from there
into the center of the bush, pulling
under ripe fruit with his teeth.

Hearing the sound a lime makes
when it comes off its sprocket
above a canyon marked by interstates
crossing and re-crossing what was once
the floor of a great ocean.

Ever since she saw the number of green citrus
held like tennis balls, bound to thick stems
in a yard so foreign it might as well
have been the moon, she can't abide
her marriage.

She would prefer to bake in the oven
of sun, to step on a rattlesnake,
a scorpion-treading the path toward
the hills that surround their arena.

There, a million sadnesses plague
the landscape, and firs blossom upward
in flames for nothing more than
a chaste wind, an errant match head.

> *-- Judith Skillman*
> *(October The Mind[less] Muse)*

Parallel as Fixation

a multiplying motive spans itself:
cannot its version, this/now
interpretation—the language's
fulcrum invites, incites what
excels within a watching version of
motivated simplicity, exceeding
virtue as rest, or visitation as
corporeal manifestation, rejoice
then when time's verbal praise
relaxes muscular tendencies, and
the purity of comprised permissions
persuades within the action of
particular interactions

-- Felino A. Soriano
(January The Mind[less] Muse)

Passing

Twilight fell like silent rain,
memories felt hallucinogenic and beautiful,
popping into existence like lightning
thrown through a lifeless sky,

visions of familiar children laughing
and tire swinging in an open yard,
the Potomac's peaceful power, a one-eyed
Tiger still hunting for love,
broken bones and friendship,

but we have become a screaming corpse
waltzing and pirouetting our way through
forgotten fractions that once comprised
a legitimately perfect equation.

We have come to rest in this residual realm
of remembrance, a place that no longer produces
any form of pleasure or protection,
much like a weeping willow earning its moniker
through a storm, a place
that like these barren days is passing
and that's alright because let's face it,

this world,

our world,

was never paradise.

-- Brandon C. Spalletta
(January Pyrokinection)

See-Saw Dialogue

She sat on this swaying plank
with quicksilver moods,
its temperament reminiscent
of a confused pendulum,
munching on peanut moments
as it weighs life's pros and cons,
with a weird boy
his hair spiked as a porcupine,
barely familiar from
earlier trysts in this park.

He wore a wide grin
as the ones seen on potato smileys,
emerging from frying pan promises~
so too intrigued to bother
about familiarity she asked him
the reason for his delight,
wondering what was so special.

With a saucy wink he recounted
a visit to an amusement park,
regaling her with descriptions
of the most amazing rides in the world,
as she felt her gaiety seep out
from her pleasant evening
making it dull and insipid
as she yearned to savor
the delight alluded by him.

She sat forlorn, wishing she could
visit this amazing place of fun n' frolic,
aware it would be deemed
a wasted, frivolous expense
by her strict and pragmatic parents,

when a girl in freckles and pigtails
peered at her to inquire
if her brother had been bragging again.

The boy had a penchant
for telling tales—the taller the better,
about things he'd heard
at his father's barber shop,
pretending to be richer and luckier
than he was just to feel grand,
making her realize
her foolish gullibility at
ignoring the joy of graffiti skies
and leisure moments with friends,
behaving as the frenzied moth
unaware of golden glow of the lamp
as it pines for an indifferent moon . . .

-- Smita Sriwastav
(September Pyrokinection)

Mist

Between lamb's wool and lion's claw
A grey mist attaches
To the air in every meadow
Winter lies in frozen ditches
Its life almost drained
But spring trapped in a bramble bush
Continues to be restrained

Fingers outstretched each ragged tree
Beckons as we tear past
Urging us south desperately
Neither first journey nor the last
But just another
Each farm fence post appearing
Like a fox breaking cover

Between cockcrow and owl screeching
A feeble sun breaks through
London's busy highways reaching
That once darker denser fog knew
Weary heads turning
We head north from railway stations
To our own lands returning.

-- *David Subacchi*
(October Jellyfish Whispers)

Horse Frightened by a Lion

-- from a painting of the same name by George Stubbs

Every sinew strained
Every muscle stretched
Every hair on end
Hooves scraping the rock
Striving to reverse

The silent lion
Calmly confident
Taking in the scene
Knows you run faster
But that you may fall

Your white coat stands out
His color blends in
With the brown landscape
He is a hunter
You are a victim

Dull trees and pale sky
Complete the background
All eyes are on you
Willing you to escape
From this encounter

-- David Subacchi
(October Jellyfish Whispers)

Greening

Spring is still sliding on the strings of a guitar
waiting on side-roads
to flash
to splash
the world in
every kind of
green.
Envious ivy—chains
Cities of glass moss
Yawning grass after a lengthy nap
The lawn mower is resting in the shed
Jaded rings of melting puddles
Jade drinks of rain-wet maples
Willow, oak, poplar: sleeping giants
but their frosty lips are already
greening with spring

-- Fanni Sütő
(September Jellyfish Whispers)

When the Writer Decided to Share Relationship Advice

when all of it shits the bed
the tumble is long,
hard.

you'll find yourself
spewing page after page

of blunt force trauma
bandaging wounds

with whiskey, and women
you'll forget by morning.

you'll never quite get it
all back

the bones
will never heal

and the smell
will never leave.

> -- *Ag Synclair*
> *(December Napalm and Novocain)*

gray ghosts of winter
a bluster of blinding snow
flakes of poetry

>   -- *Ag Synclair*
>   *(December High Coupe)*

Looking Out to Spectacle Island in April

The beach this time of year
is nothing but rocks.
She ignores the man
who is placing one
on top of the other,
trying to balance them.

She ignores his dog.

She is waiting for the summer
of bare-chested boys in shallow water,
baseball on the radio,
and the reggae ice cream truck
with its flavors
of soursop, mango, and rum raisin.

She is waiting.

-- Marianne Szlyk
(May Jellyfish Whispers)

It's For You

is going through the aging pop star's head as he pedals downhill and then across the village green, doing his five miles of cardio in case the guys reunite one last time. He imagines another life, one where he played guitar like Pat Metheny. He'd be touring with friends who loved music, not the limelight, who were musicians, not actors too typecast for another show.

But jazz wasn't for long-haired kids in jeans when he started out in the Village. Jazz was standards, something played with horns and pianos, sung by a lady in a satin sheath dress, something performed in night clubs for men who could not cry or laugh or love.

He still can't get over Mark's fingers stumbling, slowing down the beginning of their most famous song. He nearly grabbed the guitar from him then and there. From that night on, he played lead.

Taking off his helmet and locking his bike up in front of the library, he pictures himself like Metheny on stage, not looking up, bent over his guitar, playing what comes, playing with his band, building the song together with his friends, while the audience is with them, listening.

                -- Marianne Szlyk
                (January Pound of Flash)

The Song of the Mean Eyed Cat and the One Eyed Fox

Cat was a gypsy of his street,
a loose tooth vagabond
with nimble ballerina feet.

The neighbors wouldn't know this
due to his sagging old linen belly
woven threadbare from the loom,
tattered but strong and ready.

Cat was the one on the fence
eyeing you with suspicion—
a ready claw, a ready purr
hinging on his disposition.

Fox was an older soldier
medals clung to his chest
along with dirt, leaves and all the rest.

He may have had a folding limp
when the air was hung with damp
but when the sun shone fiercely
he was an acrobat.

Fox was the eyes you felt
on your back from within the trees,
he was the uneasy chill
that made you pick up speed.

Cat, the one claw killer
(perfected over time)
of the starling napping
on the washing line.

A giver of gifts left behind
on doorsteps cold at 5 am,

the prize winning fish—
a dissected corpse with a dangling eye.

Fox, the seventh cub of a seventh cub
intimate between the mists,
hands shook with comeuppance,
just another ration over chewed.

Dashing in red beret,
captain of those midnight raids
on dustbins laden with enemy supplies
destined for the home stomach.

Both roamed the bi-ways of the town
and had a paw in all things devious,
for the work of the Devil lies
not just in idle hands
but in all clean clawed creatures.

-- Grant Tarbard
(December The Mind[less] Muse)

Honey

The first time you kissed me
I should have seen it coming
You were animal-starved
pawing hungry at my hips

You were hurricane-tongued
bracing me against your mouth
I pulled up fierce to match you
claw for claw around your neck

I could not hear us breathing
deafened by your torrent eyes
I did not recognize the beast
devouring my skin like victory

I wasn't your prey or your prize
bound to be death-squandered
I had waited beyond time for you
to lay yourself down at my feet

I had hoped for honey sweet
and slow to drench my lips
with tenderness. But I—
I should have known

-- Sarah Thursday
(June Pyrokinection)

She Has A Body Like My Spirit

She has a body like my spirit
and a heart Welsh mountain sized.
Calm with a smiling tenderness
to quell the ferocity of my storm.
A tender nature ripe with giving.
A contented, caring gentle soul
Our emotions fit like puzzle pieces
the North and South sides of a whole.

-- Paul Tristram
(March Pyrokinection)

Doubtful

I watched a grey squirrel
in the park
scamper and jump around
like a lunatic
trying to shake off
yesterday's shadow.
The poor thing
really seemed
to be in a bad mood.
"How curious!" I mumbled
quietly to myself
as I left by the side gate,
into the back lanes
to avoid you.

-- Paul Tristram
(February Napalm and Novocain)

She was Insensitive to My Sensitivity

. . . so I refrained from looking
as she chose to not wave goodbye.

-- Paul Tristram
(May Napalm and Novocain)

A Naïve Trap for Love-Sick Souls

She unclasped the ornate
silver Celtic chain
from around her neck
and held up the little
coffin shaped locket
to my ear and I listened
at the little hinge upon the side
just like to the sea inside a shell
as she had instructed.

"It's faint but I can hear them.
It's like being in a back bedroom
of a terraced house late at night
when it's perfectly quiet outside
then hearing someone groaning
loudly in every consecutive house
all down the side of your road.
How fascinating and remarkable,
will you show me how it's done?"

"In its native tongue it is called
'a naïve trap for love-sick souls'
Yes, I will show you soon enough
just be patient while I finish tiring
of our present moments together!"

-- Paul Tristram
(September Napalm and Novocain)

Our last thanksgiving
Turkey stuffed with words of death
We smile and laugh

> -- *Matthew Valdespino*
> *(November High Coupe)*

Expansion

mother's crinoline
scrapes while she paces these paths
too blistered to fly

prairies built on less
breathe as though sleek hummingbirds
when she wanders past

and the silhouette
I remember twice she called
beyond mere windows

with snow slick as skin
hedgerows our blank crucible
hush the violets

all along the trees
whisper their benediction
they call her starlight

-- Michelle Villanueva
(December High Coupe)

This is how it starts:
A misplaced promise.
Old light tearing heaven.
Where the pieces land,
You're born.

Each wide, a mountain
Because of the others.
All motherless,
One way or another.
All mothers.

Marking time in the sky,
Bearing histories through
distances.
Witnessing
The drag. The skip. The mystery.

Go on, seven sisters.
Burn, muting Orion.
You ancient test of vision,
Love's beautiful ambush,
Where darkness dies to light.

-- Anne Richmond Wakefield
(March Jellyfish Whispers)

The Wolf's Trail

"Come home. Come home to the Cookson Hills,"
Mother's old Cherokee friend wrote. "I will show you where
Sumacs redden and pokeberries ripen purple-black within
Shadows of the great oaks."

There was never time for things we wanted to do. Instead, we
Sat in mixed company on straight-backed wooden chairs
Talking about mundane matters, catching up on years of
Living between visits.

"What's the name of that man you married?" Golda asked,
Acting like my mother who had already gone ahead to sit
Beside the Wolf's Trail, waiting for her old friend, Golda.

Golda never waited for my answer. She wanted to walk the long,
Dusty road to the mailbox. While the persimmon-red
Oklahoma sun bled into dust, scorching my feet, Golda kept at me.

Words, like arrows, pierced my conscience.
"Next time you come home . . . take me to town.
I want you to buy me new clothes." Promises were made going down
Dusty road and back; solemn promises never meant to be broken;
Promises impossible to keep.

Ninety-two, as supple as the slender branches of the
Wahoo tree growing in her front yard.
"They were everywhere when I was young," she said.
"Now it's the only one around here."

She squatted before her old bookcase,
Searching for The Advocate so I could catch up on all the
Happenings in The Nation since I'd been away. Finding one
She jumped to her feet, a young girl again.

I wanted Golda to be 'Spirit' in a diaphanous gown of mist to
Rise above the Cookson Hills, soar high to Sky and disappear like
Eagle, but ninety-two winters made her host to the great worm and
She went to sit with the Ancient Ones beside The Wolf's Trail.

Through the boughs of Ponderosas surrounding me
Comes my mother's voice, joining that of her old Cherokee friend, Golda.
They call with the wind.
"When are you coming home?" they ask.
"Come soon. We'll show you where to find good
Huckleberries on the slopes and where sumac reddens and
Purple-black pokeberries grow within shadows of the great oaks."

-- Nadine Waltman-Harmon
(January Pyrokinection)

icy waves spew wrath
upon a deserted shore
drowning self pity

> *-- Nells Wasilewski*
> *(September High Coupe)*

Wedding Vision

Blue jay and robins
march us down
the evergreen tree aisle way
in sister-woman-sister love.
We hold hands on the edge of a mountain
with our valley future in panoramic views.
Should we jump?
Leap away from marriage,
pretend
we don't pledge
soul mates till death,
welded by wedding bands
for all to see or not to see,
love in the eye of the beholder?

-- Diane Webster
(March Pyrokinection)

Soul Mates

On this crisp morning we walk
like children pretending to exhale
great plumes of cigarette smoke
or dragons blowing flames
to envelop the tiny knight
struggling to inject us with
the poisoned sword.
But this cold, oppressive day
your soul breathes momentarily
reaching for the clouds above . . .
when failing I feel
the whisper of your breath
like lilac in May.
We stop.
Breath, soul, fragrance
mingle, vaporize
in ever shortening gasps
until only a breath separates
our lips.
I inhale your exhale
you inhale my exhale
we breathe in visible
unison.

-- Diane Webster
(March Pyrokinection)

Puddle Passage

The puddle assimilates the girl's feet
into amputated reflection rippling
like shivers across the surface
as she crosses with shoes and socks
balanced in outstretched hands
wanting her passage unnoticed
like a mosquito surfing wind
until shore as each foot emerges
in minimal disturbance,
a seashell glistening for discovery.

-- Diane Webster
(February Jellyfish Whispers)

Deflation

I used to love the tides,
The taste of chilled salt air,
And the granite boulders scattered along the shoreline
Like dice in a glacial game of craps.
But there came a morning when
I looked for the ocean and I saw nothing but
Miles of seaweed shining in the sun,
Deflated.
I picked my way down the slope past the low tide mark
Where I swam the week before,
Now stepping carefully rock to rock.
A mackerel flapped at my feet,
The smacking sound too loud.
I stood with the fish
Until it was still.

"You disgust me,"
He said on the last night we spent together.
I sat on the floor and did not cry.
Later, the apology swooped in like a vaudeville hook,
But true things linger.

Tectonic plates drag apart
So slowly.
Solid rock splits unnoticed until
Continents are separated by an ocean
So vast the far coast is
Invisible.

The sun was hot and
The fish was dead.
Pebbles and silt underfoot
Warm and sharp,
Black grit between my toes.
I could hear the armored legs of a crab

Tottering towards the trench ahead.
It disappeared over the edge
And I followed.
Climbing down the Cliffside,
Hand over hand,
The wall slick,
Damp algae underneath my fingernails.
The abyss was drained of sea-water and
The fall, when it came, was infinite.

-- Catherine Weiss
(July Napalm and Novocain)

Monica Wanted to Be 2-D

She was okay as a centerfold.
Then she put on blue eye shadow and heels,
became a Cosmo cover.

I wanted to wrap her around books
art, philosophy, anything to add depth
but she became a crayon drawing
of a house and baby
yellow sun
lollipop trees.

I folded her into a paper airplane
and launched her into the sky.
She fluttered back as a credit card bill.

I took up origami
practiced cranes, butterflies, and elephants.
She countered with liquor ads and romance novels.

I thought a Mobius strip would satisfy both of us
but her feminist language critique cut my tongue
when I licked its adhesive edges.

Finally, she became a page from The Rules,
slipped under my door,
and skipped
away
pursued by the wind.

> *-- Jon Wesick*
> *(January Napalm and Novocain)*

I Have Seen These Stones Rise

an illusion of waves on the cliff
where gloves lie waiting for frost

fall of sunlight as winter spins
bleak tides under oak and elm

gulls soar over ragged stones
watching spiders linger in moss

night rubs grains of roiling sand
through cave of polished pale bones

steps broken in waltz-time to place
on kelp falling under an ebb-tide

these rocks have been stifled by fog
thrown against ears ringed by guitars

short messages traced by slim feet
balanced green under the solstice

broken keel slides into short grass
seaweed tangles between prayer and altar

pockets of faith in mapped oceans
dispersed in a salt-sprayed cemetery

-- Joanna M. Weston
(March Jellyfish Whispers)

Held in Forever

the year turns in my hands
from snowdrop to bluebell
through daffodil and rose
spinning pansies into chrysanthemums
and copper and gold maple leaves

I want to hold the year
so that each petal remains
distinct as the moment
of the wind's caress
each stamen waiting for a bee
in that second when sunlight cuts
shadow and a finger touches my skin
with the color of the season
imprisoned in a cup of petals

-- Joanna M. Weston
(November Jellyfish Whispers)

Never Again Hand in Hand

from the fir a whisper
the click of the answering machine

the mutations of a glacier
his girl wore running shoes

tangled spears of grass hay fields
wind takes the veil from her head

feathers strewn across the carpet
these letters written years ago

we are better strangers than friends
initials carved on a fence post

a crow drops twigs on the roof
phone call from another continent

-- Joanna M. Weston
(February Napalm and Novocain)

On Bad Days

we stretch
barbed wire
through the house
entangle ourselves
in recoil

bleed into
one another
staunch jagged
wounds before
cut   clash
again knives

-- Joanna M. Weston
(March Napalm and Novocain)

thin window shade—
my neighbor's Christmas lights
flash in my dreams

-- Kelley White
(November High Coupe)

God Visits Michelangelo at the Sistine Chapel

Michelangelo was painting on his back
God giving the spark of life
and intelligence to Eve.

God appeared next to him, lying on her back,
"they will never believe you, you know."

"I know," he admitted, applying apple cheeks
to Eve. "But I can see the truth
and I paint what I see."

"They will persecute you," God warned,
"you better paint me with a beard
and make Eve into Adam.
It is what they expect."

"You could show yourself,"
Michelangelo suggested, "show them
they are wrong."

"They would not believe me, not even
if I brought some plagues or turned salt
into wine. They would want some proof.
After seeing proof, they still would not believe.
And even if they did,
they would want to look up my skirt,
make sure I am a woman."

After making the changes, he said,
"I guess you have to give them what they expect."

-- Martin Willitts, Jr.
(December Pyrokinection)

Inanimate

I end up
watching
anime at
four in the
morning. *Cow-*

boy Bebop.
There is a
jazz sound-
track but for
some reason

Sinatra is
singing 'when
I was seven-
teen' inside
my head. It

is raining.
It is always
raining in
anime. Out-
side & in.

                               -- Mark Young
                            (October The Mind[less] Muse)

Chronometry

I kissed your morning
With mine, and held
Your night closely with mine too

Between your spring and autumn
I lay my summer
Deep in winter

From your January through February
To your March, I wrap your April and May
With my June and July

Within your August
I use my September or October
To caress both your November and December

And right from your moment
I suck my whole year

-- Changming Yuan
(July Pyrokinection)

Chinese Gentility: Four Confucian Haiku

Orchid: Deep in the valley
Alone on an obscure spot
You bloom nonetheless

Lotus: From foul decayed silt
You shoot clean against the sun
Never pollutable

Mum: Hanging on and on
Even when wishes wither
You keep flowering

Plum: Your brave bold blood dropped
As though to melt all world's snow
Before spring gathers

-- Changming Yuan
(August High Coupe)

A Hemingway Day

While on a short vacation in Havana I ran into Ernest Hemingway at the bar Floridita and he invited me to sit down with him. Of course, he did most of the talking, telling me about a recent hunting trip in Africa and marlin fishing with some movie star friends. At some point, while there was a pause, I decided to tell him about a recent event that happened to me back in New York City. I decided to tell him the story even though I doubted that a man like Hemingway, who'd been everywhere and done everything, would be much interested in what I had to say. Mainly I wanted to find out what he would have done in the same situation.

"So I was walking down the street on one of those hot, muggy days in Manhattan when I noticed a child in a stroller eating an ice cream. Stopping to watch him lick at the ball of ice cream, it was only a short time before it fell out of the cone, bounced off his knee and onto the sidewalk. Immediately the kid started crying and screaming, while his mother tried to comfort him. Seeing that we were right in front of the ice cream parlor, I walked up to the mother and asked her to wait there a moment. I then went inside and ordered a fresh strawberry ice cream on a cone. Of course, I failed to notice what flavor the kid was originally eating, but just decided on strawberry because it was the first flavor that I saw. I walked out and tried to hand it to the kid, but he just looked at it for a moment, and then started crying and screaming even louder than before. Obviously embarrassed, the mother thanked me anyway, and started pushing the stroller down the street while I stood there holding a melting strawberry ice cream. Not really caring for that flavor, I walked over to the nearest trash can and dropped it inside."

At this point, I looked closely at Hemingway and realized he was staring to the side of me at a group of people sitting at a table. Sitting with the group was a beautiful woman who seemed to have captivated Hemingway's attention. "What would you have done?" I asked him, and still looking to the side of me, he responded, "It's not what I would have done. It's what I'm going to do!" And he got up from his seat and went over to the table where the beautiful woman was sitting. He introduced himself, and because everyone knew who he was, they immediately invited him to join them.

Now sitting there alone I wondered if my story would have impressed anyone other than an average person like myself, who never had a 'Hemingway Day' in his entire life, and probably never would . . .

-- Jeffrey Zable
(October Pound of Flash)

From The Editors

Life is Like a Bag of Cheetos

Full of hard pieces, devoured
without thought of consequences. Potential
choking hazards that dissolve,
a mouthful of memories that stain
everything they touch.

-- A.J. Huffman
(June Pyrokinection)

Toes in the Wind

Baby girl waits for greyhounds to emerge,
feet swinging over railing as she holds on
to supportive hands holding her. She giggles
excitedly as the eight graceful gallopers are paraded
before the crowd, waves her arms in support
of her fast and furious friends. She knows
nothing of protests or controversy of animals
raised to race as sport. Her eight-month-old eyes
only see freedom found by four paws pacing four more,
running, streamline away from the sun.

-- A.J. Huffman
(October Pyrokinection)

Twinkle Twinkle

Little starfish
flicker beneath layers of darkening
water. Clouds of sand shift over
their shapes, a reflection
of night's sky. I touch this almost
reality, my fingers shock
its expanse. For a moment
it prickles, before settling
back into its eerie looking-glass
impersonation of what lies
beyond.

-- A.J. Huffman
(February Jellyfish Whispers)

Dawn Breaks

through remnants of midnight's rain,
illuminates the residual gray
clinging to nature's morning. Eyes
search for disruptive streak of lingering
silver, refusing to relinquish
the slick elegance of moonlight's glow.
Failure: the abysmal haze holds,
complete. I shrivel
deeper into my own
skin, an automatic escape
attempt, focus on following
a now less discernible path home.

-- A.J. Huffman
(October Jellyfish Whispers)

Your Penis Made You Do It

You could not control it. You tried, but
it would not listen to reason, drained
all the blood from your head. You blacked out,
woke with that blonde in your bed, had no idea
where she came from. You think I should
understand, forgive you for its mistake.
I don't. I am not impressed
by you or it. An erection is not monumental
in my eyes. I do not mythologize it
the way you do, the way you want me to.
I have no desire to build a temple around it,
flat out refuse to sacrifice my self
respect in its honor. You continue
your misogynistic diatribe, hoping
to charm me into swallowing something,
maybe even my pride. I eventually submit,
fall into resignation, finally accept all you have
to off is the truth: you are truly sorry
(though I prefer the term pathetic). I slam
the door and my mind shut as I leave. Thoughts
of you echo momentarily before fading
into the forgettable pile of my other past
mistakes.

-- A.J. Huffman
(January Napalm and Novocain)

Desire

is a drop of blood permeating the ocean.
An infusion of color consuming initial point
of contact, slowly spreading in wash
of tendrils. Temporary is the label
of their touch. They tickle, tease with soft
hues that distort vision, but quickly grow
weak, dissolve until there is nothing
but the original body, flowing, tainted
by memory.

-- A.J. Huffman
(May Napalm and Novocain)

With Iron

icicles carved from moonbeams, I battle
mind-monsters crawling from moments
of half-sleep. My adrenaline-junkie REM
ranger rides past me. His dune buggy
laden with long lost sleep dust. The bitter
little bastard bits his thumb at me. I string
a streak of bloody wishes, watch them erupt
just under the skyline. Spin out, double
flip. Bogey! My score is definite
ly improving.

-- A.J. Huffman
(January The Mind[less] Muse)

I Wish I Had a Donut

to sing me to sleep tonight. I have been
a good girl, making friends with celery
and carrots, really annoying vegetable sticks.
Sadly, I find them standard issue. They bore me
with their mocking selflessness. I would prefer the indulgent
sound of jelly dripping through over-sugared dough to tuck
me in, to lay itself beneath my head, a perfect pillow
to foster sweet dreams filled with visions of a dietless life,
a world where a crunchless bite doesn't echo with regret.

>   *-- A.J. Huffman*
>   *(October The Mind[less] Muse)*

Fallen leaves dissolve
beneath winter's smothering
kiss. Seasons' cycle.

Skeletal trees stretch
through morning's fog, desperate
for hint of sun's warmth.

Grey eye of winter
blinks, snowflakes fall at random,
bless the earth like tears.

-- A.J. Huffman
(January High Coupe)

Game of the Gods

Admiral Richards idly strolled the upper deck of the U.S.S. Guitarro. The ship had been stationed off the Japanese coast for three months now. He was beginning to miss his wife and daughter back in the states. *Maybe it's time to request a transfer state side,* he thought as he ran his white-gloved hand instinctively under the railing. Satisfied that the fingertips remained clean, he prepared to return to his quarters. He was intercepted by Lieutenant Commander Collins.

"Sir, the radar is picking up Japanese naval movement just beyond those cliffs," Collins indicated the steep cliffs about 4500 yards out.

"Have the men established radio contact?"

"Yes and no, sir. They have managed to isolate the ship's transmitting frequency, but they aren't getting any response."

"I see," Richards stared off towards the ridge. These situations were always difficult. If one is not careful an international incident could start because a destroyer's transmission officer had too much wine at dinner and fell asleep on the job. "Tell the men to continue trying to establish contact. I will put in a call to the base in Yokohama to see if they have any military movements in the area we need to be aware of."

The lieutenant had barely finished his departure salute when the first explosion sounded. The torpedo exploded about 1000 yards out, sending a pillar of water into the air that rained down on the admiral's head. "Sound the alarms," he demanded, wiping the water from his eyes. "Get the ship into attack position. I want all men on deck -- NOW!"

In minutes, alarms all over the ship were buzzing. Red warning lights flashed as another torpedo exploded -- only 500 yards out this time. They were getting closer. The admiral had visual on the ship now.

The Japanese destroy had moved from behind the cover of the cliffs, and was alight in full battle glory: flags raise; guns smoking.

"Red alert! Red alert!" the blow horn resonated across the deck. "All men on deck! Report to your stations immediately! Red alert!"

The admiral could feel the ship rock as the men clambered up onto the deck to man their battle stations. Collins had just returned when the third torpedo exploded. The ship rocked violently as the torpedo finally found its mark. "Damage report! I want a damage report immediately," the admiral screamed over the din. But Collins was already scrambling back up the bridge.

Collins returned within moments to report that the damage was minimal. A small breach in the hull on the starboard side. The damage was above the water line and was already under control.

"Are the men in position?"

"Yes, sire."

"Fire when ready."

The lieutenant disappeared back into the bridge. And the blow horn sounded the order: "Fire."

The ship bolted from the thrust of pressure as the torpedo was ejected. The admiral tracked its deadly path with his binoculars. It swept silently through the water. He saw the fire before he heard the explosion. "Direct hit," he whispered to himself and smiled. That transfer would be guaranteed now.

The lieutenant returned as a roar rose up from the men. "Direct hit, sir. She's sinking." And as they watched, the flaming inferno that was once a vessel of death slowly disappeared beneath the waves.

* * * * *

The moon had just sunk below the cloud line when their game ended. A frown creased Buddha's brow as he slammed his fist down hard on the table. "You sank my battleship!"

God just smiled. "What shall we play next?"

-- A.J. Huffman
(January Pound of Flash)

Referential Mania

Everything is hideously symbolic

-- Dorianne Laux, "Abschied Symphony"

The ashtray hanging above the no-smoking sign, its one eye hole
daring and inviting someone at the County Assistance Office
of Mental Health (And Retardation, both) to extinguish
a butt before entering by way of code punched
into an archaic phone pad, speaks to me. It says I should
quit smoking before I die of cancer.
It says time is running out. Life contains a code
I have yet to crack.
The book of poetry that showed up in my mailbox
says my name in it, right there in the text. This is no coincidence,
even though my name is a month and that is probably what
the poet meant. The songs on the radio,
their metallic complaint of whining electric
guitar speak to me, talking of skin graphs and war
and making peace before we all die. Before we all cease.
The approach of autumn. My dying
petunias and hibiscus. These things say to me
it is time to do something great. But I do not know what
that something is. So I light another cigarette, let its smell roll
up in waves around my hair, consume me with its aura,
look for following fire.

-- April Salzano
(January Pyrokinection)

Garden Hoe

I fuck for flowers.
He is filling my garden now
with the brightest purple pansies.
He tills the earth in the bed, better
dirt raked up to fertilize. Spores
will catch the wind and ride
to greener grasses.
Pollinating progression breeds
more blooms, spreading wide
my intention to color the world
in temporary shades of lusted hues.

-- April Salzano
(May Pyrokinection)

Weeping Willow

I am finally afraid to die, though I know
that was not my husband's intention
when he planted a willow tree at the edge
of the driveway. I know this
is where I will sit in twenty years
when the trunk has finally grown tall
enough so the embrace of branches forms
the canopy where I will wait for my grandchildren
to arrive on a day not unlike today,
autumn a mere threat against September sun.
They will say, *there is grandma under her tree.*
I know the roots my tree is forming
will ensure that it outlives me, them,
their own children, just as I know my roots
extend only just beneath the surface.

-- April Salzano
(January Jellyfish Whispers)

Running Dead

Dear people who live
in the house near my nest, today I am going
to commit squirrel suicide. Know that
it was nothing you did. Next chance
I have when the man is driving (because
the woman will risk her life not to hit me),
I am going to run headlong into your tire,
make it to the other side
of the car, run 5 feet while dead,
dive for a tree on pure instinct,
and collapse in a tail twitching tragedy.
There will be no other explanation
for what did not appear to be an accident.
It is simply too cold and I am too tired
of attempting to gather my nuts.

-- April Salzano
(May Jellyfish Whispers)

If Love Can Be Put on a Shelf

hatred can line the pantry, spin
around on the lazy Susan like cans
of kidney beans, organ pebbles held
in aluminum captivity, dusty, waiting.
Jealousy can rage in the fridge,
barking at the plastic jug of milk,
that bloated breast of sustenance,
unnecessary, conspiratorial species'
potion that slides down throats
of our young, who believe they cannot
live without it. Honesty can
be folded with the laundry, washed
clean, erased like a stain on fabric
that hides flaws, covers scars, cracked
open scabs on knees, flaking eczymatic
skin. Trust can be swept under the rug,
crumbs, bits of bread and other garbage
no one believes in anymore.

-- April Salzano
(January Napalm and Novocain)

He Loved Me Like a Whore

like he was running out
of time. His hands were
everywhere his tongue
would not go. He loved me
like an ocean that threatened
to drown us both, carry our wasted
bodies to shore, enough salt
to cleanse any wound. He loved me
like I was no longer
breathing. The air he exhaled
was a breeze from that moment
he was just passing through.

-- April Salzano
(November Napalm and Novocain)

Out of Thin Air

I must choose my words, carefully
and quietly, so they do not hear me coming
with a butterfly net and a straight jacket.
I am diving up/through loose threads of sleep.
Neither will not come willingly & Both/
is too heavy for me to lift//on my own, what
goes unhomogenized will settle at the top
to be skimmed/from another dream.

-- April Salzano
(January The Mind[less] Muse)

The Girl of My Dreams

She is thin in the morning and fat
by nightfall, loose seams tearing apart, death
a wish that comes as much as it goes,
a passing fancy, a fancy passing.
She watches a string dance, umbilicus
of dust laced from ceiling to cupboard,
she is sure it is not the reverse.
She watches it blow but never fall.
Falling and mingling with the rest of the filth,
it will go undetected. Her skin has a mouth
that eats everything in sight. Careful,
she thinks you look delicious.
Dust bunnies romp in the garden of her
dreams, unflowered, save the dandelions
with all their heads popped off
because of people who had babies
and made rhyme out of reason,
not the reverse. Laughter is her echo,
a paralyzing fit of convulsions.
She is contradicted.
Look into the mirror. Her
reflection is yours. Now read this
backwards and see
how lovely she is.

-- April Salzano
(May The Mind[less] Muse)

Rote answer robot
programmed with your ABA.
Independent thoughts?

Undeniable
truth rests in what you say that
you think I can't hear.

Limit what is fun.
Electronics, narcotics,
poison for my brain.

Zipper weighted vest,
offer sensory fidget,
thing to bite or pull.

-- April Salzano
(January High Coupe)

Days of Our Lives

Sometimes I say it aloud, though in a whisper, the way they do on soap operas. As if the actors could hear them anyway. As if they wouldn't just act like the replacement actor was the regular character. But saying it helps me make it real. "Today April will be playing the part of a good mother."

Other days I actually feel it without having to say it. These are the days of cookies baked from scratch. They are just Nestle Tollhouse pan cookies, but you would be surprised how many people have never heard of them. Once at a BBQ hosted by my best friend for her new husband's family, the retarded brother in law who loved milk and home movies asked on a reconnaissance mission for his chain-smoking, wax-eared mother if he could have the recipe. He simultaneously insisted the cookies were "from a mix." I do not attribute his lack of manners to his being retarded. I didn't give him the recipe though I am pretty sure it's a matter of public record. It may even be printed on the bag on chocolate chips. I bake the cookies and play outside with my two sons on the swing set and only sneak off to smoke a couple cigarettes, answer only half my text messages and keep my F-bombs to an absolute minimum. I may even suggest a board game after dinner.

Then there are days I plan to play the role and fail miserably. There are no cookies. The television serves as babysitter and my ashtray overflows. I admit to hoping my kids don't notice the poor substitute for a mother the casting agency has sent, that neither of them will sting me with a "what's the matter mommy?" or worse, an "are you happy, Mom?" These are the kind of days I can only wait for bedtime to come and pray everyone wakes the following morning unscathed. I tell myself these are not the days that translate into memory, though I remember my fair share of them, a locked screen door and the smell of smoke on my mother's breath.

-- April Salzano
(May Pound of Flash)

Author Bios

Sheikha A. hails from Pakistan and United Arab Emirates and is the author of a short poetry collection titled *Spaced* [Hammer and Anvil Books, 2013]. Her work appears in over 40 literary zines/journals/magazines such as *Red Fez, The Muse, Ygdrasil, A New Ulster, Pyrokinection, Mad Swirl, Carcinogenic Poetry, ken*again, American Diversity Report* to name a few, and several anthologies by Silver Birch Press. Her recent publications have been in *Switch [the Difference]* anthology by Kind of a Hurricane Press and *Twenty Seven Signs – Poetry Anthology* by Lady Chaos Press.

Jonel Abellanosa resides in Cebu City, the Philippines. His poetry is forthcoming in *Anglican Theological Review, The Lyric, Ancient Paths,* and has appeared in *Windhover, PEN Peace Mindanao anthology, Star*Line, Liquid Imagination, Mobius Journal of Social Change, Inwood Indiana Press, Golden Lantern, Poetry Quarterly, New Verse News, Qarrtsiluni, Anak Sastra: Stories for Southeast Asia, Fox Chase Review, Burning Word, Barefoot Review, Red River Review, Philippines Free Press, Philippine Graphic.* He is working on his first poetry collection, *Multiverse.*

Carol Amato has had her poetry appear in several magazines and journals. She feels the goal of much of her poetry is to help the reader to visualize and appreciate the interconnectedness between humans and nature. She is also the author of several nature-based children's books and a natural science educator in the greater Boston area. Her 'Let's Find Out Program' carries her across the state in pursuit of the wonder of children! As an evaluator of children's books for Barron's Educational Series (one of her publishers), she is devoted to encouraging writers to also inspire wonder.

Amanda Anastasi is a poet from Melbourne, Australia, and is a two-time winner of the Williamstown Literary Festival's *Ada Cambridge Poetry Prize*. Amanda's first poetry collection *2012 and other poems* was named in Ali Alizadeh's Top Ten Poetic Works of 2012 in Overland Literary Journal. She is also the co-writer of *Loop City*, a spoken word/music show about Melbourne, which was commissioned by MSO violinist Sarah Curro for the *Volume* concert series.

Janet Shell Anderson writes flash fiction, has published a "flash" novel, has been published by decomP, Vestal Review, FRIGG, Convergence, Grey Sparrow, Cease Cows and others and has been nominated for the Pushcart Prize for fiction. She is an attorney.

Steve Ausherman is an artist, photographer and writer whose poetry has thrice been nominated for the Pushcart Prize in poetry. His first chapbook entitled *Creek Bed Blue* (Encircle Publications, 2012) has been nominated for a 2014 New Mexico Book Award and celebrates farming, family heritage and a connection to place. His forthcoming chapbook entitled, *Marking the Bend* (Encircle Publications) is scheduled for 2015 publication and celebrates travel, spirit in the landscape, and a love of wilderness. His poetry has recently been in the literary journals *Decanto, Bear Creek Haiku, the Aurorean, Cheap Seats: Ticket to Ride, Pilgrimage* and *Shemom*. As well, his work recently appeared in the poetry anthology *Mo'Joe* (Beatlick Press, 2014). Free time finds him exploring the hiking trails of the American West with his wife Denise.

Mary Jo Balistreri has two books of poetry, *Joy in the Morning*, and *gathering the harvest*, both published by Bellowing Ark Press. A chapbook, *Best Brothers*, is forthcoming in spring, 2014 from Tiger's Eye Press. Mary Jo has published widely, and has three Pushcart nominations and two Best of the Net. She is a founding member of Grace River Poets, an outreach for schools, women's shelters, and churches. Please visit Mary Jo on her website maryjobalistreripoet.com

Pattie Palmer-Baker discovered, after exhibiting her work, a combination of her poetry in calligraphic form and collages of paste paper, that most people, despite what they may believe, do like poetry, and in fact many like the poetry better than the visual art. She now concentrates on poetry. She still creates artwork but not as often. She finds poetry is more engaging. She loves words.

Donna Barkman was born into a family of actors, and started performing in kindergarten and has been writing for a dozen years. Recent productions: "What Goes Around" and a solo play, "Sticks and Stones and Women's Bones," produced in NYC and Peekskill, NY. Her poetry has been published in The Westchester Review, Pennsylvania English, Chautauqua, Common Ground, Adrienne Rich: A Tribute Anthology, and others. She's enjoyed two artist residencies in Wyoming.

Amy Barry writes poems and short stories. She has worked in the media, hotel and Oil& Gas industries. Her poems have been published in anthologies, journals, and e-zines, in Ireland and abroad. Her poems have been read and shared over the radio in Australia, Canada and Ireland. Trips to India, Nepal, China, Bali, Paris, Berlin and Tramore-have all inspired her work. When not inspired to write, she plays Table Tennis.

David J. Bauman has been printed in various student and faculty journals. His awards include the Savage Poetry Prize from Bloomsburg University and the Academy of American Poets. He has recent poems published or forthcoming in T(OUR), The Blue Hour Magazine, Word Fountain and Watershed, a Journal of the Susquehanna. He writes regularly about the joys of fatherhood, nature and poetry in his blog The Dad Poet, http://dadpoet.wordpress.com

Sarah Bence is a senior English and Creative Writing major at Kenyon College, where she also works as the Community Outreach Intern for the *Kenyon Review*. Her poetry has previously been published in *The Dunes Review*, *The Round*, and *Apeiron Review*.

Karen Berry lives and works in Portland, Oregon. Her poetry has been published in Goblin Fruit, Fireweed, Seek It, Prairie Poetry, and many more journals and anthologies. Her poem "Ceres" was nominated for the Dwarf Star Poetry Prize, and her piece "Caught" was a runner-up in The Binnacle's ultra-short fiction competition. Her first novel, Love and Mahem at Francie June Memorial Trailer Park, was published in June of 2014.

Aaron Besson is a writer of horror and dark fiction from Seattle, Washington. His writing has been published in the Weird Fiction Review from Centipede Press, James Ward Kirk Publishing, J Ellington Ashton Press, and Spinetinglers.

Byron Beynon has appeared in several publications, including Jellyfish Whispers, Montucky Review, Worcester Review, Poetry Wales, Poppy Road Review and London Magazine. His most recent collection is The Echoing Coastline (Agenda Editions).

Ali Carey Billedeaux is a Midwestern writer, but she doesn't usually write about what she knows. For more information about her work, follow her blog at aliwriteswords.wordpress.com.

Jane Blanchard lives and writes in Georgia. Her work has recently appeared in *Boston Literary Magazine, The Enigmatist, Halycon, Kigo,* and *Leaves of Ink.*

Sam Bockover is a writer and poet from the American Midwest.

Andrew M. Bowen works as a sales manager. He is trying to publish his first novel. He has appeared in eight independent films and five stage productions.

Shirley J. Brewer is a poet, educator, and workshop facilitator. Her poetry has appeared in *The Cortland Review, Comstock Review, Passager, New Verse News, Innisfree Poetry Journal, Manorborn,* and other publications. Her poetry chapbook, *A Little Breast Music,* was published in 2008 by Passager Books. A second book of poems, *After Words,* was published in 2013 by Apprentice House/Loyola University. www.apoeticlicense.com

Alan S. Bridges began writing haiku in 2008, with encouragement from poet John Stevenson after the pair met on a cross-country train ride. Alan was subsequently included in A New Resonance 7,

Emerging Voices in English-Language Haiku, Red Moon Press, 2011. An avid fisherman, he is currently compiling fishing-related haiku for an anthology. He resides in Littleton, Massachusetts.

Michael H. Brownstein has been widely published. His latest works, *Firestorm: A Rendering of Torah* (http://booksonblog35.blogspot.com/) (Camel Saloon Books on Blogs) and The Katy Trail, Mid-Missouri, 100F Outside and other poems (http://barometricpressures.blogspot.com/2013/07/the-katy-trail-mid-missouri-100f.html) (Barometric Pressures--A Kind of Hurricane Press). The Katy Trail, Mid-Missouri, 100F Outside And Other PoemsHis work has appeared in *The Café Review*, *American Letters and Commentary*, *Xavier Review*, *Hotel Amerika*, *Meridian Anthology of Contemporary Poetry*, *The Pacific Review*, and others. In addition, he has nine poetry chapbooks including *The Shooting Gallery* (Samidat Press, 1987), *Poems from the Body Bag* (Ommation Press, 1988), *A Period of Trees* (Snark Press, 2004), *What Stone Is* (Fractal Edge Press, 2005), and *I Was a Teacher Once* (Ten Page Press, 2011: (http://tenpagespress.wordpress.com/2011/03/27/i-was-a-teacher-once-by-michael-h-brownstein/). He is the editor of *First Poems from Viet Nam* (2011).

J.J. Campbell has given up the farm life and is currently trapped in suburbia. He's been widely published over the years, most recently at The Camel Saloon, Your One Phone Call, Pink Litter, 48th Street Press and Dead Snakes. His latest collection, *Sofisticated White Trash*, is available wherever people buy books these days. You can find J.J. most days polluting the world with his thoughts at his highly entertaining blog, evil delights. (http://evildelights.blogspot.com)

Andrew Campbell-Kearsey is a former headteacher/principlal who now writes short stories. His first anthology was printed last year by Spinetinglers, called 'Centurionman.' Two of his stories have been filmed and screened at Cannes and at the Hollyshorts Film Festival, Los Angeles.

Theresa A. Cancro writes poetry and short fiction from Wilmington, Delaware. Many of her poems have been published in online and print journals, including Kind of a Hurricane Press anthologies, The Artistic Muse, Kumquat Poetry, Birds By My Window, The Rainbow Journal, Lost Paper, Brass Bell, A Handful of Stones, A Hundred Gourds, Cattails, Chrysanthemum, Shamrock Haiku Journal, and Presence, among others.

Seamas Carraher was born in Dublin, Ireland in 1956. He lives on the Ballyogan estate, in South County Dublin, Ireland, at present. Kind of a Hurricane Press published his chapbook *South Dakota Suite* online, in July 2014. http://www.seamascarraher.blogspot.ie/

John Casquarelli is the author of two full-length collections, *On Equilibrium of Song* (Overpass Books 2011) and *Lavender* (Authorspress 2014). He serves as Editor for *Otter Magazine* (http://ottermagazine.com/) and *Overpass Books* (http://overpassbooks.org/). He was awarded the 2010 Esther Hyneman Award for Poetry and the 2015 Petite Kafka Award. John is a member of a literary and art community called the Unbearables. His work has appeared in the International Higher Education Teaching and Learning Association's (HETL) anthology,*Teaching as a Human Experience* (Cambridge Scholars Publishing). Other publishing credits include *Storm Cycle: Best of Kind of a Hurricane Press*, *Suisun Valley Review, Ginosko Literary Journal, Pyrokinection, Visceral Brooklyn, Flatbush Review,* and *Kinship of Rivers.*

Alan Catlin has been publishing since the seventies earning him the title Venerable Bard, not to be confused with the Venerable Bede, an entirely different kind of writer. He has published a number of chapbooks and full length book including a chapbook of surreal poems illustrated by collage artist Michael Shores titled, "The Insomniac's Gift", which was nominated for a Bram Stoker Book Award. He has a new full length book, *Alien Nation.* It is a collection of four thematically related chapbooks of poetry.

Cathleen Chambless is a Miami native. She is an MFA candidate in poetry at FIU, and also a visual artist and activist. Her work has appeared in MPC's 10 Cent Journal, the anthology A Touch of Saccharine, and she was a poetry finalist for the Bellingham Review's 2014 Parallel Award for poetry. She co-authors a queer/feminist zine called Phallacies.

David Chorlton came to Phoenix from Europe in 1978 with his wife Roberta, an Arizona native. He quickly became comfortable with the climate while adjusting to the New World too longer. Writing and reading poetry have helped immensely in that respect, as has exposure to the American small presses. Arizona's landscape and wildlife became increasingly important to him both as a source of pleasure and a measure of how precarious the natural world is. Thirty years ago he regarded the idea of "nature poetry" as one tainted with sentimentality but today it appears ever more necessary as an element of resistance to the conformity that Edward Abbey confronted so well in his writings on the Southwest. FutureCycle Press recently published his Selected Poems.

Aidan Clarke has been a writer for more than 3 decades during most of which he has lived, worked and walked around in Newcastle Upon Tyne. He has been performing his poetry at Spoken Word events for 4 years. His USP is a menu of around 140 poems each of which he can perform off by heart on request.

Daniel Clausen has been published in Slipstream Magazine, Zygote in my Coffee, Leading Edge Magazine, and Spindrift, among other literary journals. You can learn more about his newest novel, The Ghosts of Nagasaki, at: ghostsofnagasaki.com

Mike Cluff is a writer living in the inland section of Southern California. He is now finishing two books of poetry: "The Initial Napoleon" and "Bulleted Meat" -- both of which are scheduled for publication in late 2013/early 2014. He believes that individuality is the touchstone of his life and pursues that ideal with passion and dedication to help the world improve with each passing instance .He also hopes to take up abstract painting in the next several months.

Cathleen Cohen is Education Director of *ArtWell, (www.theartwell.org)*, which brings poetry and arts workshops to thousands of children of diverse cultures and faiths in the Philadelphia area and abroad. Cathleen's poems have appeared in such publications as *Apiary, Baltimore Review, East Coast Ink, Ember, The Four Quarters Magazine, Ishaan Literary Review, Moment, Layers of Possibility, Philadelphia Stories, 6ix, The Breath of Parted Lips,* and *Bridges: A Jewish Feminist Journal*. She has received the *Interfaith Relations Award* from the Montgomery County Advisory Board to the PA Human Rights Commission and the *Public Service Award* from the National Association of Poetry Therapy. Her paintings have been exhibited in Philadelphia, New Jersey and NYC at *Rosenfeld Gallery, RiverArts Gallery,* and *Soho20 Chelsea Gallery.*

SuzAnne C. Cole holds an MA from Stanford, is a former college English instructor, and writes from a studio in the Texas Hill Country. Her flash fiction has been published in many anthologies and magazines including The World's Best Shortest Stories (of all time), has been listed on The Best of the Web del Sol, and nominated for Pushcart Prizes in both fiction and poetry. Her book *To Our Heart's Content: Meditations for Women Turning Fifty* was published by Contemporary. She's also published more than 400 essays, plays, and poetry in venues ranging from *Newsweek, Baltimore Sun, Houston Chronicle, San Antonio Express-News* to literary and commercial journals. She and her husband have traveled the world— Iceland, China, Nepal, Panama, Peru, Chile, Australia, New Zealand, Britain, Ireland, Turkey, Slovakia, Costa Rica, France, Italy, Switzerland, and Russia. That being said, she also likes to imagine future worlds of exploration and imagination.

Kelly Cressio-Moeller has new poems forthcoming in *Gargoyle, Iodine Poetry Journal, Spillway,* and *THRUSH Poetry Journal*. Previously, her work has appeared in *Boxcar Poetry Review, Cha: An Asian Literary Journal, Crab Creek Review, Crab Orchard Review, Poet Lore, Rattle,* and *ZYZZYVA* as well as the anthology *First Water:*

Best of Pirene's Fountain, Diane Lockward's book, *The Crafty Poet*, and elsewhere. Her poems have been nominated for the Pushcart Prize and Best New Poets. You can visit her website here: www.kellycressiomoeller.com

Larry Crist has lived in Seattle for the past 20 years and is originally from California, specifically Humboldt County. He has lived in Chicago, Houston, London, and Philadelphia where he attended Temple U receiving an MFA in theatre. He's been widely published. Some of his favorites are Pearl, Rattle, Slipstream, Evening Street Review, Dos Passos Review, Alimentum, Floating Bridge Press and Clover. Larry is publishing his first poetry collection in March '14, Undertow Overtures.

Betsey Cullen resides in West Chester, Pennsylvania. She views the natural world with reverence tempered with realism. Her work has appeared in two anthologies published by Kind of a Hurricane Press. She earned a B.A. from the University of Rochester and an M.A. from Cornell University and began writing poetry in retirement. She is married with two grown children and three granddaughters. She can be reached at ewcullen@yahoo.com.

Peter Dabbene has seen his poetry published in many online and print literary journals, and collected in the book *Optimism*. His stories can be found online at www.defenestrationmag.net, www.mcsweeneys.net, www.piginpoke.com, www.wordriot.org, and elsewhere, and his comic book work can be seen in the graphic novels *Ark* and *Robin Hood*, and the magazine *Futurequake*. He has published two story collections, *Prime Movements* and *Glossolalia*, and a novel, *Mister Dreyfus' Demons*. His latest book is the humor collection *More Spamming the Spammers (with Dieter P. Bieny)*. He writes a monthly column for the *Hamilton Post* (viewable at www.mercerspace.com/blog/pdabbene) and reviews for BlueInk Review and Foreword Reviews. His plays have been performed in New Jersey and Philadelphia venues. His website is www.peterdabbene.com.

Dah has appeared, most recently, in The Sandy River Review, Stone Voices Magazine, Diverse Voices Quarterly, Orion headless, Words & Images In Flight, and Miracle Magazine, and is forthcoming in Eunoia Review, Perfume River Review, River & South Review, and Literature Today. The author of two collections of poetry from Stillpoint Books, his third collection is due for publication in 2014, also from Stillpoint. Dah lives in Berkeley, California, where he is currently working on the manuscript for his fourth book.

Susan Dale has had her poems and fiction published in Hurricane Press, Ken *Again, Penman Review, Inner Art Journal, Feathered Flounder, Garbanzo, and Hurricane Press. In 2007, she won the grand prize for poetry from Oneswan.

Cassandra Dallett occupies Oakland, CA. Cassandra writes of a counter culture childhood in Vermont and her ongoing adolescence in the San Francisco Bay Area. She has published in *Slip Stream, Sparkle and Blink, Hip Mama, The Chiron Review, Bleed Me A River, Ascent Aspirations, Criminal Class Review, Enizagam, The Delinquent and The Milvia Street Journal* among many others. Look for links and chapbooks on cassandradallett.com

J.P. Dancing Bear prefers to let the work speak for itself.

Tim Dardis grew up in Northbrook, Illinois and lives in Boulder, Colorado. He earned a Bachelor of Special Studies from Cornell College, in Mt. Vernon, Iowa, and a Master of Arts in English-Creative Writing from the University of Colorado Boulder. In past lives he's been a special education teaching assistant, a wilderness canoe guide, and an adaptive ski instructor. He currently works as a Content Services Specialist for Vertafore and competes as an Expert mountain bike racer. His poems have appeared in *Flatirons Literary Review, Toad Suck Review, Exquisite Corpse, Chicago Literati, Fat City Review, Midnight Screaming, Whetstone, Hudson Valley Echoes, Grasslands Review, Kinesis, Sierra Nevada College Review,* and *Poetry Motel*. He is the author of *Road Rash – Selected Poems,* forthcoming from Shakespeare & Company - Toad Suck Press.

Theresa Darling has been published in The Green Hills Literary Journal, Baily's Beads, Hellbender Journal, Kind of a Hurricane Press, and The Cellar Door. Her poem "Another Departure" was nominated for the Pushcart Prize. She recently fulfilled a lifelong dream by moving to Vermont, where she hopes to live happily ever after with her husband Reg, and two shelter cats.

William G. Davies, Jr. lives in a town surrounded by dairy farms. He has been happily married for thirty-eight years. His work has appeared in the Cortland Review, Bluepepper, The Wilderness House Review, Gloom Cupboard and many others.

Pijush Kanti Deb is a new poet with 60 published poems and haiku in different national and international magazines and journals-print and online.he is an Associate Professor in Economics.He lives in India.

Darren C. Demaree is living in Columbus, Ohio with his wife and children. He is the author of "As We Refer To Our Bodies" (2013) and "Not For Art Nor Prayer" (2014), both collections are to be published by 8th House Publishing House. He is also the recipient of two Pushcart Prize nominations.

James Diaz lives in New York. His poems can be found in Pismire, Epigraph, Negative Suck, Abramelin, and My Favorite Bullet.

Bruce Louis Dodson is an American expat living in Borlänge, Sweden, where he practices photography and writes fiction and poetry. Some of his most recent work has appeared in: Breadline Press West Coast Poetry Anthology, Foreign & Far Away – Writers Abroad Anthology, Sleeping Cat Books – Trip of a Lifetime Anthology, The Crucible, Blue Collar Review, Barely South Review, 3rd Wednesday, The Path, Northern Liberties Review, Pirene's Fountain, Sounds of Solace – Meditative Verse Anthology, Tic Toc Anthology, High Coupe, Vine Leaves, and Cordite Poetry Review.

Liz Dolan was nominated for both the Robert McGovern Prize, Ashville University, and a Pushcart for her poetry manuscript, *A Secret of Long Life*. She has been published by Cave Moon Press. Her first poetry collection, *They Abide,* was published by March Street. An eight-time Pushcart nominee and winner of Best of the Web, she was a finalist for Best of the Net 2014. She recently won The Nassau Prize for prose. She has received fellowships from the Delaware Division of the Arts, The Atlantic Center for the Arts and Martha's Vineyard. Liz serves on the poetry board of *Philadelphia Stories*.

Melissa Duclos is the founder of the Clovers Project, which provides mentoring for writers at various stages of their careers. Her work has appeared in *Salon*, *The Offing*, and *Electric Literature*, among other venues. She received her MFA from Columbia University and now lives in Portland, OR, with her husband and two children. She works as a freelance writer, editor, and writing instructor.

J.K. Durick is a writing teacher at the Community College of Vermont and an online writing tutor. His recent poems have appeared in *Write Rome, Black Mirror, Third Wednesday, Foliate Oak,* and *Orange Room*.

Liz Egan holds an MFA in fiction writing from George Mason University. Her writing has been published in *ink & coda* and *Sliced Bread*. She teaches writing and directs the writing center at Millsaps College in Jackson, Mississippi.

Chiyuma Elliott is an Assistant Professor of African American Studies at the University of California, Berkeley. A former Stegner Fellow, Chiyuma's poems have appeared in the African American Review, Callaloo, the Notre Dame Review, the PN Review, and other journals. She has received fellowships from the American Philosophical Society, the James Irvine Foundation, and the Vermont Studio Center. She is currently at work on a poem cycle called Vigil.

Neil Ellman writes from New Jersey, and has been nominated for the Pushcart Prize, Best of the Net, and the Rhysling Award. More than 900 of his poems, many of which are ekphrastic and written in response to works of modern and contemporary art, appear in print and online journals, anthologies and chapbooks throughout the world.

Eric Evans is a writer and musician from Buffalo, New York with stops in Portland, Oregon and Rochester, New York where he currently resides. His work has appeared in *Artvoice, decomP magazinE, Tangent Magazine, Posey, Xenith Magazine, Anobium Literary Magazine, Pemmican Press, Remark* and many other publications and anthologies. He has published seven full collections and three broadsides through his own small press, Ink Publications, in addition to a broadside through Lucid Moon Press. He is the editor of *The Bond Street Review* as well as the proud recipient of the 2009 Geva Theatre Center Summer Academy Snapple Fact Award.

Alexis Rhone Fancher is the author of *"How I Lost My Virginity To Michael Cohen and Other Heart Stab Poems,"* (Sybaritic Press, 2014). You can find her work in *Rattle, The MacGuffin, Fjords, Broadzine!, Slipstream, H_NGM_N, The Chiron Review, Menacing Hedge, Ragazine, Cactus Heart, Carbon Culture Review, The Literary Underground*, and elsewhere. Her poems have been published in over twenty American and international anthologies. Alexis is Photography Editor of *Fine Linen Literary Journal.* Her photos have been published worldwide, including spreads in *River Styx, Blue Lyra, Blink-Ink*, and the covers of *The Mas Tequila Review* and *Witness*. Since 2013 she's been nominated for three Pushcart Prizes and a Best of The Net award. Alexis is poetry editor of *Cultural Weekly*, where she also publishes *The Poet's Eye*, a monthly photo essay about Los Angeles. www.alexisrhonefancher.com

Cyd Ferree is a songwriter (as Cyd Ward) and graphic designer. She lives in the Sunshine State, and attends the Savannah College of Art and Design in Georgia full-time, where writing revives her between storms.

Claire T. Feild has had 286 poems accepted for print publication in 101 journals and anthologies such as *The Tulane Review*; *Chinaberries and Crows: An Anthology*; *Palimpsest: A Creative Journal of the Humanities*; *Zymbol Magazine*; *Folio*; *The Path: A Literary Magazine*; *Pinyon Review*; *Dewpoint Literary Magazine*; *Birmingham Arts Journal*; *Kudzu*; *Words Dance*; *Coup d'Etat; Folio*; *San Pedro River Review*; *The Homestead Review*; and *The Carolina Quarterly*. Her first poetry book is *Mississippi Delta Women* in Prism. Her second collection of poetry is titled *Southern Aunts: The 1950s*. Indigo Blues, a micro-book, was published by the Origami Poetry Project. Her fourth book is a creative non-fiction book titled *A Delta Vigil: Yazoo City, Mississippi, the 1950s*.

Daniel N. Flanagan is a Worcester, MA native. He is the author of three short stories, including the popular "Daddy's Girl," along with twenty poems, featured in *Poppy Road Review, Three Line Poetry*, etc. He has one chap-book, four stories and six poems scheduled for publication by various journals, including *Stone Path Review*. Check him out at www.DanFlanagan.webs.com and follow him @DanielNFlanagan.

Ryan Quinn Flanagan has published thirteen collections of poetry and one joint chapbook through various small presses. He is a Pushcart Prize nominee, and a 2010 Sundress Best of the Net finalist. His poetry has appeared in nearly a hundred online and print journals spanning five continents.

Pattie Flint is an uprooted Seattle native toughing it out in Scotland binding books by hand. She has been published in *Five [Quarterly]*, *Hippocampus* and *TAB,* amongst others. She is currently working on her MFA at Cedar Crest College.

Sarah Flint lives in the West Country of the UK and for several years has written about diverse interests including gardening, cooking and climbing. At present she likes to write poetry . She enjoys playing with words and tries to put them in an interesting order. Her poetry has been published by The Pygmy Giant, Message in a Bottle and she has been runner-up in the Mountaineering Council of Scotland poetry competition.

Nancy Flynn grew up on the Susquehanna River in northeastern Pennsylvania, spent many years on a downtown creek in Ithaca, New York, and now lives near the mighty Columbia in Portland, Oregon. She attended Oberlin College, Cornell University, and has an M.A. in English from SUNY at Binghamton. Her writing has received an Oregon Literary Fellowship and the James Jones First Novel Fellowship. Poetry chapbooks include *The Hours of Us* (2007) and *Eternity a Coal's Throw* (2012); her book-length collection, *Every Door Recklessly Ajar*, was published by Cayuga Lake Books in June 2015. Her website is www.nancyflynn.com.

Vernon Frazer is a poet and author. His most recent books of poetry include *T(exto)-V(isual) Poetry* and *Unsettled Music*. Enigmatic Ink has published Frazer's new novel, *Field Reporting*. Frazer's web site is http://www.vernonfrazer.net. *Bellicose Warbling*, the blog that updates his web page, can be read at http://bellicosewarbling.blogspot.com/ His work, including the long poem *IMPROVISATIONS*, may also be viewed at Scribd.com. In addition to writing poetry and fiction, Frazer also performs his poetry, incorporating text and recitation with animation and musical accompaniment on YouTube. Frazer is married.

Linda Gamble is a retired reading specialist from New Jersey. She has previously published poems in Edison Literary Review, US1 Worksheets, Mused, A Kind of Hurricane, A Long Story Short, Camel Saloon and Jellyfish Whispers.

Sue Mayfield Geiger is a freelance writer living on the Texas Gulf Coast.

Phil Ginsburg is a performance poet/playwright. His two poetry chapbooks "Psychotropic Poems" and "The Choreography of Corn" are available at Poor Richards Bookstore in Colorado Springs, CO. His poetry work can be discovered at indiefeedpp.libsyn.com. His short play "Anonymous, Anonymous" was also performed in 2014 at the Confetti Stage Short Play Fest in Albany, NY. Another short play, "Another

Day in Polka-Topia," was the winner of the 2011 Alan Minieri Playwright Award at the American Globe Theater in NYC. He lives in Colorado Springs and is active in the poetry and theater community there.

Jessica Gleason writes because Bukowski no longer can. Gleason has two published books, "Madison Murphy, Wisconsin Weirdo" and "Sundown on This Town." Her work can also be found in Nefarious Ballerina, Fickle Muses, Postcard Shorts, Misfits Miscellany, Citizens for Decent Literature and Verse Wisconsin. If you want to read more of her work, google her. She also, occasionally, likes to sleep in a Star Trek uniform and has mastered The Song of Time on her Ocarina.

Patricia L. Goodman is a widowed mother and grandmother, a graduate of Wells College with a degree in Biology and is a member of Phi Beta Kappa. Her career involved breeding and training horses with her orthodontist husband on their farm in Chadds Ford, PA. She has had poems published in the likes of *Aries, The Broadkill Review, Sugar Mule, Requiem Magazine, Jellyfish Whispers, Fox Chase Review; Mistletoe Madness , Storm Cycle, Poised in Flight* (all from Kind of a Hurricane Press) *On Our Own* (Silver Boomer Books) and *The Widow's Handbook.* Her first book, *Closer to the Ground* was a finalist in the 2014 Dogfish Head Poetry Competition and she has twice won the Delaware Press Association Communications Award in poetry. She lives on the banks of the Red Clay Creek in Delaware, where she is surrounded by the natural world she loves.

Taylor Graham is a volunteer search-and-rescue dog handler in the Sierra Nevada. She's included in the anthologies Villanelles (Everyman's Library, 2012) and California Poetry: From the Gold Rush to the Present (Santa Clara University, 2004). Her book The Downstairs Dance Floor was awarded the Robert Phillips Poetry Chapbook Prize. Her latest book is What the Wind Says (Lummox Press, 2013), poems about living and working with her canine search partners over the past 40 years.

Allison Grayhurst is a full member of the League of Canadian Poets. She has over 600 poems published in more than 300 international journals, magazines, and anthologies. Her book *Somewhere Falling* was published by Beach Holme Publishers, a Porcepic Book, in Vancouver in 1995. Since then she has published ten other books of poetry and four collections with Edge Unlimited Publishing. Prior to the publication *of Somewhere Falling* she had a poetry book published, *Common Dream*, and four chapbooks published by The Plowman. Her poetry chapbook *The River is Blind* was recently published by Ottawa publisher above/ground press December 2012. She lives in Toronto with family. She also sculpts, working with clay.

John Grey is an Australian born poet. Recently published in The Lyric, Vallum and the science fiction anthology, "The Kennedy Curse" with work upcoming in Bryant Literary Magazine, Natural Bridge, Southern California Review and the Oyez Review.

Carl James Grindley grew up on an island on Canada's pacific coast but now lives and works in the south Bronx. His last book of poetry, Lora and The Dark Lady, was published in 2013 by Ravenna Press.

Cristine A. Gruber has had worked featured in numerous magazines, including: *North American Review, Writer's Digest, Writers' Journal, Ascent Aspirations, California Quarterly, Dead Snakes Online Journal, The Endicott Review, Garbanzo Literary Journal, The Homestead Review, Iodine Poetry Journal, Kind of a Hurricane Press: Something's Brewing Anthology, Miller's Pond Poetry Magazine, The Penwood Review, Poem, Thema, The Tule Review,* and *Westward Quarterly*. Her first full-length collection of poetry, Lifeline, was released by Infinity Publishing and is available from Amazon.com

Ahab Hamza is a university student born in Birkenhead on 27th November 1993. He has been featured in the several publications including The Recusant's "The Robin Hood Book"

anthology and the Spring 2012 issue of Inclement Magazine. Most recently he has been featured in Kind of a Hurricane Press's Pyrokinection, the "What's Your Sign" anthology and Forward Poetry's "Love is in the Air" anthology of 2014. He was also shortlisted for the 2012 erbacce prize for poetry.

Patricia Hanahoe-Dosch has been published in *The Atticus Review, War, Art and Literature, Confrontation, The Red River Review, San Pedro River Review, Marco Polo Arts Magazine, Red Ochre Lit, Nervous Breakdown, Quantum Poetry Magazine, The Paterson Literary Review, Abalone Moon, Apt, Switched-On Gutenberg, Paterson: The Poets' City* (an anthology edited by Marie Mazziotti Gillan), and *MALALA: Poems for Malala Yousafzai* (a Good Works anthology by FutureCycle Press to raise money for the Malala Fund), among others. Articles of hers have appeared in *Travel Belles, On a Junket*, and *Wholistic Living News*. Her story, "Sighting Bia," was selected as a finalist for A Room of Her Own Foundation's 2012 Orlando Prize for Flash Fiction. My story, "Serendip," was published in *In Posse Review*.

Margery Hauser is a New York City poet whose work has appeared in Point Mass, Poetica Magazine, Umbrella, The Jewish Women's Literary Annual, Mobius, and other journals, both print and online. She is the author of Fairyland Mail (NoNet Press, 2013) and a member of the Parkside Poets Collective.

Nancy J. Hayden is a writer, artist, and organic farmer living in northern Vermont. She is also fascinated with World War I. The story in this anthology was inspired by one of the letters her great uncle Harry sent to his family while he was in France during WWI. He had a real sweet tooth. Nancy had four fiction and three nonfiction pieces published or accepted in 2014 including the WWI stories "Unknown Soldier" in the anthology, *Kneeling in the Silver Light, Stories from the Great War* (released in September, 2014, Alchemy Press), and "No Man's Land" in the upcoming 2015 anthology *Enter at Your Own Risk: Dreamscapes Into Darkness* by Firbolg Publishing. She is currently working on an historical novel and a dark fantasy short story collection set during WWI. She earned an MFA in creative writing from the

Stonecoast Writer's Program at the University of Southern Maine in 2012. She also has degrees in English, studio art, ecology and environmental engineering. Her website is www.northwindarts.com with a link to her WWI Collage Blog that presents her art, stories and research related to WWI.

Damien Healy is from Dublin in Ireland but now lives in Osaka, Japan. He teaches English and writes textbooks for the Japanese tertiary market. He doesn't have much free time to read or write poetry, especially with a two year old son, but on those happy occasions when life is not so hectic he can be found reading many wonderful poetry journals from the four corners of the world. He was nominated for the Pushcart Prize 2013 and has been published in Jellyfish Whispers, Napalm and Novocain, The mind[less] Muse, Poetry 24, In other words Merida, The Ofi Press Mexico, Poetry Scotland's Open Mouse, Spinozablue and The Weekenders.

Heather Heyns is a freelancer writer from Southern California. Her work can be found in Howl Literary Magazine and upcoming issues of Literary Orphans, Thick Jam, and Yellow Mama.

Christopher Hivner writes from a small town in Pennsylvania surrounded by books and the echoes of music. He recently won 1st place in Eye on Life Magazine's poetry contest for the second consecutive year. A chapbook of poems, "The Silence Brushes My Cheek Like Glass" was published by Scars Publications.

Harmony Hodges lives in the Pacific Northwest and writes poetry and fiction. More of her work can be found in several poetry anthologies on Amazon, edited by A.J. Huffman.

Trish Hopkinson has always loved words—in fact, her mother tells everyone she was born with a pen in her hand. She has two chapbooks *Emissions* and *Pieced Into Treetops* and has been published in several anthologies and journals, including *The Found Poetry Review*, *Chagrin River Review*, and

Reconnaissance Magazine. Trish is co-founder of a local poetry group, Rock Canyon Poets. She is a project manager by profession and resides in Utah with her handsome husband and their two outstanding children. You can follow her poetry adventures at http://trishhopkinson.com/.

Liz Hufford takes regular doses of the Sonoran desert and the tall pines of Arizona to avoid what Richard Louv has labeled "nature-deficit disorder." She has published poems, articles, essays, and short stories. Recent publications include the poem "Living with Scorpions" (2014) and the short story "No Man" (2013).

Wendy Elizabeth Ingersoll won the 2010 National Federation of Press Women Contest with her book, *Grace Only Follows,* and was a finalist for Drake University's 2012 Emerging Writer Prize. Her poems have appeared in Naugatuck River Review, Passager, Caesura, Controlled Burn, Broadkill Review, and been nominated for a Pushcart Prize. She is a retired piano teacher.

Diane Jackman has had her poetry appear in magazines and anthologies, including The Rialto, Outposts and Words-Myth and a short story in "Story" (Happenstance Press). She was winner of the Liverpool Poetry Festival competition 2006. She wrote the libretto for "Pinocchio", for the Kings' Singers/LSO performed at The Barbican, has published seven children's books and many stories. She lives in Norfolk.

Miguel Jacq is a French-Australian poet. He lives in Melbourne, Australia where he runs (some say ruins) an I.T business. His work has been published by The Blue Hour Press, Dagda Publishing, Deep Water Literary Journal, Kind Of A Hurricane Press, The Poetry Jar, Vox Poetica and Visible Ink. In 2013, he was shortlisted for the Australian Science Poetry Prize, and published two poetry collections 'Black Coat City' and 'Magnetics'. He is co-editor of the online literary journal, 'The Blue Hour Magazine'.

David James has produced more than thirty of his one-act plays from New York to California. He teaches for Oakland Community College.

His third book, *My Torn Dance Card,* is forthcoming from FCNI Press in 2015.

Bill Jansen lives in Forest Grove, Oregon, two blocks from the building where he was born in 1946. Recent work appeared in Gap-Toothed Madness and Asinine Poetry. In addition to a self published collection titled Soft Thorns, about 40 poems have been published in various ezines and journals.

Ivan Jenson is a pop artist painter and contemporary poet whose artwork was featured in *Art in America, Art News,* and *Interview Magazine* while selling at auction at Christie's. Jenson was commissioned by Absolut Vodka to make a painting titled "Absolut Jenson" for the brand's national ad campaign, and his "Marlboro Man" was collected by the Philip Morris corporate collection. Jenson wrote two novels, *Dead Artist* and *Seeing Soriah,* both of which illustrate the creative and often dramatic lives of artists. Jenson turned to poetry as an outlet for artistic expression, and he is now a prolific writer who is widely published (with over 450 poems published in the US, UK and Europe) in a variety of literary media. Jenson's poems were recently published by Hen House Press in a book titled *Media Child and Other Poems,* which can be acquired on Amazon. Two new novels by Ivan Jenson entitled, *Marketing Mia* and *Erotic Rights,* have now been published hardcover and are available for purchase at bookstores worldwide. Ivan Jenson's website is: www.IvanJenson.com

Sonja Johanson attended College of the Atlantic, in Bar Harbor, ME. She has recent work appearing in The Albatross, Off the Coast, and Out of Sequence: The Sonnets Remixed, and was a participating writer in the Found Poetry Review's 2014 Oulipost Project. Sonja divides her time between work in Massachusetts and her home in the mountains of western Maine.

Michael Lee Johnson lived ten years in Canada during the Vietnam era. Today he is a poet, freelance writer, amateur photographer, small business owner in Itasca, Illinois. He has been published in more than 850 small press magazines in twenty-seven countries, and he edits nine poetry sites. Author's website http://poetryman.mysite.com/. Michael is the author of The *Lost American: From Exile to Freedom (136 page book) ISBN: 978-0-595-46091-5,* several chapbooks of poetry, including *From Which Place the Morning Rises* and *Challenge of Night and Day,* and *Chicago Poems.* He also has over 73 poetry videos on YouTube as of 2015: *https://www.youtube.com/user/poetrymanusa/videos*

Ken L. Jones has been a professional writer for the past thirty plus years. He has published in practically every medium that a writer can appear in. Among his earliest and most noteworthy accomplishment was as a cartoonist of note whose scripts appeared in the titles of such major publishers as Disney Comics and Harvey Comics where he was a lead writer for The New Kids On The Block family of titles. In the last few years he has shifted his emphasis to writing speculative fiction and horror short stories as well as very well received poems of horror which have appeared many times in anthologies and online and which also resulted in his first solo book of poetry Bad Harvest and Other Poems which was released by Panic Press. He also recently had a poem published in Poised In Flight from Kind Of A Hurricane Press. In addition to all this he currently is constantly turning in new horror poems to George Wilhite's Long Intervals of Horrible Sanity blog which features regularly updated selections of his latest visions of terror. You can find it at the following link http://georgewilhite.blogspot.com/p/poetry-by-ken-l-jones.html. In spare moments he is also preparing several books of his non-horror poetry work for possible future publication.

Larry Jones lives in Utah. He has poetry at The Camel Saloon, Dead Snakes and Clutching at Straws.

B.T. Joy is a free verse poet whose work has appeared in journals, magazines, e-zines and podcasts worlwide. He has also practiced as a haiga artist and has had work featured with World Haiku Association, Haiga Online and Daily Haiga. He currently works as a high school English teacher. He can be reached through his website http://btjooo5uk.wix.com/btjoypoet or on tumblr http://btjooo5uk.tumblr.com/

Amanda Kabak holds an MFA Pacific University, and her stories have been found in Midwestern Gothic, The Quotable, Perceptions Magazine, and other print and online periodicals. Amanda has been the winner of the Betty Gabehart prize, issued through the Kentucky Women Writer's Conference, a finalist in december magazine's Curt Johnson prose contest, and a finalist in Iron Horse Literary Review's chapbook contest. She is a denizen of the Windy City, and when she's not writing fiction, she compose scientific software aimed at changing the way cities work.

Babo Kamel has had her poetry appear in The Greensboro Review, Alligator Juniper, California Quarterly, The Grolier Poetry Prize, and Contemporary Verse 2 among others. She was a winner of The Charlotte Newberger Poetry Prize, which was published in Lilith Magazine. She has poems forthcoming with Purple Passion Press. Originally from Montreal, Quebec, she now resides in Venice, Florida.

Clyde Kessler from Radford, Virginia is a regional editor of Virginia Birds, a publication of the Virginia Society of Ornithology. He is also a founding member of Blue Ridge Discovery Center, an environmental education organization with programs in North Carolina and Virginia. His poetry has been published in many magazines.

Marla Kessler is embarking on her passion for fiction after a successful career in consulting and economics, where she published business articles. Marla has already written two novels (unpublished), but she is looking to refine her style and find her true voice through short fiction. Her first award was for *Lipstick*, a 400 word piece of flash fiction that reflects her desire to take readers on an emotional journey while leaving them with something to think about later. Her writing style is faced-paced and usually centers around strong women who need to find strength within themselves. She has been publishing a blog –www.inmarlaswords.com – to help her readers and fellow writers understand her writing process but more interestingly, the inspiration behind it. While she is working to become a professional writer, Marla still channels her creativity through her consulting and marketing responsibilities at work as well through the creative imaginations of her twin boys.

Steve Klepetar has received several nominations for the Pushcart Prize and Best of the Net. His most recent collections include *Speaking to the Field Mice* (Sweatshoppe Publications, 2013), *My Son Writes a Report on the Warsaw Ghetto* (Flutter Press, 2013) and *Return of the Bride of Frankenstein* (forthcoming from Kind of a Hurricane Press).

Irene Koronas has a fine arts degree from Mass College of Art Boston. She is a multi media artist working with paint, collage, mono-printing, artists books, poetry and photography. She is currently the poetry editor for Wilderness House Literary Review. Her poetry has appeared in journals and magazines, on line zines and Clarion 13. She has seven chap-books: work among friends, where words drip; perception; tongue on everyday; species; flat house; and, to speak the meaning of being. her work is in 8 anthologies, she has two full length books, 'self portrait drawn from many' ibbettson street press; "pentakomon cyprus," Cervena Barva Press. "Emily Dickinson," Propaganda Press; "Zero Boundaries" Cervena Barva Press. The release of "Turtle Grass" a full length book of poems is expected March 2014, Muddy River Books.

John Kross is an aspiring poet living and working In Dallas, TX. His poems have recently appeared in *Napalm and Novocain*, *The Mind[less] Muse*, *Pyrokinection* and the 2012 edition of *Storm Cycle*. You can read more of John's work and interact with him as the poet "V" at Hello Poetry. www.hellopoetry.com/v/

Martha Landman was born in South Africa, and currently writes in North Queensland, Australia. Her latest work has appeared in *egg poetry*, *Beakful* and *Jellyfish Whispers*.

Ron. Lavalette is a cranky poet from Barton VT. He has been widely published in both ink and pixel form. A reasonable sample of his published work can be found at Eggs Over Tokyo (http://eggsovertokyo.blogspot.com).

Lyn Lifshin has published over 130 books and chapbooks including 3 from Black Sparrow Press: *Cold Comfort, Before It's Light* and *Another Woman Who Looks Like Me*. Before *Secretariat: The Red Freak, The Miracle*, Lifshin published her prize winning book about the short lived beautiful race horse Ruffian, *The Licorice Daughter: My Year With Ruffian* and *Barbaro: Beyond Brokenness*. Recent books include *Ballroom, All the Poets Who Have Touched Me, Living and Dead. All True, Especially The Lies, Light At the End: The Jesus Poems, Katrina, Mirrors, Persphone, Lost In The Fog, Knife Edge & Absinthe: The Tango Poems*. NYQ books published *A Girl Goes into The Woods*. Also just out: *For the Roses* poems after Joni Mitchell and *Hitchcock Hotel* from Danse Macabre. *Secretariat: The Red Freak, The Miracle*. And *Tangled as the Alphabet,-- The Istanbul Poems from* NightBallet Press Just released as well *Malala*, the dvd of *Lyn Lifshin: Not Made of Glass. The Marilyn Poems* was just released from Rubber Boots Press. An update to her Gale Research Autobiography is out: *Lips, Blues, Blue Lace: On The Outside*. Also just out is a dvd of the documentary film about her: *Lyn Lifshin: Not Made Of Glass*. Just out: Femme Eterna *Eneduanna, Schererzade and Nefertiti* and *Moving Through Stained Glass: the Maple Poems* and *Dega's Little Dancer*.

Duane Locke lives in Tampa, Florida near anhinga, gallinules, raccoons, alligators, etc. He has published 6,763 poems, including 31 books of poems. His latest book publications: April 2012, *Duane Locke, The First Decade,* 1968-1978 (Bitter Oleander Press). This book is a republication of his first eleven books, contains 333 pages. Available at www.bitteroleander.com or on Amazon.

Jack e Lorts is a retired educator living in a small town in eastern Oregon. He has published widely, if infrequently, over the past 40+ years, in such magazines as *Arizona Quarterly, Kansas Quarterly, English Journal, Agnostic Lobster, Quantum Tao, High Desert Journal* and elsewhere. Author of several chapbooks, his most recent is *Dear Gilbert Sorrentino and Other*

Poems, from Finishing Line Press. Active in local, state and national Democratic politics, he is currently Mayor of Fossil, OR (population 479).

Laura Lovic-Lindsay left Penn State with an English degree in hand in 1993, but only began writing in earnest a few years ago. She writes in darkly forested Western Pennsylvania where she resides with her two children and a long-lived hermit crab.

Chad W. Lutz was born in 1986 in Akron, Ohio, and raised in the neighboring suburb of Stow. His works have been featured in Diverse Voices Quarterly, The Dying Goose, Haunted Waters Press, and prominently on AltOhio.com, of which he serves managing editor. Chad currently works in North Canton writing web content for an online job resource website. An avid athlete, Chad runs competitively for a Northeast Ohio running club and swims in his spare time. He aspires to run the Olympic marathon at the 2016 games.

Iain Macdonald was born and raised in Glasgow, Scotland, and currently lives in Arcata, California. He has earned his bread and beer in various ways, from flower picker to factory hand, merchant marine officer to high school teacher. His chapbooks, *Plotting the Course* and *Transit Report*, are published by March Street Press. A third chapbook, *The Wrecker's Yard*, has been accepted for publication by Kattywompus Press.

Stacy Lynn Mar is a 30-something American poet. Inspired by the works of Sharon Olds and Anne Sexton, her work is primarily confessional. She holds three graduate degrees in psychology and attended Lindsey Wilson College of Human Sciences as well as Ellis College of NYIT for a BA in English. Shacy divides her time between her young daughter, her forays into writing, a genuine love of books, film, coffee, vintage things, and her life partner. She is founder and masthead of a new literary ezine for women, Pink. Girl. Ink, and also has a book review blog. She invites you to visit her personal blog www.warningthestars.blogspot.com

Jacqueline Markowski is currently working on a compilation of short stories and a collection of poetry. Her poetry and short stories have appeared in numerous publications including *Cochlea/The Neovictorian, Permafrost Literary Journal, The Camel Saloon, Pyrokinection* and *Jellyfish Whispers*. Her work has been anthologized in "Backlit Barbell," "Storm Cycle" and "Point Mass" (Kind of a Hurricane Press*)*. She is a Pushcart prize nominee and was awarded first place in poetry at The Sandhills Writers Conference.

Denny E. Marshall has had art and poetry published, some recently. He does have a personal website with previously published works. The web address is www.dennymarshall.com.

Grace Maselli is at work on a collection of essays and poems. She studied for seven years in New York City at The Writers Studio founded by American poet and author, Philip Schultz. Her work has appeared in *Cleaver Magazine, Poydras Review, Streetlight Magazine* and *The Penmen Review*. Her poem, *What the Hair Is Going On?* was recently published as a mini chapbook by *Phafours Press, Ottowa, Canada*. She lives in North Tampa, FL, with a husband, two kids, two dogs, and a Coronet guinea pig.

Anna McCluskey is a fresh new voice in the poetry world. She studied creative writing at Saint Louis University, and currently lives in Portland, OR.

Bradley McIlwain lives in Ontario, Canada where he is inspired by the songs in nature, and examining our relationships within it. His poems have appeared in the *New Verse News, The Open Mouse, Wilderness Interface Zone,* and anthologies including *Something's Brewing*, Kind of a Hurricane Press (2014), The 5-2 Crime Poetry Weekly Vol. 2 (2013) and in *Love Notes: A Collection of Romantic Poetry* from Vagabondage Press (2012). His micro-chapbook *Philosophers Walk* was published in 2014 by the Origami Poems Project, and is available for a free download at: http://www.origamipoems.com/poets/215-bradley-mcilwain

Joan McNerney has had her poetry included in numerous literary magazines such as Seven Circle Press, Dinner with the Muse, Blueline, Spectrum, three Bright Spring Press Anthologies and several Kind of A Hurricane Publications. She has been nominated three times for Best of the Net. Poet and Geek recognized her work as their best poem of 2013. Four of her books have been published by fine small literary presses and she has three e-book titles.

Bruce McRae is a Pushcart nominee and a Canadian musician with over 800 publications, including Poetry.com and The North American Review. His first book, 'The So-Called Sonnets' is available from the Silenced Press website or via Amazon books. To hear his music and view more poems visit his website: www.bpmcrae.com, or "TheBruceMcRaeChannel" on Youtube.

Jim Meirose has had his work appear in numerous journals, including the Fiddlehead, Witness, Alaska Quarterly review, and Xavier Review. Two collections of his work and three novels have been published. A new novel, "Mount Everest", will come out in 2015 from Montag Press. Reach Jim at www.jimmeirose.com

Karla Linn Merrifield is a nine-time Pushcart-Prize nominee and National Park Artist-in-Residence. She has had over 500 poems appear in dozens of publications with twelve books to her credit, the newest of which, from FootHills Publishing, is *Bunchberries, More Poems of Canada*, a sequel to her award-winning *Godwit: Poems of Canada* (FootHills). She is assistant editor/ poetry book reviewer for *The Centrifugal Eye*. Visit her blog, *Vagabond Poet*, at http://karlalinn.blogspot.com.

Les Merton has always been interested in writing; he had his first short story published in the Manchester Evening News in 1968. He started to write more prolifically in 1995 and is the author of 20 books. His poetry has been published in over 120 UK magazines and in 15 different countries. In 2002 he became the founder editor of Poetry Cornwall / Bardhonyeth Kernow which is still going.

Jane Miller is a writer of poetry and short fiction from Delaware. Her work has appeared or forthcoming in *In Gilded Cage, Connected:*

What Remains as We all Change, Wanderings, and *Halfway Down the Stairs.* She was awarded a 2014 Individual Artist Fellowship as an emerging artist in poetry from the Delaware Division of the Arts.

James Mirarchi grew up in Queens, New York. In addition to his poetry collections, Venison, Dervish, and Shards, he has written and directed short films which have played festivals. His poems have appeared in several independent literary journals. Links to his work can be found at: www.thehydratedpoet.blogspot.com/

Mark J. Mitchell studied writing at UC Santa Cruz under Raymond Carver, George Hitchcock and Barbara Hull. His work has appeared in various periodicals over the last thirty five years, as well as the anthologies, It has also been nominated for both Pushcart Prizes and The Best of the Net. Good Poems, American Places, Hunger Enough, Retail Woes and Line Drives. A length collection, Lent 1999, was ,just published by Leaf Garden Press. His chapbook, Three Visitors has been published by Negative Capability Press. Artifacts and Relics, another chapbook, was just released from Folded Word and his novel, Knight Prisoner, was published by Vagabondage Press and a another novel, A Book of Lost Songs is coming soon from Wild Child Publishing. He lives in San Francisco with his wife, the documentarian and filmmaker Joan Juster.

Ralph Monday is an Associate Professor of English at Roane State Community College in Harriman, TN., where he teaches composition, literature, and creative writing courses. He has had hundreds of poems published in over 50 journals including Agenda, The New Plains Review, New Liberties Review, Fiction Week Literary Review and many others. His poetry has been nominated for a Pushcart Prize and Houghton Mifflin's "Best of" Anthologies, as well as other awards. A chapbook, *All American Girl and Other Poems*, was published in July 2014. A book *Empty Houses and American Renditions* was published May 2015 by Aldrich Press. A Kindle chapbook *Narcissus the Sorcerer* was published June 2015 by Odin Hill Press. When not gardening, painting, or writing he listens to the coyotes and owls calling in the woods behind his house.

Jude Neale was shortlisted for the Gregory O'Donoghue International Poetry Prize (Ireland), The International Poetic Republic Poetry Prize (U.K),The Mary Chalmers Smith Poetry Prize (UK), The Wenlock International Poetry Prize(UK), the RCLA short story and poem competition and she was nominated for the Canadian ReLit Award and the Pat Lowther Award for her book *Only the Fallen Can See*.

Emily Pittman Newberry is a poet, speaker, writer and performance poet. After living a life in hiding she finally came out as the transgendered woman she lives as today. Her writing and performances explore the challenges of living as spiritual beings in a human world, of the paradox of life. Emily wrote songs and poetry during the mass movements of the 1960's and did street theater. One Spirit Press has published two books of her poetry; Butterfly A Rose, in 2010 and the chapbook Nature Speaking, Naturally with artist Adelaide Beeman White, in 2012. She lives in Portland Oregon. In 2014 her collaboration with Shu-Ju Wang, a limited edition artist's book titled Water was published. Her web site is www.butterflyarose.com.

Mary Newell is a writer and educator and lives in the lower Hudson Valley. She has taught literature and writing at the college level. She received a doctorate from Fordham University in American Literature and the Environment, as well as MAs from Teachers College and Columbia University. Her publications include poems published or forthcoming in About Place, First Literary Review East, Jivin' Ladybug, and Howling Dog Press, as well as essays and reviews. Her poem, "The Traffic in Old Ladies" will appear as an honorable mention in the Best of 2014 Anthology of Kind of a Hurricane Press.

BZ Niditch is a poet, playwright, and fiction writer. His work is widely published in journals and magazines throughout the world, including: *Columbia: A Magazine of Poetry and Art*; *The Literary Review*; *Denver Quarterly*; *Hawaii Review*; *Le Guepard* (France); *Kadmos* (France); *Prism International*; *Jejune* (Czech Republic); *Leopold Bloom* (Hungary); *Antioch Review*; and *Prairie Schooner*, among others. His latest poetry collections are *Lorca at Seville* and *Captive Cities*. He lives in Brookline, Massachusetts.

ayaz daryl nielsen is husband, father, veteran, x-roughneck (as on oil rigs), x-hospice nurse, editor of print publication *bear creek haiku* (23+ years/115+ issues). His poetry's homes include *Lilliput Review, Yellow Mama, Verse Wisconsin, Shamrock* and *Shemom*. He has earned cherished awards, and, participated in anthologies. His poetry ensembles include *Concentric Penumbra's of the Heart* and *Tumbleweeds Still Tumbling* and has released a selection from 36 poets titled *The Bear Creek Anthology*. His beloved wife/poet Judith Partin-Nielsen, assistant Frosty, and! <u>bearcreekhaiku.blogspot.com</u> translate as *joie de vivre*.

Cristina M. R. Norcross is the author of 5 poetry collections including, *Land & Sea: Poetry Inspired by Art* (2007), *The Red Drum*(2008, 2013), *Unsung Love Songs* (2010), *The Lava Storyteller* (2013) and *Living Nature's Moments: A Conversation Between Poetry and Photography* (2014) with co-author, Patricia Bashford. Her works appear in print and online in North American and international journals, such as *The Toronto Quarterly, Red Cedar, Verse Wisconsin, The Moon Magazine, Your Daily Poem, Lime Hawk,* and *The Nervous Breakdown*. Featured in the BVAG show, ARTiculate (2011, 2012), Cristina's work also appears in the anthologies, *Contemporary Women's Literature* (2007), *Verse & Vision* (2011, 2012), *Sounds of Solace* (2013), *A Touch of Saccharine*(2014) and the *Ariel Anthology* (2014). She was the co-editor for the project *One Vision: A Fusion of Art & Poetry in Lake Country*(2009-11) and is currently one of the co-organizers of Random Acts of Poetry & Art Day. Cristina is also a contributing member of the Art Abandonment group. Cristina is the founding editor of, *Blue Heron Review* (http://www.blueheronreview.com), an online poetry journal. Find out more about this author at: www.FirkinFiction.com. Cristina's poem, "The Red Drum," inspired a short film by Marie Craven. Available to watch on Vimeo: http://vimeo.com/115796426

Agholor Leonard Obiaderi lives in Nigeria. He loves poetry and crime novels though he has no criminal friends. He has been featured as poet of the week in *Poetry Super-Highway* and *Wild Violet Literary Magazine*. His poems have been published in Storm Cycle Anthology of Kind of a Hurricane Press.

Vincent O'Connor has been a published writer since fourth grade, when his poem about protozoa was first published. Over the years he has published poetry in various print and online publications, as well as magazine articles, training material for various organizations, technical manuals for software companies, and a play, "Nearly Departed."

Mary Orovan is the author of "Green Rain" (Poets Wear Prada, 2008) available on Amazon.com. She has current or recent poems on line at 2River.org, Winter issue, and First Literary Review www.rulrul.4mg.com. Print journals include, "San Pedro River Review", "Poetry East", and many other publications. She's been writing poetry for about 12 years.

Scott Thomas Outlar hails from the heart of Atlantis where he kneels atop intricately designed rugs woven from prediluvian cloth, praying to the Holy Spirit Vibration for courage, grace, humility and discernment during this epic time of history at the edge of a new epoch. When not caught up in such passionate fervor, he spends his time writing such things as poetry, essays and rants. His work can be seen at Dissident Voice, Common Line Journal, Oracular Tree, Daily Anarchist, and Ascent Aspirations.

Coco Owen is a stay-at-home poet in Los Angeles. She has published poems in the *Antioch Review*, *1913*, *CutBank*, *The Journal*, *Rio Grande Review* and the *Feminist Wire*, among other venues. She has been a finalist in several recent book contests and has a mini chapbook with Binge Press. Owen serves on the board of Les Figues Press in Los Angeles. Find more of her work at: www.cocoowenphd.com.

Mangal Patel is a Director of Information Technology (IT) and a Governor of a school. She is married, has twins and lives in London, UK. Relatively new to writing, her published stories include *Revolving Lives* (anthology Boscombe Revolution Issue 2, Hesterglock Press), *Dramatic Encounters* (The Casket), *Lightening Force* (Wordland3), and *Thunder Smoke* (The Little Gold Pencil). Publications in Kind Of A Hurricane anthologies include: "Time's Up" in *Tic Toc* (also selected to be in the 2014 Best Of anthology, *Storm Cycle)*, "Mischief Moments" in *Just a Touch of Saccharine,* "Gilt Edged Trappings" in *Life Is A Rollercoaster* and soon to be published "Happily Ever After" in *Twice Upon A Time*.

Simon Perchik is an attorney whose poems have appeared in Partisan Review, The Nation, Poetry, The New Yorker, and elsewhere. His most recent collection is *Almost Rain,* published by River Otter Press (2013). For more information, free e-books and his essay titled "Magic, Illusion and Other Realities" please visit his website at www.simonperchik.com

Richard King Perkins II is a state-sponsored advocate for residents in long-term care facilities. He lives in Crystal Lake, IL with his wife Vickie, and daughter, Sage. He is a three-time Pushcart nominee and a Best of the Net nominee whose work has appeared in hundreds of publications including The Louisiana Review, Bluestem, Emrys Journal, Sierra Nevada Review, Roanoke Review, The Red Cedar Review and The William and Mary Review. He has poems forthcoming in Sobotka Literary Magazine, The Alembic, Old Red Kimono and Milkfist. He was a recent finalist in The Rash Awards, Sharkpack Alchemy, Writer's Digest and Bacopa Literary Review poetry contests.

Kushal Poddar is a native of Kolkata, India. He writes poetry, scripts and prose and is published world wide. He authored "All Our Fictional Dreams," published in several anthologies in the Continent and in America. The forthcoming book is "A Place for Your Ghost Animals." Find more at https://www.facebook.com/pages/Kushal-The-Poet/166552613396144

Ben Rasnic is a native of Jonesville, a small rural town in Southwest Virginia with a population <1000. A Pushcart Prize nominee in 2011, Rasnic still considers as his greatest literary achievement, electing to publish two short poems by Yusef Komunyakaa while serving as editor of his college literary magazine, Jimson Weed, in 1978—16 years before Komunyakaa received the Pulitzer Prize for Poetry. He is the author of two volumes of poetry, "Artifacts and Legends" (2012) and "Puppet" (2013), both available on amazon.com.. Ben currently resides in Bowie, Maryland.

Jendi Reiter is the author of the poetry collections *Bullies in Love* (Little Red Tree Publishing, 2015), *Barbie at 50* (Cervena Barva Press, 2010), *Swallow* (Amsterdam Press, 2009), and *A Talent for Sadness* (Turning Point Books, 2003). Awards include a 2010 Massachusetts Cultural Council Artists' Grant for Poetry, the 2013 Little Red Tree International Poetry Prize, the 2012 Betsy Colquitt Award for Poetry from Descant magazine, the 2011 James Knudsen Editor's Prize in Fiction from Bayou Magazine, the 2011 OSA Enizagam Award for Fiction, the 2010 Anderbo Poetry Prize, and second prize in the 2010 Iowa Review Awards for Fiction. She is the editor of WinningWriters.com, an online resource site for creative writers. Visit her blog at www.jendireiter.com and follow her on Twitter @JendiReiter.

henry 7. reneau, jr. writes words in fire to wake the world ablaze & illuminated by courage that empathizes with all the awful moments: a freight train bearing down with warning that blazes from the heart, like a chambered bullet exploding inadvertently.

Brad Rose was born and raised in southern California, and lives in Boston. He is recipient of Camroc Press Review's, Editor's Favorite Poetry Award, a Pushcart nominee in fiction, and the 2014 winner of unFold Magazine's "FIVE (5) Contest" for his found poem "Signs of Reincarnation at Le Parker Meridien Hotel, NY, NY." Brad's poetry and fiction have appeared in *The Los Angeles Times, Posit, The Baltimore Review, San Pedro River Review, Off the Coast, Third Wednesday, Boston Literary Magazine, Right Hand Pointing, The Potomac, Santa Fe Literary Review, The Common Line Journal, The*

Molotov Cocktail; Sleetmagazine, Monkeybicycle, Camroc Press Review, MadHat Lit, Burning Word and other publications. His book of poetry and micro fiction, *Pink X-Ray*, is forthcoming from Big Table Publishing in Spring, 2015. Links to Brad's poetry and fiction can be found at: http://bradrosepoetry.blogspot.com/ His chapbook of miniature fiction, "Coyotes Circle the Party Store," can be read at: https://sites.google.com/site/bradroserhpchapbook/ Audio recordings of a selection of Brad's published poetry can be heard at: https://soundcloud.com/bradrose1

Sy Roth comes riding in and then canters out. Oftentimes, the head is bowed by reality; other times, he is proud to have said something noteworthy.cRetired after forty-two years as teacher/school administrator, he now resides in Mount Sinai, far from Moses and the tablets. This has led him to find words for solace. He spends his time writing and playing his guitar. He has published in many online publications such as BlogNostics, Every Day Poets, The Weekender, The Squawk Back, Dead Snakes, Bitchin' Kitsch, Scapegoat Review, The Artistic Muse, Inclement, Napalm and Novocain, Euphemism, Humanimalz Literary Journal, Ascent Aspirations, Fowl Feathered Review, Vayavya, Wilderness House Journal, Aberration Labyrinth, Mindless(Muse), Em Dash, Subliminal Interiors, South Townsville Micropoetry Journal, The Penwood Review, The Rampallian, Vox Poetica, Clutching at Straws, Downer Magazine, Full of Crow, Abisinth Literary Review, Every Day Poems, Avalon Literary Review, Napalm and Novocaine, Wilderness House Literary Review, St. Elsewhere Journal, The Neglected Ratio, The Weekenders and Kerouac's Dog. One of his poems, *Forsaken Man*, was selected for Best of 2012 poems in *Storm Cycle*. Also selected Poet of the Month in Poetry Super Highway, September 2012. His work was also read at Palimpsest Poetry Festival in December 2012. He was named Poet of the Month for the month of February in BlogNostics.

Walter Ruhlmann works as an English teacher, edits mgversion2>datura and Beakful, and runs mgv2>publishing. His latest collections are *The Loss* through Flutter Press, *Twelve Times Thirteen* through Kind of a Hurricane Press, 2014, and *Crossing Puddles* through Robocup Press, 2015. His blogs http://thenightorchid.blogspot.fr and http://nightorchidswork.blogspot.fr

Fain Rutherford has worked as a soldier, lawyer, university lecturer, rock-climbing guide, survival instructor and at-home-dad. He currently resides in the desert of central Washington State. His recent poems appear or are scheduled to appear in Right Hand Pointing, Pyrokinection, Poetry Quarterly, Jellyfish Whispers, Halfway Down the Stairs, Furious Gazelle, Front Porch Review, Eunoia Review, Connotation Press, and Apeiron Review.

Richard Schnap is a poet, songwriter and collagist living in Pittsburgh, Pennsylvania. His poems have most recently appeared locally, nationally and overseas in a variety of print and online publications.

Leland Seese lives in Seattle, Washington, with his wife, Lisa Konick, and the younger three of their six foster-adopted and biological children. He earned a B. A. in English Lit/Creative Writing from the University of Washington, and a M. Div. from Princeton Theological Seminary, and was ordained to the ministry. He has served churches in the Detroit, Michigan, area as well as Seattle. After successful treatment for a bout of cancer, he felt compelled to try to say something meaningful about his life through poetry writing. He is grateful for inclusion in this anthology and in Pyrokinection. His work has also appeared in The East Bay Review, Clerestory Journal, and The Christian Century. Seese can be contacted at leeseese@gmail.com

John W. Sexton lives in the Republic of Ireland and is the author of five poetry collections, the most recent being *The Offspring of the Moon*, (Salmon Poetry, 2013). He also created and wrote *The Ivory Tower* for RTI radio, which ran to over one hundred half-hour episodes from 1999 to 2002. Two novels based on the characters from this series have been published by the O'Brien Press: *The Johnny Coffin Diaries* and *Johnny Coffin School-Dazed*, which have been translated into both Italian and Serbian. He is a past nominee for The Hennessy

Literary Award and his poem "The Green Owl" won the Listowel Poetry Prize 2007. Also in 2007 he was awarded a Patrick and Katherine Kavanagh Fellowship in Poetry.

Sunil Sharma is a Mumbai-based college principal, is also widely-published Indian critic, poet, literary interviewer, editor, translator, essayist and fiction writer. He has already published three collections of poetry, one collection of short fiction, one novel and co-edited five books so far. His six short stories and the novel Minotaur were recently prescribed for the undergraduate classes under the Post-colonial Studies, Clayton University, Georgia, USA. He is a recipient of the UK-based Destiny Poets' inaugural Poet of the Year award -- 2012.

Lance Sheridan prefers to let his work speak for itself.

Terri Simon has degrees from Sarah Lawrence College (Writing/Literature) and Virginia Tech (Computer Science) and works in IT. She lives in Laurel, Maryland with her husband and dogs. She organizes a poetry Meetup, plays hand drums, and has more projects started than she will ever finish. Her work has appeared in "Aberration Labyrinth," "Three Line Poetry," "Black Mirror Magazine," and the anthologies "A Mantle of Stars: A Queen of Heaven Devotional" and "Bright Stars: An Organic Tanka Journal (Volume 1)."

Bobbi Sinha-Morey is a poet living in the peaceful city of Brookings, Oregon. Her poetry can be seen in places such as *Pirene's Fountain, Bellowing Ark, Plainsongs, Taproot Literary Review,* and *Orbis,* among others. Her books of poetry, *The Glass Swan* and *Candle Song,* are available at Amazon.com and www.writewordsinc.com. Her website is located at http://bobbisinhamorey.wordpress.com.

Judith Skillman has a new book entitled *House of Burnt Offerings* from Pleasure Boat Studio. The author of fifteen collections of poetry, her work has appeared in *J Journal, Tampa Review, Prairie Schooner, FIELD, The Iowa Review, Poetry,* and other journals. Awards include grants from the Academy of

American Poets and Washington State Arts Commission. Skillman taught in the field of humanities for twenty-five years, and has collaboratively translated poems from Italian, Portuguese, and French. Currently she works on manuscript review. Visit www.judithskillman.com

Felino A. Soriano is a poet documenting coöccurrences. His poetic language stems from exterior motivation of jazz music and the belief in language's unconstrained devotion to broaden understanding. His work has been nominated for the *Pushcart Prize* and *Best of the Net* anthologies. Recent poetry collections include *Forms, migrating, Of isolated limning, Mathematics, Espials, watching what invents perception,* and *Of these voices*. He lives in California with his wife and family and is a director of supported living and independent living programs providing supports to adults with developmental disabilities. Visit <u>felinoasoriano.info</u> for more information.

Brandon C. Spalletta is a poet from Herndon, Virginia who lives with his beautiful wife and best friend. Since discovering his passion for words in his early twenties his poetry has appeared in the journals Pyrokinection and Jellyfish Whispers, and in the international anthology series These Human Shores, and Prism.

Smita Sriwastav is an M.B.B.S. doctor with a passion for poetry and literature. She has always expressed her innermost thoughts and sentiments through the medium of poetry. A feeling of inner tranquility and bliss captures her soul whenever she pens her verse. Nature has been the most inspiring force in molding the shape of her writings. She has published two books and has published poems in journals like the Rusty Nail (Rule of Survival)and Contemporary Literary Review India (spring lingers),four and twenty, Paradise Review, Literary Juice, Blast Furnace and many more and one of her poems "Unsaid Goodbyes" was published in an anthology called 'Inspired by Tagore' published by Sampad and British Council. She has written poetry all her life and aims to do so forever.

Tom Sterner wrestles with creativity: graphic art, music, photography, & WORD. A native Coloradoan, he lives in Denver. Tom's artwork, music, photography, & written word have been published in magazines

& on the internet by various folk, including *Howling Dog Press/Omega, Carpe Articulum Literary Review, Skyline Literary Review, The Storyteller, & Flashquake*. Published work includes five novels: *~momma's rain~*, *~spiders 'n snakes~*, *~gordian objective~*, *~after earth~*, *~cranial loop~* & the epic book-length poem *~quodlibet~*. He is winner of the Marija Cerjak Award for Avant-Garde/Experimental Writing & was nominated for the Pushcart Prize in 2006 & 2008. email: wordwulf@gmail.com website: http://wordwulf.com

Kevin Strong is from Winnipeg, Canada. He writes music, scripts, stories and poetry when he is not doing accounting or doting on his wife and 2 children. Kevin takes inspiration from current events, famous poems, novels and even song lyrics. Kevin hopes to someday publish his own poetry book. Kevin's work has been published by Amulet Magazine, Conceit Magazine, Expressions by Skyline, Falling Star Magazine, Joe Brainard's Pyjamas, Kind of a Hurricane Press (Tic Toc Anthology, Life is a Roller Coaster Anthology and Storm Cycle Anthology), languageandculture.net, Lone Stars Magazine, Mystical Muse Magazine, Pink Mouse Pub, Rhubarb Magazine, Sage of Consciousness, The Taylor Trust, Weekly Poem, and Word Slaw.

David Subacchi lives in Wrexham (UK) and studied at the University of Liverpool. He was born in Aberystwyth of Italian roots and writes in both English and Welsh. Cestrian Press has published two collections of his poems. "First Cut" (2012) and "Hiding in Shadows" (2014).

Fanni Sütő is a 24-year-old writer, poet, dreamer who believes in fairy tales even if they are dark, disenchanted and deconstructed. She writes about everything which comes her way or goes bump in the night. She has been published in Hungary, the US, the UK, and Australia.

Anne Swannell lives in Victoria, BC, where she writes, paints, makes mosaics, and is a scenic painter/set-designer for local theatre companies.

Ag Synclair is an unapologetic pessimist, rule breaker, and rebel without a clue. When he isn't editing *The Montucky Review* and serving on the editorial staff of *The Bookends Review*, he is drinking from glasses that are perpetually half empty and collaborating with his partner in crime, the artist and poet Heather Brager. Despite being extensively published around the globe, he flies under the radar. Deftly.

Marianne Szlyk is the editor of The Song Is... and a professor of English at Montgomery College. Recently, she published her first chapbook with Kind of a Hurricane Press: http://barometricpressures.blogspot.com/2014/10/listening-to-electric-cambodia-looking.html Her poems have appeared in a variety of online and print venues, including Long Exposure, Bottlec[r]ap, ken*again, Of/with, bird's thumb, Carcinogenic Poetry, and Black Poppy Review as well as Kind of a Hurricane Press' anthologies from Of Sun and Sand on. She hopes that you will consider sending work to The Song Is.... For more information about the spring/summer contests, see this link: http://thesongis.blogspot.com/2015/04/contests-for-springsummer.html

Grant Tarbard has worked as a journalist, a contributor to magazines, an editor, a reviewer and an interviewer. He is now the editor of The Screech Owl and co-founder of Resurgant Press with Bethany W. Pope. His work can be seen in such magazines as *The Rialto, Ink, Sweat & Tears, Bone Orchard Poetry, BLAZE, The Journal, Southlight, Sarasvati, Earth Love, Mood Swing, Puff Puff Prose Poetry & Prose, Postcards Poetry and Prose, Playerist 2, Lake City Lights, Medusa's Kitchen, The Open Mouse, Weyfarers, Miracle, Poetry Cornwall, I-70, South Florida Review, Stare's Nest, Zymbol, Synchronized Chaos, BLUEPEPPER, Every Day Poetry, Tribe, Verse-Virtual* and *Decanto*.

Yermiyahu Ahron Taub is the author of three books of poetry, Uncle Feygele (Plain View Press, 2011), What Stillness Illuminated/Vos shtilkayt hot baloykhtn (Parlor Press, 2008; Free Verse Editions series), and The Insatiable Psalm (Wind River Press, 2005). He was honored by the Museum of Jewish Heritage as one of New York's best emerging Jewish artists and has been nominated twice for a Pushcart

Prize and twice for a Best of the Net award. Please visit his web site at www.yataub.net

Judith Terzi has had her poetry appeared widely in journals and anthologies including *Myrrh, Mothwing, Smoke: Erotic Poems* (Tupelo), *Raintown Review, Times They Were A-Changing: Women Remember the 60s & 70s* (She Writes), *Trivia: Voices of Feminism*, and *Wide Awake: The Poets of Los Angeles and Beyond* (Beyond Baroque). She is the author of *Sharing Tabouli* and *Ghazal for a Chambermaid* (Finishing Line). *If You Spot Your Brother Floating By* was just published by Kattywompus Press.

Talaia Thomas lives, works, and writes in Vermont's Northeast Kingdom. Her writing has been published in 4 Legs and a Tail, Catkin On!, and The Transcript.

Sarah Thursday is a music obsessed, Long Beach poetry advocate, editor of CadenceCollective.net, and teacher of 4th and 5th graders. She is honored to have forthcoming or been published in The Long Beach Union, The Atticus Review, East Jasmine Review, Ishaan Literary Review, Napalm and Novocain, Mind[less] Muse, Pyrokinection, Something's Brewing Anthology, and Mayo Review. Her full length collection, All the Tiny Anchors, is in the works. Follow her at SarahThursday.com.

Paul Tristram is a Welsh writer who has poems, short stories, sketches and photography published in many publications around the world. He yearns to tattoo porcelain bridesmaids instead of digging empty graves for innocence at midnight. This too may pass, yet.

David Turnbull lives in South East London. His short fiction has previously appeared in Salt Publishing's Best British Fantasy 2014. His recent publications include Girl at the End of the World II (Fox Spirit) and Horror Uncut (Grey Friar Press) Solstice Shorts (Arachne Press) and Sensorama (Eibonvale

Press). He is member of the Clockhouse London group of genre writers. His website can be found at http://www.tumsh.co.uk/

Matthew Valdespino is a 23 year old graduate of the University of Pennsylvania currently living in Tacoma. After spending the past year working on farms in Lynden, Washington and Central Chile, he has moved into the Seattle-Tacoma area to pursue his interests in Poetry on a more full time basis. His work tends to explore limitations, both of himself and those around him, the virtue of struggle, and the city of Seattle.

Jessica Van de Kemp is a 2014 *Best of the Net* nominee and the author of the poetry chapbook, *Spirit Light*, from *The Steel Chisel*. The recipient of a BlackBerry Scholarship in English Language and Literature and the winner of a TA Award for Excellence in Teaching, Jessica is currently pursuing a PhD in Rhetoric at the University of Waterloo. Website: jessvdk.wordpress.com | Twitter: @jess_vdk

Michelle Villanueva is a student finishing up an MFA in Creative Writing - Poetry at the University of Nevada, Las Vegas. She is the author of one chapbook, Postcard: Lions (forthcoming 2015, Etched Press), and her poetry has been published in Foothill Poetry Journal, The Tower Review, The Camel Saloon, and other print and online publications.

Anne Richmond Wakefield lives and writes in Austin, Texas. When not painstakingly composing her first novel, she's enjoying the outdoors with her husband, two sons, and decrepit Lab-mix.

Tamara K. Walker dreams of irrealities among typewriter ribbons, stuffed animals and duct tape flower barrettes. She lives near Boulder, Colorado with her wife/life partner and blogs irregularly about writing and literature at http://tamarakwalker.wordpress.com. She may also be found online at http://about.me/tamara.kwalker. Her writing has appeared or is forthcoming in A cappella Zoo, Identity Theory, Apocrypha and Abstractions, Gay Flash Fiction, the Tic Toc themed poetry anthology released by Kind of a Hurricane Press, and a variety of poetry zines including nin: a journal of erotic poetics, LYNX: A

Journal for Linking Poets, Scifaikuest, A Hundred Gourds, and Eucalypt.

Nadine Waltman-Harmon is a retired teacher of 42 years, who grew up in northeastern Oklahoma. In the 1960's she taught African teachers in Tanzania, East Africa Nadine lives in a log house in the Pacific Northwest with her cat, Mama Chai.

Nells Wasilewski lives in a small southern town, seventy miles southeast of Nashville, Tennessee with her husband, Walter. She retired from the mortgage industry in 2011 and began pursuing her lifelong dream of writing. Her writing has been greatly influenced by her faith in Jesus Christ, her own experiences and nature. She is currently working on daily devotionals. Her work has appeared in *Haiku Journal, Three Line Poetry, 50 Haikus, Poetry Quarterly, Barefoot Review,* and *Dual Coast Magazine.*

Mercedes Webb-Pullman graduated from IIML Victoria University Wellington with MA in Creative Writing in 2011. Her poems and the odd short story have appeared online, in print and in her books *Food 4 Thought, Numeralla Dreaming, After the Danse, Ono, Looking for Kerouac, Tasseography, Bravo Charlie Foxtrot* and *Collected poems 2008 - 2014.* She lives on the Kapiti Coast, New Zealand. www.benchpress.co.nz

Diane Webster spends many nights falling asleep, juggling images to fit into a poem. Her goal is to remain open to poetry ideas in everyday life or nature or an overheard phrase and to write from her perspective at the moment. Her work has appeared in *ken*again, Illya's Honey, Red River Review* and other literary magazines.

Catherine Weiss is a poet and author living in Northampton, MA. In her spare time she enjoys ping pong, monopoly, and audiobooks. Her website with more info can be found at http://catherineweiss.com.

Jon Wesick is the host of the Gelato Poetry Series, instigator of the San Diego Poetry Un-Slam, and an editor of the San Diego

Poetry Annual. He has published nearly three hundred poems in journals such as the Atlanta Review, Pearl, and Slipstream. He has also published over seventy short stories. Jon has a Ph.D. in physics and is a longtime student of Buddhism and the martial arts. One of his poems won second place in the 2007 African American Writers and Artists contest.

Joanna M. Weston is married, has two cats, multiple spiders, a herd of deer, and two derelict hen-houses. Her middle-reader, *Those Blue Shoes*, was published by Clarity House Press; and her collection of poetry, *A Summer Father*, was published by Frontenac House of Calgary. Her ebooks are at http://www.1960willowtree.wordpress.com/

Denise Weuve has recently appeared in *Bop Dead City, Curio Poetry, Emerge Literary Journal, Gutter Eloquence, Red River Review,* and *San Pedro River Review*. She teaches English and Creative Writing in Cerritos, California and collects paper cuts, and other miscellaneous damage to display in glass cases (her blog http://deniserweuve.wordpress.com/). Contact her at Inkdamage@gmail.com or follow her on Facebook or Twitter.

Kelley White worked in inner city Philadelphia and now works in rural New Hampshire. Her poems have appeared in journals including *Exquisite Corpse, Rattle* and *JAMA*. Her most recent books are *Toxic Environment* (Boston Poet Press) and *Two Birds in Flame* (Beech River Books). She received a 2008 Pennsylvania Council on the Arts grant.

Emma Whitehall is a writer and spoken-word performer based in the North East of England. She specialises in Flash Fiction and poetry, focusing around horror and dark fantasy themes. Her work has been featured in literary and genre magazines on both sides of the Atlantic; her paranormal love story "Waiting" has been translated into Spanish, and her short story "Shed" was featured in a charity anthology for the American independent publishing company, Hazardous Press.

Martin Willitts, Jr. is a retired Librarian living in Syracuse, NY. His poems have appeared in Bitter Oleander, Blue Fifth, Conclave, Kind of a Hurricane, Comstock, Stone Canoe, and numerous others. Winner of the 2012 *William K. Hathaway Award*; co-winner of the 2013 *Bill Holm Witness Poetry Contest*; winner of the 2013 *"Trees" Poetry Contest*; winner of the 2014 *Broadsided award*. He has 6 full-length collections including contest winner "Searching for What is Not There" (Hiraeth Press, 2013) and over 20 chapbooks including contest winner "William Blake, Not Blessed Angel But Restless Man" (Red Ochre Press, 2014). He has a forthcoming web book "A is for Aorta" with *A Kind Of Hurricane Press*.

Deborah L. Wymbs prefers to let her work speak for itself.

Ron Yazinski is a retired English teacher who, with his wife Jeanne, lives in Winter Garden, Florida. His poems have appeared in many journals, including The Mulberry Poets and Writers Association, Strong Verse, The Bijou Review, The Edison Literary Review, Jones Av., Chantarelle's Notebook, Centrifugal Eye, amphibi.us, Nefarious Ballerina, The Talon, Amarillo Bay, The Write Room, Pulsar, Sunken Lines, Wilderness House, Blast Furnace, and The Houston Literary Review. He is also the author of the chapbook HOUSES: AN AMERICAN ZODIAC, and two volumes of poetry, SOUTH OF SCRANTON and KARAMAZOV POEMS.

Dana Yost was an award-winning daily newspaper editor for 29 years. He is the author of four books, and a two-time nominee for a Pushcart Prize in poetry. This is the second consecutive year his work has been selected for *Storm Cyc*le. He lives in Forest City, Iowa.

Mark Young is the editor of Otoliths, lives in a small town in North Queensland in Australia, & has been publishing poetry for more than fifty-five years. His work has been widely anthologized, & his essays & poetry translated into a number of languages. He is the author of over twenty-five books, primarily poetry but also including speculative fiction & art history. A new collection of poems, *Bandicoot habitat*, is due out from gradient books of Finland later this year.

Changming Yuan is an 8-time Pushcart nominee and author of Chansons of a Chinaman (2009) and Landscaping (2013) grew up in rural China, holds a PhD in English, and currently tutors in Vancouver, where he co-edits Poetry Pacific with Allen Qing Yuan and operates PP Press. Since mid-2005, Yuan has published poetry in Asia Literary Review Best Canadian Poetry, BestNewPoemsOnline, London Magazine, Threepenny Review and 889 other literary journals/anthologies across 30 countries.

Jeffrey Zable is a teacher and conga drummer who plays Afro-Cuban folkloric music for dance classes and Rumbas around the San Francisco Bay Area. He's published five chapbooks including Zable's Fables with an introduction by the late great Beat poet Harold Norse. Present or upcoming writing in Toad Suck Review, Clarion, Kentucky Review, Edge, The Alarmist, Skidrow Penthouse, Uppagus, Ishaan Literary Review, Clackamas Literary Review, Futures Trading, Chrome Baby and many others.

About The Editors

A.J. Huffman has published seven solo chapbooks and one joint chapbook through various small presses. Her eighth solo chapbook, *Drippings from a Painted Mind,* won the 2013 Two Wolves Chapbook Contest. She is a Pushcart Prize nominee, and her poetry, fiction, haiku, and photography have appeared in hundreds of national and international journals, including *Labletter, The James Dickey Review, Bone Orchard, EgoPHobia, Kritya, Offerta Speciale,* in which her work appeared in both English and Italian translation, and *Chrysanthemum,* in which her work appeard in both English and German translation. She is also the founding editor of Kind of a Hurricane Press. www.kindofahurricanepress.com

April Salzano teaches college writing in Pennsylvania where she lives with her husband and two sons. Most recently, she was nominated for two Pushcart prizes and finished her first collection of poetry. She is working on a memoir on raising a child with autism. Her work has appeared in journals such as *Convergence, Ascent Aspirations, The Camel Saloon, Centrifugal Eye, Deadsnakes, Visceral Uterus, Salome, Poetry Quarterly, Writing Tomorrow* and *Rattle.* The author also serves as co-editor at Kind of a Hurricane Press.

Made in the USA
Middletown, DE
27 August 2015